W9-BBE-332

AVIGNON IN FLOWER

1309–1403

Decorated by
Pauline Baynes

DC 801
A96
G3

APR 27 1982

316626

AVIGNON
IN FLOWER
1309-1403

BY MARZIEH GAIL

HOUGHTON MIFFLIN COMPANY BOSTON
THE RIVERSIDE PRESS CAMBRIDGE : 1965

FIRST PRINTING   W

COPYRIGHT © 1965 BY MARZIEH GAIL
ALL RIGHTS RESERVED INCLUDING THE RIGHT TO
REPRODUCE THIS BOOK OR PARTS THEREOF IN ANY FORM
LIBRARY OF CONGRESS CATALOG CARD NUMBER: 65-13169
PRINTED IN THE UNITED STATES OF AMERICA

for Harold

CONTENTS

vii

AVIGNON IN FLOWER

1309–1403

· THE ROOM OF
THE STAG

A BRIDGE going nowhere, spanning nothing, snapped off in the middle of the
river. A bridge where even in the wind,
even from the nonexistent part of the
span, you can hear the thump of dancing feet. Now point-
less, it stretches between two structures equally without present meaning: Philip the Fair's square tower, across the river
in what used to be the beginning of France; and here on the
Avignon side, the massive Palace of the Popes. Beside the
Palace is a garden growing on the Rock, blowing up there
high above the river. Look down, way down at the blue-
green Rhône, at the small open boat that sidles over the river,
hanging to a wire overhead; at the flat plains laid out, green
and gold like a page just opened in a Book of Hours; crisp,
unchanged since the Popes looked down. Away off, slanting

across a low hill, are the bisque, precise and rounded towers of the Fort St.-André, standing these six hundred years.

Perhaps in many minds the town is only a nursery song today: "On the bridge at Avignon, that's where they dance, that's where they dance . . ." But when in the fourteenth century the Popes moved here from Rome, it was Christendom's throne city, and it rivaled Rome. Its very being led to the Great Schism of the West, so that on this massive Rock the Church was split.

Nine Popes were here at Avignon: Clement, and John, and Benedict, and Clement; Innocent and Urban; Gregory, and Clement, and Benedict. The seven of this book were Popes in the usual way; but the last two, whose status, we believe, can never be resolved, are called "Popes in their obedience": valid, shall we say, for those who found them so. Secretly, a common word preserves the nine's joint memory: poplin, first made here, named from the Italian *papalino*. They came to Avignon, exchanging the Tiber for the Rhône; for ninety-four years, from March to March, from 1309 to 1403, they made this place the core of the Western world; and because they were here instead of back in Rome, they changed that world for always.

☙ ☙ ☙

The big icy Mistral sweeps down the Rhône and bangs at the city. Why couldn't the Pope have stayed in gentle Rome? His robes might almost have sailed him off his feet in this wind. And how could the ladies of his Court keep the jewels from blowing out of their hair? The sun would be soft and warm, if it weren't for this ever-drumming wind. Stay out of the deep blue shadows, keep in the warm patches of sun.

Here before the Papal Palace, two Muslim-looking minarets grow out of the massive wall, that is pierced with narrow openings, aptly cross-shaped though meant not for worship but warfare: they are slits for the archers to shoot through. Gargoyles, away up there in infinity, lean over you, ready to spit down rain. Two Popes, Benedict XII the baker's son and Clement VI the noble, built this stronghold, in only eighteen years. One of them raised a Romanesque sort of barracks, the other added a graceful Gothic pile. After them, their successors worked on the fortress for another five decades. The sky turns suddenly black dark and the wind hammers.

Follow the rest into the great, somber place. Like so many medieval strongholds, this too is best seen from the outside. It has the same lonely bareness of many another reconstruction, such as those often noticed in bombed-out European towns, where the rebuilding is solid and correct, and only the soul has been bombed away. There is, however, one notable exception here, although many a tourist will never find it out. Coming, summertimes, in great tramping hordes, people are no longer (unless the rule changes again) allowed to look at the one special thing: the private apartment of Clement VI. It is in the Wardrobe Tower, and they call it the Room of the Stag.

This Clement VI was the captain jewel, the most magnificent in the chain of Avignon's nine Popes. He is the one you think back to, like him or not, and because of him you want to know the story of them all. Gaze at his image fast asleep in the Palace, at his sleek jaws and puffy eyelids, his hands in prayer, his feet pressed against a small stone lion that is sleeping too.

Up here in this hidden room, this aerial, field-and-forest hideaway, rests his real heart. Trying to evoke, now, that secret study of Clement's, with its frescoes done by Matteo di Giovanni about 1344, is like trying to bring back a perfume out of memory. It is almost the only thing inside the gigantic pile that stirs you. The Gobelins, the empty money room, the high vaulted hall with long windows letting in the southern light, where the guide shouts to make echoes (marvelous acoustics, up to twelve reverberations), the narrow twisting stairways — none quite reaches you, not even when you shut your eyes and think how the whole place once glowed with painted frescoes, with bright hangings and deep carpets and exotic birds. Remember that Froissart named it "the loveliest, vastest house in the world."

But here in Clement's tower room is a human being, not a dead Gothic man on a slab. Here on the walls, with whitish mottled patches from the damp, are the things he liked when he was on earth.

Field, thicket, stream, under a circle of blue sky. Background of leaves, fruits, flowers, each jewel-sharp. The walls are like a magic velvet tapestry, softly rubbed by time, but with people and objects still emerging from it. Men with nets by a green fishpond with swimming pike. Brittany spaniels. A young noble standing, poised, easy, with a cap on his long smooth hair, a cloak hanging from one shoulder, brandishing a falcon in his gloved right hand; facing him another, in a light overgarment also knee-short, wearing a gem-studded belt with a dagger at the side; these are Clement's brother and nephew, some will tell you. A slim white greyhound. A child in a tree. Grasses, bright birds, a stream and bathers. Colors still shine here; greens and browns; an orange dress; blue fish; oranges in a tree. People, serene, quiet, unfevered, doing pleasant things. An impression of leafiness in this hidden place. A happy world that is perhaps about to be blotted away; some of the figures look different from the way they were a few years before. Has a bather been clothed? There are the white splotches where, it seems, restoration is going on.

Best of all, the mind was not compelled to stay, even in this loveliness. The eye could escape; the room has a view that soars and dips, out over flat green plains, down across the little rooftops of the city.

As revealing as what the Pope liked is what he left out of his private apartment; nowhere in all this lavishly painted Room of the Stag, this real home of Clement VI, is there a single religious symbol of any kind.

In Avignon, during Clement's reign, this Palace foreshadowed Versailles. There were feasts and tournaments and balls for the beautiful ladies (the vanished Doucette; Blanchefleur; Almodie) and the lords of "Europe's most polished court." Not the haphazard, slightly bemused, incurious tourists that people it today, but elegant priests and princes and pages and beauties, in a choice assortment of damasks, silks and velvets, embroideries in gold thread, peacock feather hats, long, pointed shoes, curls, jeweled crowns and ivory combs, ermine and that squirrel fur called *vair* (which may have been what Cinderella's slipper was made of after all, instead of glass or *verre*). All these, the wearers and the things they wore, now piled into a heap and swept away.

The accounts remark, casually and as if back of the hand, that Clement received too often in this apartment the lovely Countess of Turenne. Just how often was too often is not recorded. But the Palace like these walls was also crowded with fair young boys.

※ ※ ※

And there was someone else besides, when the Pontiffs built their Palace here. A lady walked through Avignon, one different from the rest because she was reflected in the mind of a poet. Where she once passed, the city is still a hodgepodge of medieval streets: dark gray walls, high, carved wooden doors; foot-wide sidewalks; a glimpse of old courtyards; arches, tunnels, a gray canal running along. And in the somber rue de la Masse, where once stood the Church of Saint Claire, a plaque says: "Here there was, in the fourteenth century, the Church of Saint Claire, in which at dawn on the 6th of April, 1327, Petrarch conceived for Laura a sublime love, which made them both immortal."

Today as tokens of it all, the Palace, the Bridge and a Book are left.

※ ※ ※

· THE POPE'S RUBY

PHILIP of France created the Avignon Popes. That is, he made the first one, a weapon to his purpose; so that in a way his ambitions generated all the nine. The one he fastened on for Pontiff and called to a secret encounter was the French Archbishop of Bordeaux.

To an abbey built deep in the pine forests, so the story runs, in the neighborhood of Saint-Jean d'Angély, the men traveled stealthily, disguised, by separate ways. After preliminaries Philip said: "How would you like to be Pope?"

"To be Pope," the Archbishop soundlessly repeated. His hands unclenched. The fingers of the right one moved to make a hidden papal blessing. Controlling his lips he gazed at Philip. There would, surely, be more to come.

Philip's eyes narrowed. He saw before him a figure stooped,

hollow-cheeked, wrapped up for warmth and somehow lost in a wide cloak.

"But there are six conditions," the King said.

The Archbishop stood like stone. Then, slowly, he nodded his head. To reconcile Philip with the Church; well, that was easy and must be done. But as the voice hurried on, still low but heavy with authority, he felt his hands turning to fists, the nails cutting into his soft palms. How could he agree to defame a dead Pope?

"Sire," he attempted at this point, but the word was soundless.

He knew that Philip had fought the dead Boniface VIII toe to toe. For Boniface claimed to be ruler of this world as well as the spiritual one, and this world included Philip. Angered at the steady flow of gold from all over Europe to Rome, which had become habitual, what with the Crusades and their continuous emergencies, Philip had tried to tax the clergy. Boniface promptly issued a bull excommunicating monarchs who should do anything of the kind. Philip jailed a Papal Nuncio. Bulls flew. One of them, the *Ausculta fili*, Philip caused to be burned in Paris to the sound of a trumpet. France stood with Philip, and Boniface answered with still another bull, the *Unam sanctam*, which asserted that to be saved, one must believe "that every human being is subject to the Pontiff of Rome."

Philip thereupon wilily summoned a States-General, the first to include all three orders: clergy, nobles and bourgeoisie, and four propositions were there debated: that Boniface was not the true Pope; that Boniface was a heretic; that Boniface was a simoniac; that Boniface was a criminal.

The Archbishop guessed that Philip had been revolving the thing in his mind: it was a curious problem for the King, because what was a Pope? A Pope was at the same time both

weak and strong; as with any man, an iron gauntlet slapped
across his face drew blood — and yet, he could place a whole
people under an interdict, and thus starve it out. Philip had
apparently decided such power should be his as well; he
wanted a Pope and would buy one.

The Archbishop shivered under his big cloak. It was damp
in the cloister and the thick walls muffled sound. In his mind's
eye, the tiara hung and glittered. He would probably say yes
to all the six conditions, whatever they might be. After the
long struggle between the Papacy and the French King, he
knew who was losing now. He would never say to Philip
the Fair what Boniface had written him: "My predecessors
have deposed three Kings of France . . . If you do not mend
your ways . . . I will put you out like a little boy!"

Word had got to the Archbishop, off in Bordeaux, of how
they tried to make Boniface abdicate, and how he replied:
"Rather would I die, than cease to be Pope!" And how even
as the soldiers of Philip and the Colonnas were scaling the
fortress walls at Anagni, breaking in, ripping up his private
apartments, the aging Boniface had dressed himself in his
papal robes. He had sat himself down on the papal throne
and awaited them, the crown of Constantine on his white
head, the Keys in one hand, the Cross in the other.

The Archbishop of Bordeaux was not of this stamp. But
on one great occasion in the past, he had opposed the will of
Philip. It was that act of intransigence, ironically turned now
by a stratagem of the King to his royal advantage, which
made possible the echoing question: "How would you like
to be Pope?"

That was the time when Philip — who had no intention of
letting Boniface give France to Albert of Austria as planned
— desired the prelates of France to endorse an edict deposing
the Pontiff, and one man present had refused to sign. Today

he stood before the King, but he was not now the same man.

Things had come to a pretty pass, if a King could appoint a Pope. It happened because the Conclave was at swords' points: some for the dead Boniface (after whom an interim Benedict reigned only briefly), some for France. When the Holy See had been vacant nine months, they at last agreed that among three names, the choice would be left to Philip. How he must have smiled when he read the name of the Gascon Archbishop of Bordeaux; the Italian Cardinals thought this priest was Philip's enemy, whereas Philip owned him. "Find out each man's thumbscrew," a Jesuit has written. Philip knew this one's impulsions.

The royal lips were moving: "Reconcile me with the Church; revoke all censures against me and mine; yield me, for five years, the tithes of my realm; condemn utterly the memory of Boniface, root and branch; bring back to the Cardinalate Pietro and Giacomo Colonna, adding some of my friends."

The King stopped. The room was quiet, except for the shifting of the Archbishop's feet on the cold stone floor.

"It was six conditions," the priest ventured, glancing aside. He did not remember that when the Devil had offered Jesus all the Kingdoms of the world and the glory of them, Jesus had chosen instead to possess His own soul.

"The last one I reserve," said Philip, "to tell you in my own good time. But to be Pope, you must accept them, one and all."

He almost saw the tiara glittering in the King's two hands. Only a word more, and he would feel it on his brows. What if the last condition was, as had been whispered, to move the Holy See away from Rome, and over the mountains to France? He would name himself Clement V. The future exploded in his mind, bright as Greek fire.

※ ※ ※

For a while everybody was happy about the new Pope. The late Boniface's nephew and his allies thought they had managed to name a man who would stand firm against Philip, while the King himself knew otherwise. It was not long before the Italians did too. One day, when Clement was celebrating, he let slip the news that he and King Philip were on the best of terms. Then he delivered another mortal blow: he would not be crowned in Rome.

Bitterly, Cardinal Matteo Orsini complained to Cardinal Alberti: "Well, you carried out your plans, and now look at us. Either I know nothing of the Gascon character, or it will be a long, long time before the Holy See gets back to Rome." Even he could hardly prophesy, however, that (with two brief exceptions) the span would stretch out till the Council at Constance, over a hundred years.

Thus the day came when they told the Archbishop of Bordeaux that he was ruler of the world, and in a way it was true.

But what was the world? Rome's Empire of the early time had vanished, split into East and West, four centuries after Jesus. The eastern part, Byzantium, was dying (although it would live on until 1453, when the Muslims would take Constantinople). The western part had fallen in fragments to savage tribes, and for three hundred years and more, had been under the Emperors of the East. Then on Christmas Day, 800, the Holy Roman Empire was born, when Pope Leo III crowned Charlemagne Emperor of the West. This Holy Roman Empire was in essence an important dream: a dream of political power linked with spiritual, of Pope and Sovereign working together to build the State of God. The dream might have come true once, who knows, under such as Gerbert the King-Maker and the young Otto III, a millennium after Christ, but Otto died. Mostly, instead of working together they wrestled, with the secular power getting stronger all the time, and the Pope flashing his two keys, symbolizing, he said, that he was Lord of spirituals and temporals alike. In practice the Empire was hard to understand. A mosaic of Kingdoms, it was; the ruler of one piece of mosaic, elected Emperor by princes both lay and of the Church, was in theory Suzerain of them all. France, now causing so much trouble, had left the Empire in 887. Her star began to rise (but by 1337 she was fighting a fateful, intermittent war with England, which would go on for more than a hundred years, and dim her waxing light).

No, Clement's world was not a monolith. There was Eastern and Western Christianity, the East with no overall Pope, they having separated from the Bishop of Rome in 1054. Then there was a multitude of those on-again, off-again Kings and Queens, those Principalities and City Republics, each with its claims and shifting loyalties. The Pope himself was one of those secular rulers among the rest, owning, for example, his Italian States, about one-third of the Peninsula. Beside him ruled the cities, and also the great houses: the Scaligeri at Verona; the Visconti at Milan; the Princes of Este at Ferrara.

You looked at the map and the countries bled into each other like running paint. A whole people would go as some bride's dowry, or on someone's deathbed pass under another flag: thus England would claim to have inherited France. Nationals would be moved around in job lots, the way Bela IV of Hungary, who founded modern Budapest in 1247, repeopled Pest, newly destroyed by the Mongols, and filled it up with Germans.

Aside from all these bits and pieces there were in any case two separate worlds: the Christian and the Muslim. The Kings of Castile fought the Moors of Granada, their country's name deriving from the castles built to shut the Muslims out. Much alive in Spain, the Muslims had won the Crusades under Saladin about a hundred years before, throve in Asia and the Middle East and pressed at the gates of Constantinople; on a day far ahead they would camp by Vienna.

Then there were these universities, and these lawyers supplanting priests: an issue would come to be posed, the howls of the torture chamber would slowly give way to judgments of the appraising mind. Speaking of those on whom it was necessary to inflict pain, there was also the flourishing world of the sects. Again, there were the traveling, armed "Companies" with their own kind of rule. At the base of it all, you had the people: often miserable, in tears, robbed bare by anyone — individual tyrants, the dreaded *fisc*, the roving bands.

Some of these things were known to Clement, some he took for granted or left unresolved, much was veiled from him. What he did not see was that — by coming away from Rome on a day when men studied the mystical properties of numbers — there were going to be two hearts, Rome and Avignon; and a battle would be joined between two winds, the Sirocco and the Mistral; between two rivers, the Tiber and the Rhône; and two rocks, Tarpeia's and the Rock of the Lords. There would also be two contending wines, vernaccia wine and that of Beaune.

He did not understand that by displacing the Holy See, he was in a way displacing the world, which meant displacing Western man. The future, if it wished to, could look back and, *mutatis mutandis*, compare his act to that of Copernicus two hundred years later; he also would displace the world.

※ ※ ※

It was a brilliant ceremony, the day they crowned Clement V at Lyons, on November 14, 1305, in the Church of Saint Just. To satisfy enormous crowds, come to witness this first crowning of a Pope on French soil, and his own emotions, Clement had decided on a magnificent processional. Dressed in his robes, wearing the tiara brought from Rome, he was helped on to a splendid mare and gave its bridle into Philip's hands. The King, after proceeding for a time on foot, turned the bridle over to his brother and mounted a charger at the Pontiff's side.

However, as the procession poured down the steep slopes of the Gourgillon, cutting its way through masses of people, an ancient wall suddenly crumpled under its load of spectators and thundered to the ground in the Pope's path. Clement was knocked from his horse and his tiara rolled away. Attendants leaped forward to raise him up. He was unharmed. His robes were shaken free of dust; his symbol was brought back to him, wiped and replaced, only now it had a gaping hole where a great wine-colored ruby had glowed before. Philip and his brother, Prince Charles of Valois, were badly hurt. Other injured writhed and twisted on the ground; within a few days, twelve would die, one of them Clement's own brother, Gaillard de Goth. As for the Pope's ruby, nothing was ever heard of it again.

The omen was plain, for all to read.

※ ※ ※

Accompanied by a swarm of friends and servants, Clement V made a triumphal — and expensive — progress from Lyons to Bordeaux. It cost him little, his hosts much. He established himself for a while at Bourges in the quarters of the Archbishop there, whom he disliked. The luxury of the papal suite ruined the Archbishop of Bourges most satisfactorily. To keep on living at all after this, the Archbishop reportedly had to attend all the choir services to get a share of the daily distributions.

Everywhere that Clement went, the fair Brunissende, Countess of Talleyrand-Périgord, was sure to go. No one was able to explain her away.

Now that he was Pope, however, Clement began to be more his own man. He did carry out some of Philip's conditions, but he took his time about condemning the departed Boniface; he staunchly refused to burn Boniface's bones, a punishment visited on atheists and heretics and repeatedly urged on him by Philip, whose attitude was that by dying, Boniface himself had unfairly gotten away.

Nevertheless, that secret encounter at the Abbey of Saint-Jean d'Angély cast a long shadow "over the city and over the world," for the King's sixth condition was undoubtedly this: that the Pope should give up Rome for France.

When Clement wandered to Poitiers with the idea of getting Philip off on a Crusade, he did find himself almost physically the King's prisoner. But Philip was much more interested in defaming the late and Christian Boniface and in another, secret plan — to smash the present, no less Christian Knights Templars — than in carrying the Cross against Islam.

Clement tried to escape. Disguised, his yellowish face covered, he set out from town, and might have gone free. But he was betrayed by the mule train of treasure which he could not bear to leave behind. They seized the Pope on the highway and hustled him back to Poitiers, where they guarded him more closely than ever.

Two years passed. The King saw that after all he could not keep the head of Christendom under physical restraint. Besides, so far as he could see, Clement was moving in the desired direction, however reluctantly. He had actually be-

gun to review the charges against the Templars — charges
which, earlier, he had termed "incredible" — and he had even
unleashed the Inquisition against that doomed Order.

This time Clement did not need to slink away.

He called a meeting of his Cardinals. It was their advice to
make for Avignon. The beauty and easy living of the South
was not their only reason: more important was the fact that
Avignon lay out of France, and bordered on the Comtat
Venaissin, land which had come to the Popes in 1274, as a
valuable by-product of the Crusade against the Albigensians.
The swift currents of the Rhône provided the city with an
effective moat; the Pope, anchored to the massive Rock of
the Lords, could watch France from across the river.

They remembered, too, that Avignon stood close to Italy,
and felt that this should reinforce the Papacy against France,
while still not entirely committing the Holy See to Italy's
embroilments. That their stratagems would provide a basic
life theme for a poet named Petrarch, then five years old,
did not occur to them. Nor could they hear the doomcrack
of the Great Schism of the West, nor see, a century beyond
that, the shadow of Luther towering.

And so began that fateful time mistakenly known as the
"Babylonian Captivity," when the Popes arrived in Avignon
and stayed. Mistakenly because Avignon, however dubious
its morals became, was not Babylon; for that matter, neither
was Rome a font of purity — Avignon's corruption was
better publicized, that was all. And the Popes were not
prisoners there. Nobody had carried them off. Nothing
chained them, except their own desires.

Was it a part of Clement's sin, was this the reason that he
lost his ruby, that he took the Papacy away from Rome?
Christ named no definite city as the center of His Church.
Peter taught in many cities. But Rome was the capital of the

Empire, and the congregation of Rome naturally stood out. In 381 the Bishop of Rome had taken the title "Pope," and the fifth century Emperor Valentinian III had recognized the Roman See as first.

By now, however, it was France, not Italy, that the West was spinning around. So why not Avignon?

Against this view are spokesmen stretching through Thomas Aquinas to Pius XII, who maintain it is Christ's will that the Church's head should be in Rome.

Remember that many in those days regarded the Pope as modern Europeans do an important bureaucrat whose functions are essential to their projects. Whether he was personally successful or not; whether they revered him or not, liked him or not — he was the Pope; he had the forms, the rubber stamps, the permits; they needed him in their daily affairs, and they had to get past him to Heaven.

To others, like Catherine of Siena, he was, as she often declared, Christ on earth. "We are no mere mortal man," said Innocent IV; "we have the place of God on earth." And Petrarch writes of one going to Rome "to contemplate the image of Him whom he hopes later on to behold, out yonder in the sky."

To everyone, he loomed very large.

· KILL THEM ALL

LEMENT got to Avignon on a day in March, 1309. He looked dispiritedly at what awaited him. Behind their Magistrates, boatmen and fishermen, clothmakers and tanners, crowded to stare. He saw cramped and muddy lanes, interweaving for chance, forgotten reasons, some bordered by ditches of viscous water, clogged with slow-moving garbage. At the town's edge he had passed hovels with thatched roofs. Here the houses were mostly narrow stone ones, and the rest of pounded and shaped earth, called *pisé*. Hardly a building with a second story to it, except for the non-descript, fortified palace of the Bishop, and the huddled Cathedral of Our Lady of the Lords. Nothing that foreshadowed the great churches and mansions, the lovely châteaux and private houses and gardens of Europe's future capital.

Already sick, Clement was nauseated by local smells, which the inhabitants could endure only because the wind would so often blow the town clean. He murmured the proverb: *Avenio ventosa, cum vento fastidiosa, sine vento venenosa.* Windy Avignon, with the wind loathsome, without the wind poisonous. Well, the poisonous part was true, at any rate.

It was cold and the city had no walls. They had been torn down a century before, following a siege by the French. Clement knew vaguely that besides the walls, which were double, with a moat of running water before each one, some three hundred fortress-mansions had also come dustily down. This helped to account for the general dreariness. Those houses of the nobility had been as much fort as home, with towers and battlements and connecting galleries. Well, Avignon had sinned, taking in the Albigensians like that — no wonder Louis the Lion had punished them for it. First of all Louis had laid siege to the place for three months. Then he and the Papal Legate got in by promising the Avignonese a full amnesty, and once inside, he brought the city down. One wondered, Clement mused, at the power of the broken word over the sword.

Clement could look that far back in time, to the Albigensians. Other things about this town he could not know. Deep and silent in the earth under his palfrey's hooves was a woman's head, and by it a carved inscription telling who she had been: a woman like another to begin with, but at death made into a Queen of Heaven. Her brother, who was also her husband and the Emperor of Rome, had ordained that his people should worship her in the same way they did Venus. A senator of his, Livius Geminius, saw her mounting up into the sky, and received one million sesterces — a sesterce being a brass coin equal to four asses — for having the vision. Born about the same time as Jesus Christ, she had a gold statue in the Forum, this statue here at Avignon and many others throughout Italy and the Provinces besides. Her name was Drusilla. Her brother's, Caligula.

The shovels would not bring her to light for many hundreds of years.

※ ※ ※

People had sheltered on this big Rock here before written time began. The Rhône had hugged closely around it, like a moat. Once it had belonged to a Gallic people called Cavares. Its name meant "City of the River" or "City of the Rushing Wind," and they spoke it variously in the old time: Aouennion — Avenion — Avennio. Celtish or Ligurian, this would have been antedating the Romans.

They had liked this place, the Romans, because it was strong, available by easy stages from Italy, on one river and only about three miles from another, the Durance. In their day it spread down from the Rock, and its towers, walls and citadel could be seen from far away. Strabo, living under Augustus and Tiberius, had called it one of the region's main cities. Long after him, when the Avignonese dug down to build themselves a theater, they came to the foundations of a vast edifice, some basilica or temple, and other vestiges of opulence. Awed, perhaps, the mayor of the day hurriedly filled it all in again without so much as making a sketch. In the third century a Bishopric was founded here. In the fifth a Greek, Stephen of Byzantium, wrote of the place as a city of Marseilles.

After Roman days, Avignon shrank back almost to the Rock again. Like the classic Persian's description of the world, it was bride to a thousand grooms. It was assailed by Vandals and Goths, Burgundians, West Goths, Goths, it belonged for a while to the Frankish Kings, was attached to

Austrasia (the Rhineland), was Burgundian. At Avignon, Clovis, he who was baptized at Rheims and established the French monarchy in Gaul, laid siege to the King of the Burgundians in 500. In the sixth century the city was known for its intellectuals, and there was a Saint Domnulus from the North, who refused to be Bishop here because he was "too plain a man for all those sophisticates and philosophers."

And then there had been the Arabs. Setting their flags over Lyons, Besançon and Sens, leaving garrisons behind them, they had marched on Tours. And they were smashed somewhere on the plains of Tours in 732, destroyed not so much by the horsemen of Charles the Hammer, and his foot soldiers in wolfskins and long matted hair, as by the love of their own heaped-up loot; for they were winning when they broke from the battle to protect their spoils. On that day, like all who choose the material world instead of the other, they had seen it slip from their fingers. And — as Clement never would have believed — that was a defeat not only for them but for the victors too, and it set back the western clock by several hundred years.

The Arabs name the place between Poitiers and Tours the Pavement of Martyrs (Balátu'sh-Shuhadá) and they say that if you listen at twilight you can still hear the angels there, calling the Muslim faithful to evening prayers.

Anyhow, the Moors ruled in Septimania, the old Seventh Legion's territory between the Mouths of the Rhône and the Pyrenees. They invaded Provence, an area which shifts somewhat with time but is roughly the Rhône basin beginning with Lyons, and the land south of the Isère, down to the sea. They stood before Avignon in 735, and the citizens, Christians in the world of Charles the Hammer, willingly opened their gates, and Maurontius, Duke of Marseilles, led them inside.

These people of the Midi had never liked the alien and

barbarian Franks. Close to Spain, they were aware that the
warriors of the Prophet brought with them a kind of New
Deal, the code of Islam. For about two years, Avignon was
an Arab town, the citizens enjoying a freedom from forcible
conversion, for the Qur'án says "Let there be no compulsion
in religion" (2:257), and "Wilt thou compel men to become
believers? No soul can believe but by the permission of God."
(10:99, 100.) If, like previous Faiths, Islam was many times
spread by the sword, still it did not live by the sword.

Then down from the North pounded Charles the Hammer.
The Avignonese and their newfound allies, the Moors, waited
confidently for Charles. Their city was strong, with a high-
walled citadel on the Rock of the Lords. But the Hammer
came down with the newest machines of war. His siege
never let up; he dealt blow after blow; again and again he
returned to the attack and in the end courage was only a
shout carried off by the wind. He broke into the town.
Every Saracen died. Thousands of Christians lay in the streets
with grinning circular wounds cut into their throats by fellow Christians. The houses were violated, the women raped.
The town went up in flames, the churches went down. It
was all a far cry from the bloodless Muhammadan entry two
short years before.

For a long time after, contrary to general opinion, the
Arabs were not far away. To contain them, the Hammer
made a great wasteland out of the places they had taken and
beautified: he leveled down Béziers and Agde, burned
Nîmes, and annihilated Maguelone.

※ ※ ※

Afterward, Avignon was part of the Kingdom of Arles
and came under the rule of the Counts of Provence. In the
eleventh century there was a renaissance here, and various

old buildings were rebuilt, including Our Lady of the Lords, standing today. As for the magical twelfth century *pont d' Avignon*, it was for a time the only bridge across the Rhône between Avignon and the sea, and brought merchants and pilgrims through the city, joining Provence to Languedoc.

These people got about the world more than we give them credit for. Like procreation, no matter what else is happening, buying and selling always seems to go on. There were traders from the southern part of what is now France signing good commercial treaties with the Muslims in the early thirteenth century, having consuls to represent them, dealing with North Africa, Barcelona, the Balearic Islands, the western coast of Italy. Spices, aromatic essences, dyes and silks, wool and leather came in, and were sold at great fairs such as that of Beaucaire. Chestnuts, Provençal coral, cloth from Avignon or Montpellier, went out. African markets, disobeying the Qur'án, even proffered French wines. The shipowners of Provence sailed under their own flag. They had counting houses in Syria, and in Acre — described by a contemporary as "the resort of all people from all countries, and of the eastern nations of every different tongue; so that it might be considered as the aliment of the world" — there was at the beginning of the thirteenth century a street called "The Street of the Men of Provence." Here natives of Marseilles and no doubt of related towns like Avignon abounded.

Toward the close of the twelfth century the city became a republic. It had the right to coin money, elect magistrates, raise an army, make treaties of alliance and commerce. But now it showed its independent spirit in matters of religion once again: this time it welcomed in the Albigensians.

If, behind Clement's pale, somewhat yellowed forehead, the rest of Avignon's past was fuzzy, here he was on home ground. He knew that the Albigensians had been expunged by the Church. That much he was sure of; as to who they had been and where they had come from, he was too busy with his own troubles to care.

Actually Mani, the Albigensians' progenitor, was a Persian, a long way off in space and time. In his own country ten centuries before, King Bahram had carefully listened to him and his dualism, hearing him out. Mani said that this material universe, resulting from the admixture of the Light with the Darkness, was essentially evil; that the Light must be released from the Darkness and go back to its Paradise; that for this reason marriage and the begetting of children was sin, since it further entangled the Light and mired it down with the Darkness. At which King Bahram pronounced his considered view: "This man has come forward and is calling upon people to destroy the world."

Accordingly Mani was flayed all night in preparation for real torture the next day, but he cheated his executioners by dying at dawn.

Four religions were against Mani, three did their best to get rid of him, two created an inquisition for the purpose. The second of these was *the* inquisition, established by Pope Gregory IX to root this people out. The Church fell upon them with fire and sword, and in seven hundred years the South of France has not recovered from the blow.

Manicheism, which owed the good in it to the Holy Writ of Zoroaster and Christ, appeared in many forms: it was spread in Spain by Priscillian, Bishop of Avila, duly beheaded in 384. It influenced the fourth century Paternians who said the Devil, not God, made the inferior or lower parts of the body and reasoned from this that sensual pleasures were no sin. In Italy it showed itself in secret societies called Patarini, described as Manichean immigrants from Bulgaria, who settled in Milan's Pataria quarter. In Germany its adherents were known as Bulgars which the chronicles variously give as Bolgre or Bougre — whence the English bugger, buggery having been attributed to the Bulgarian heretics. (The Albigensians, often confused with these, and all being, in the popular belief, against marriage and having children, were naturally charged with the same unnatural procedures.)

It was through the Arabs of Spain that these doctrines came up to flourish around Albi, and Mani's Southern French followers were particularly suspect because they, or at least the Cathari or Perfecti among them — the higher ranks — were set against wealth and worldliness. To desire the material was sin; to pursue possessions, vile; all nonspiritual aspects of life, evil. The Albigensians were thus early "protestants" against the luxury of the clergy. They seem to have opposed the Church, the hierarchy, the ritual, and not surprisingly, the idea of Mary as the Mother of God. It is reported that Saint Dominic had them write down their doctrines in a book, while he wrote the true Catholic ones in another; the two books were then thrown into a bonfire, and the Albigensian book burned. Saint Dominic's not only did not burn, but jumped out of the flames, yo-yo like, as often as it was cast in.

Their big protector was the cheerful Raymond VI, Count of Toulouse, who had three wives and apparently no fanaticism, since he was charged by the Pope of the day with giving emoluments to the Jews, as well as with sheltering heretics. He was Avignon's feudal lord, but it was not until after the Fourth Lateran Council of 1215 that the Republic of Avignon took his side. This was the Twelfth Ecumenical Council, called the greatest of the Middle Ages, and it relieved Raymond VI of a substantial part of his domains. The Count passed through Avignon on his way back from Rome, and as the people poured out of their houses to welcome him and his

son, they shouted "God with us!" and "Toulouse!" And they
sang a song against the Pope's crusaders, vowing to stand or
fall with their liege:

Lord both by law and by love, whatever betide,
Give out with free hands!
For you with our goods, with our bodies, each one of us stands,
Till either you get back your lands,
Or we die at your side.

But the might of the North and the Church prevailed.
When half a million men took arms against him, Raymond
was forced to submit. Naked to the middle, a rope around
his neck, he was whipped at the altar.

This ignominy might have been enough to satisfy the Pope.
The army, however, felt otherwise. It was a strange, ecclesiastical army, its officers French and Roman prelates, its
generals Bishops, and with an Archdeacon for an engineer.
It wanted blood; spoils and blood. Man has made the sun look
down on hideous things since life began, but the historian
says of these horrors that the orb of day had never seen
their like. Trampling on the dead at the taking of Béziers, a
soldier asked the Abbot Arnold how he could tell Catholics
from heretics, and spare the good. And the Pope's Legate
cried, "Kill them all! God will know His own!"

※ ※ ※

That is how Avignon came to be seized by Louis the Lion,
as part of the Pope's Albigensian crusade, and Louis dis-
mantled it and pulled its towers down. Wall-less, a proud
republic no more, it submitted in 1251 to the Counts of
Provence.

Some of this history, perhaps a hundred years' worth,
could have been in Clement's mind as he rode into Avignon

that day. He happened to be suzerain of the Counts of Provence, who owned the place, and he happened to choose it as his throne city. Other Popes beside him had lived out of Rome, but he was the first to make a different place his capital.

He could not, of course, know that after forty years, another Clement would buy the town from his beautiful ward, Queen Joanna, and that from then until the French Revolution, Avignon would belong to the Holy See. And he could hardly guess, as he was helped down from his palfrey, that he was heading for Martin Luther, and ninety-five theses nailed to a door.

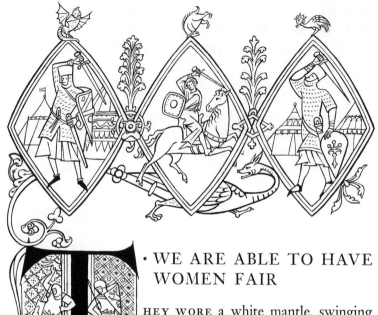

·WE ARE ABLE TO HAVE WOMEN FAIR

HEY WORE a white mantle, swinging rich and full, and it bore a great red cross. Under it they had a close-fitting coat to the knees. A sword at the side, they galloped by on magnificent mounts. They were all nobles, and proud of it; no plebeian could come among them, except for large numbers of serving brethren, dressed in sober brown mantles and looked down on by the Knights.

These "Poor Knights of the Temple" were the greatest of the military orders and had been founded in 1118. Their symbol was a child being devoured by a serpent; it is still to be seen in the arms of Austria's royal house. Their duty had long been to protect the pilgrims going to Jerusalem. Their wealth stretched across the map, from Cyprus to Ireland, from Denmark to Spain. When the victorious Saladin drove the Christians out, at the end of the Crusades, these Knights, rich and mysterious, spread to the West. Here they met their match in Philip the Fair and Clement, his French Pope.

History has not yet declared for or against Philip. Agreeing only as to his physical beauty and his courage, the accounts do not establish whether he was luckily impulsive or a master-planner or merely blessed with those brilliant ministers who are known in France as "the lawyers" — *les légistes* — bolstering up his power through their knowledge of Roman law; his, or their, aim being absolutism for the Prince and a consolidated France.

He had robbed the Jews and expelled them; he had done as much to the Lombard bankers; to Dante's disgust, he had inflated his currency in 1302 — and was thereafter known as "the Counterfeiter." Then there had been the business with Boniface. Captured at Anagni the Pope was ridden off to prison on a nag, with his face toward the tail. Afterward, Villani says, "the heart of Boniface being petrified with grief . . . he gnawed himself as one frantic, and in this state expired." This fulfilled the prophecy of his predecessor, Celestine V (the Pope who abdicated), that Boniface would enter on the Papacy like a fox, reign like a lion, and die like a dog.

(Celestine's view of the future may have been colored by emotion, since he himself was held prisoner by Boniface in the Castle of Fumone, and gradually starved to death. It seems he had expressed the wish to retire and meditate, and Boniface had helped. One day three Cardinals came in to see the captive. They found the abdicated Pope saying Mass, but what really took them aback was that he was standing on the air. Saint Peter Celestine was given to levitation.)

Meanwhile, Philip still needed money. He looked around and noticed — who could fail to? they were at the height of their power — the Knights Templars.

They were great bankers then. Their Paris Temple was the world's Bourse. Popes and Kings banked with them; having strongholds everywhere, they made possible the exchange of money with the East. And they were known as both strong and honest. To take interest was of course unlawful, being usury, but they apparently got around this with a fourteenth century prototype of modern under-the-table methods. Ostensibly the borrower paid back only as much as he had borrowed. Actually, he paid back more, and the difference — in effect, the interest — was not recorded.

Philip was good to them at first. He extended their many privileges and liked them enough to borrow 5200 pounds of Tours from them. As late as 1307 he was present at the reception of a new Templar.

The Poor Knights of the Temple were admittedly rich. This fact had somehow to be distorted into meaning that they were guilty of unmentionable crimes in an age when everything was mentionable. They were foredoomed; Philip, aside from funds, wanted the three military Orders reduced to one, the Knights of Jerusalem, to be headed by a French Prince of the blood, to match the French Pope. Suddenly the Templars were heretics, apostates, immoral. A "leak" was arranged; their secrets, long rumored, were supposedly divulged. All France was then under the Inquisition, and the Grand Inquisitor, William of Paris, was Philip's confessor. But Clement put things off.

Even the Abbé André, far from their partisan, is willing to say that the 15,000 Knights of the Order could not *all* have been perverts. He loyally cries, however, "Without the shadow of a doubt, it would be mad to try and justify the Order in the face of these crushing depositions made by more than four hundred Templars, duly registered by public notaries, depositions obtained by the benevolent, gentle and

moderate investigations of the Pontifical commissioners."
And he adds, "Let everyone cease, then, from calling that
sodomist, Jacques de Molay, a martyr."

The Templars themselves said, "We are able to have
women fair and beautifully-adorned, nor do we fail in this,
for we are rich and powerful; why then should we go against
the bent of nature?"

Jacques de Molay, their last Grand Master, was summoned
from Cyprus by the Pope. On October 13, 1307, at dawn,
all the Templars in France were simultaneously arrested.
Jacques was taken along with sixty Knights, and they were
tortured, first by the royal officers and then over again by the
Inquisitors. Thirty-six of them died in the process. Many
Templars confessed to anything: that they belonged to the
Order body and soul; that upon joining they renounced all
else, in token of which there had been the initiate's obscene
kiss (similar to the kiss given the Devil at Black Sabbaths
and still retained in schoolboy slang); that they had wor-
shipped a three-faced head.

De Molay's letter was the worst, if anyone thinks that confessions obtained under torture are of value: he wrote, in
tears, a letter addressed to all the Templars in France, stating
that he had denied Jesus and spat on the Cross.

In his bull of November 22, 1307, Pope Clement had already committed himself to the Templars' guilt. ". . . he,
as well as they, was on trial before Christendom," says Lea,
"and their acquittal by the council would be his conviction.
He was, therefore, no judge, but an antagonist, forced by
the instinct of self-preservation to destroy them . . . As
the council [of Vienne, the Fifteenth Ecumenical Council]
drew near his anxiety increased, and he cast around for means
to secure the testimony which should justify him by proving
the heresy of the Order."

England looks good in this affair. Clement had to write and chide King Edward for having prohibited torture as contrary to the law of the land. In 1309 the Pope's Inquisitors examined the Templars in the Bishop of London's palace, but no one was able to find them guilty; the Inquisitors were baffled; without brutalities they could not make the confessions come right. The Pope now affirmed that no law could override the Canons, and after some threats he offered Edward remission of his sins if he would stop being obstinate about torture. More than once thereafter, Edward sent out orders to Bishops and Inquisitors to "employ ecclesiastical law"; in later orders the word "torture" was used, the King explaining that he was acting out of reverence for the Holy See. The English, however, muddled along; their Templars were not convicted. They were parceled out among various monasteries and a daily provision was allotted them. They have left their place names behind them: London's Inner Temple and Middle Temple, among others.

An example shows how the torture system worked. There were in Florence thirteen Templars who had been duly investigated by the Inquisition in 1310, and some of them had confessed. Under renewed urging by Clement, these were reassembled in 1311 and put through the procedure again. Six yielded satisfactory testimony, confessing to the adoration of idols, cats, and all the rest. Seven, however, stubbornly maintained that the Order was innocent. The Inquisitors sent the Pope only the six confessions; they reported that the other seven Knights had been duly retortured but had produced nothing worth reporting.

Without dwelling on the dark old scenes, we remember this, from Templars who had been subjected to Philip's men: "Brother Bernard du Gué declared that he had been so tortured and exposed to the fire that the flesh of his heels was charred to powder, and that, a few days later, the heel bones fell out . . . At the same time he took out of his pocket two of these bones. Brother Robert Vigier stated that the torments to which they had been subjected were so intolerable that three of his companions in captivity died of them . . . Brother Jean de Cormèle exhibited four teeth that had been torn out of his mouth in the course of horrible torment . . . Brother Gérard du Passage, trembling with dread that it all would begin again, told the Commissioners that the royal bailiff of Mâcon had tortured him by having weights tied to his genital organs . . ."

In his bull *Vox in excelso* (March 22, 1312) Clement "admitted that the evidence did not canonically justify the definitive condemnation of the Order," but said it had now "been so scandalized that no honorable man could enter it hereafter . . ."

The Council of Vienne (1311–1313) did not pass judgment on the accusations against the Templars. Nevertheless their Order was abolished (1312), and Clement's bull *Ad providam* transferred much of their property to their rivals, the Knights Hospitallers of Saint John of Jerusalem, it was thought for an enormous douceur.

Dante was one of those who believed the Templars. The *Purgatorio* (20: 92) says of Philip:

> Lo! the new Pilate, of whose cruelty
> Such violence cannot fill the measure up
> With no decree to sanction, pushes on
> Into the Temple . . . .

They were not convicted in England, as we saw, or in Cyprus, and were acquitted in Germany, Bologna, Aragon, Majorca, Castile and Portugal. Only in France had there been general confessions of guilt.

What is the true story of the Templars? The acts of the Council of Vienne have reportedly vanished from the papal archives, stolen — who knows? — by Clement's nephew, Bertrand de Goth. Or they could have been lost later during the Great Schism when Benedict XIII carried off some of the archives to Peñiscola, or in transporting the Curia from Avignon back to Rome. In 1810 Napoleon had the papal archives brought to Paris, where they were kept five years. At that time there were 3239 boxes full of them and the papal archivists maintained that many were never returned, while the French answered that they had returned them all to the Pope's agents, but these had sold great quantities of the records to grocers, presumably for wrapping up vegetables.

It will probably be shown, some day, that the Knights' real crime was their sympathy for the Muslims and Islam. Among many accusations leveled against them, a key might be found in these words: *"frequenter conversabuntur cum Saracenis."*

The Satan pact was invoked as usual: the Pope purportedly believed that the Devil was back of them — Islam was equated with the Devil — and because they spread Islamic doctrine in the West they brought on their own ruin. Europe at the close of the Crusades was disillusioned: in what had been considered a trial by battle, the winner to be surely right, Christendom had lost to the Muhammadans. And now, riding through Europe, were these haughty and indeed superior Lords, who knew the East, and who reported in secret that Muhammad was a true Prophet and Saladin no brute, but a verray, parfit gentil knight. All this was unforgivable, particularly in an Order that was so rich.

Thus it came about that many an evening in Paris was sweetened, for some, with the smoke from one hundred and thirteen Templars, being slowly burned, one after another, out at the Porte St.-Antoine. As for de Molay, he asserted, to his last moment, the Order's innocence and his own: "Before Heaven and earth, on the verge of death, when the least falsehood bears like an intolerable burden on the soul."

In 1314 his stake and a fellow prisoner's were put up on an island in the Seine. It was early evening and the vesper bells were ringing and King Philip was looking on. The fires were set, and rose. Then out of the crackling flames the voices came, swearing to innocence; and there were those who said that de Molay cried out at the last: "Clement! Thou wicked and false judge, I summon thee to meet me within forty days at the bar of God!"

There were many portents then, in the sky and on the earth; eclipses of the sun and moon, parahelia, paraselenae, fires darting up out of the ground, thunder in blue sky. A mare dropped a foal with nine feet; flocks of unknown birds came down. A little longer, and both Clement and Philip would pass from the scene.

· THE SAVING OF
BONIFACE'S FACE

HAD the deceased Boniface actually been brought to trial, as Philip planned, he having chosen Clement to pull this ecclesiastical chestnut out of the fire, it would not have been the first such case in Church history: Pope Stephen VII had disinterred the ninth century Formosus, clothed the body in papal robes, sat it in a chair, had it tried before a Council, and pronounced judgment: three of its fingers were chopped off and it was dumped into the Tiber.

Like many who do not argue from strength, Clement, in his fight to save the memory of Boniface VIII, nevertheless had a trusty weapon: delay. He set Boniface's trial in motion, but his Cardinals, hurrying to the dead Pontiff's rescue, brought in troops from England and Germany and helpfully threatened to have Clement carried off to Rome unless he stopped. "You see what I am going through" was the burden of the Pope's complaints to the French Ambassadors.

The delays engineered by Clement made it possible for the resentment of the Christian world to mobilize. Philip sensed the cold air of protest; too late, he saw that in this Clement had outmaneuvered him and had patiently built up the papal power while seeming to do the will of the King.

Surer now of his position, Clement declared Boniface innocent on all counts. He also absolved Philip of any complicity in the actions of his subordinates, de Nogaret and the Colonnas. Financially, Philip did not escape. He had to pay 100,000 florins (a gold florin was about the equivalent of a sheep) as costs of the proceedings. Thus Clement rescued Boniface, failed to observe the King's guilt, and blandly made Philip foot the bill.

※ ※ ※

The fourteenth century was a sort of vast Los Angeles of cults. Ideas, too many to list, would disappear and reappear under other names: a continuous erosion and transformation of belief, much of it owing to the impact of Islam. Besides, secularization and indifference became the offspring of disunity, as a philosopher of Elizabeth's day was going to remark: ". . . nothing doth so much keep men out of the Church, and drive men out of the Church, as breach of unity." Many minds escaped gratefully into the Classics.

Typical of sectarians confronting Clement was a society of religious laymen, the "Brothers of Penitence of the Third Order." These were derisively nicknamed Beghards, or if women, Beguines, after their founder Lambert le Bègue — the Stammerer, a twelfth century priest of Liège. They were sometimes loosely called, along with other groups, Fraticelli

(Little Brothers). Some of these announced the reign on earth of the Spirit — which should, in view of the times, have caused them to be charged with ungovernable optimism, rather than heresy. The Beghards had advanced the doctrine that a man could in this world reach such a state of perfection as to render him free from sin, and achieve grace in such great measure that more could not be had even in Heaven.

One of the writing Beguines carried this a step further, promulgating a theory which became widely diffused and offered many interesting applications: she maintained that a soul overwhelmed with the love of its Creator could and should accord to nature without remorse all that nature might demand. (The later Adamites of Paris were not the only ones to practice this literally; these wandered naked through the streets, perpetrating turpitude. In 1373 Charles V discovered a way to quiet them down. He burned them alive.)

Looking backward across the century, a French cleric deplores what he sees: in Germany, the Bishop of Halberstadt preaching "the Turkish dogma of predestination." The German barons were all for it, he reports. And Holland and Hungary were "infested with Beghards teaching Oriental gnosis," while Bosnia and Bulgaria and the Danubian provinces — let alone Southern France — teemed with Manicheans.

There were also such phenomena as the Waldensians or Poor Men of Lyons, followers of a kind of early-day Tolstoy, Peter Waldo, a living affront to the rich Church. Innocent III, the same Pope who annulled the Magna Charta, had unleashed a horrible crusade against them, before Clement's time. There were the Apostolics simplifying Christianity down to the single principle of charity, and the Flagellants whipped away at themselves and drew blood then, as they still do today in New Mexico (apparently having gotten no better).

And there was a friar called Dolcino, living up in the mountains beyond Novara with 3000 disciples, teaching the community of property and of wives, and denouncing Clement. The Pope's Legate and the people of Novara finally destroyed him. In the popular mind he was thought of as Islamic. Dante, who like some modern scholars regarded Muhammad as a heretic, and whose treatment of the Prophet symbolizes Christendom's terror of Muslim might, has Muhammad send a message to Dolcino; with Dante's usual prophetic hindsight, the message warns Dolcino to lay up a store of food and beware of Novara.

Thousands upon thousands of such sectarians were delivered up to the Inquisition. The property involved normally found its way into the papal treasury.

※ ※ ※

It was no use denying it, Clement was not well. He dragged his mysterious sickness here and there, growing more and more somber and unquiet. He favored solitude now, and desert places. He did not trust his Cardinals and held few Consistories. He could not rest. He finally left Avignon and set out for Carpentras, which the Church had owned for many years and which he had recently provided with good water. But he could not stop. He thought that perhaps the place of his birth and the focus of his childhood memories would help, and he had them carry him westward toward Bordeaux. On April 20, 1314, in the village of Roquemaure, a few leagues out of Carpentras on the high road, he died.

Twenty-three Cardinals then came together at the Episcopal Palace in Carpentras. Instead of electing a new Pope, however, they started a wild dispute on the Rome vs. Avignon

question. As they wrangled, their palace was attacked by a
shrieking, sword-waving mob, at its head Bertrand de Goth.
This Bertrand, "a Baron treacherous, brutal, sneering, indif-
ferent, a sharp lawyer, a tricky clerk," was the nephew of the
late Clement.

First to be cut down this day were the Italian merchants
who had spread out their wares near the place of the Conclave. After them the servants went, and then the Cardinals'
familiars. The town blew up in flames. Clement's guards vanished and his body lay unheeding on its bier. Looters ran in
and pulled away what they could take: rings from the stiff
fingers, the rich outer robes; only a thin tunic was left on the
naked form. The thieves fled too as the corpse went up in
smoke and crackling fire.

Hemmed in by Bertrand's soldiers, the terrified Cardinals
burst out of the palace — now falling to a heap of rubble —
through a small opening hastily made at the back, and the
Italian ones betook themselves to Valence.

Trying to recover here they received a letter from Dante,
urging them to get the Holy See back to Rome. They even
wrote in desperation to Philip the Fair: Clement had deceived
them, they said. "Under his Pontificate, Rome crumbled to
ruin . . . all Italy is filled with trouble and sedition; all benefices, all Bishoprics, are sold there for money. The late Pope
treated us with contempt, us Italians who had raised him to
the Papacy . . . God took pity on us; because Pope Clement wanted to reduce the Church to a corner of Gascony . . ."

They as much as threatened Philip against having a successor who would be like Clement. "It was never our intention
to transfer the Holy See from Rome, nor to desert the sanctuaries of the Holy Apostles. We wish for a Pope whose life
would be saintly and edifying, and who, having the necessary

qualities, would be attached to your realm and your person; who would correct abuses, banish the simony which has flourished up to now, and not enrich his relatives with the spoils of the Church, as did the late Pope."

But Philip also had a mysterious disease, one that could not be located in any part of his body. In the prime of life, and even without a fever, to the stupefaction of his doctors — but not of those who remembered de Molay's curse on him and Clement — he died. Others maintain that Philip died when his horse was thrown to the ground by a wild boar, which jibes with Dante's description of the King as one "who by the tusk will perish." Either way, the Templars could now rest in peace.

A son of Philip's ascended the throne of France, but — was it still de Molay's malediction? — in eighteen months Louis the Quarrelsome was also struck down, when his heir was still in the womb. And the baby died soon after birth.

As to the Papacy, for two years there was no Pope at all.

· KINGS HAVE LOVED ME

BESIDES the public worlds, there were the private ones, for the proverb says: Every head is a world. We can take up and handle one of the best of fourteenth century heads, Petrarch's, and look out at the day as he saw it. Poet, lover, ecclesiastic, scholar, and diplomat, he began life as a fop.

"Do you remember," he wrote his brother Gherardo in later years, "all the care we took about the style of our clothes, and how clean we kept them! What precautions, so that passersby would get no spot on them, nor disarrange the graceful drape we gave them. What fears we had, that the wind would ruffle up our hair and undo the set of it! What shall I say of our shoes which tore our feet instead of covering them!"

Every night, Petrarch and his brother would spend a long session before the looking glass — which had two wings enabling a person to see the back of his head — curling their hair, putting it up in a bandage against the morning, wrapping it so tightly that forehead and temples would show the red marks. Their clothes, fresh and perfumed, were changed twice a day.

Together the young men walked through Avignon, shielding their well-groomed heads from the Mistral, keeping their pointed toes out of the dirt, protecting the hang of their garments, trying all the while to avoid being trampled by horses, crushed by heavy-wheeled vehicles, knocked into by overburdened donkeys, pushed about by passersby, tugged at by hawkers, sideshow freaks and beggars, thrown by holes and unevenness underfoot. Besides pigs, they further risked encounters with packs of dogs, not the aristocratic hunting dogs and lapdogs of the Papal Court, but belligerent outcasts and scavengers. All this traffic crowding, straining and bumping together and in season generously spattered with mud.

Petrarch was the handsome one, with a quick and active body, a searching look and keen sight. His face was brown, his cheeks blooming, his eyes on fire.

Looking back at his family group, we can make out the mother hardly at all, although Petrarch writes of her that she was "the best of all mothers he ever had seen." Some say her name was Eletta, and that he composed his first verses at her death, to promise her that "together we shall live forever, together we shall be remembered." She seems to have died soon after the father, Petracco, when Petrarch was about twenty-two. There was, too, a shadowy sister, who is never spoken of, apparently for a tragic reason, as we shall see.

Why Petrarch altered his family name, when his brother Gherardo kept it, is not known. Certainly Petracco was a man of some distinction: once sent on public missions for the Florentine Republic, he was a friend of Dante, exiled out of Florence like him, then obliged through poverty to abandon his studies, which had included Cicero.

We know of Petrarch's father that once, at least, he took his boys on an outing to Vaucluse, the Closed Valley which later became the center of Petrarch's life. But he remains in memory mostly because of a lifesaving anecdote: when past fifty, he picked up a mirror and discovered a single gray hair — whereupon he filled his house and the neighborhood with lamentation. Petrarch comments on this that his own hair began turning before he was twenty-five.

⚜ ⚜ ⚜

All geniuses are displaced persons, and this must be allowed for when we look at an age through their eyes. Petrarch remained, by bias, an anti-French Italian all his life — perhaps because Italy was not there. He was born already banished. He came into the world at Arezzo, near dawn, between July 19 and 20, 1304, his family then being in horrifying circumstances for which a French Prince, Charles de Valois, was directly to blame. For Petracco, Petrarch's father, was one of six hundred persons who had been put out of Florence, their home city, by the Black Guelphs, the Pope's party, led by the victorious Charles.

A fellow exile of Petracco's was Dante Alighieri. Thus ruined, both Dante and Petracco — White Guelphs who had sided with the Emperor against the Pope — were condemned to be burned alive.

Petrarch's first words were Tuscan, because his family had a little property at Incisa not far from Florence, and here his mother remained with her babies, Petracco visiting her in secret. The family stayed on here about seven years.

By this time, Petracco despaired of seeing Florence again. He made a detour to Pisa, where the boy Petrarch spent his eighth year. After that Petracco managed to transport his household away to the Provençal town of Carpentras. They came a long journey, from Arezzo to Genoa, and from there to Marseilles, and from there northward to Avignon. Here, trying to rebuild his life, the exiled onetime lawyer stayed on in the crowded papal metropolis, while his family lived quietly in nearby Carpentras, then capital of the Comtat Venaissin. Afterward Petrarch was to go back longingly in his mind to those four years.

"Do you remember the days? That peace in the house, that freedom without; the hush in the fields, the utter quiet. Thank God for giving me a space of tranquil time, so that out of the whirlwind of events I could, at least to the extent that my frailty of mind would let me, suck in the sweet milk of childhood's learning, and develop strength for more solid substance later on."

As a child in Carpentras, he began his study of the trivium — grammar, logic, and rhetoric. Later at his father's insistence he went on to learn the law at Montpellier and after that at Bologna. He and Gherardo, a year younger, were both at the University of Bologna in 1320 when they were saved from their hated studies by Petracco's death. Repeatedly, death was to release Petrarch from one burden after another.

Freed from the law, he returned to Avignon and began his ecclesiastical career. In other words, his presence and abilities and good looks brought him to the attention of the powerful Colonnas, Princes of the Church, who at Avignon received as a matter of course all the Pope's prominent visitors, that is, all the great of their day. From then on, for the rest of his life, Petrarch was wooed by the leaders of that century.

He tells us quite simply: "The greatest Kings of this age have loved and courted me. They may know why; I certainly do not." He adds that they always seemed to be his guests rather than he theirs.

Summing up this early part of his life, he wrote, "On the windy banks of the river Rhône I spent my boyhood, guided by my parents, and then, guided by my own fancies, the whole of my youth."

※ ※ ※

· WAS JESUS POOR?

T WAS 1316 and the Holy See was still
vacant. Pope Clement V was ashes
and Philip the Fair had died too soon
after him to choose another Pontiff.
The Cardinals now had to be lured into a Conclave, but after
escaping with their lives from the riots at Carpentras, they
were reluctant to be locked up again. Philip's son, another
Philip who was Count of Poitiers, finally convoked them
himself, swearing a great oath that they would be safe from
molestation and would not be jailed. Oaths and promises were
in order, for not only were the Cardinals locked up in Conclave, like a modern jury (conclave means with a key),
but worse yet, in order to hasten a vote the portions of food
served to them could be progressively diminished. It is said
that Philip managed to get them together by means of a pri-

vate understanding with each one that he would help him secure the vacant Chair.

After coaxing the Cardinals into the Convent of the Preaching Friars at Lyons, Philip shut them in, and told them they would not get out till they elected a Pope. This was perfectly correct procedure: he was only carrying out the decree *Ne Romani* inserted in the *Corpus Juris Canonici*. This directs the civil authority, where the Conclave meets, to use force against such Cardinals as show reluctance to enter the Conclave. The lay authority, whoever he be, not only should but must exercise such coercion.

The Count's brother, King Louis the Quarrelsome, then died, and with the Cardinals safely locked up, the Count hurried north to Paris where he became Regent. Then Louis's baby was born and died, all in a few days, and the Regent ascended the throne of France as Philip V the Long. Meanwhile this Philip tired of being understanding with the Cardinals. He informed them that they were his prisoners and would continue as such until they produced a new Pope. It still took them forty days of fasting, under armed guard, before they elected Jacques d'Euse.

They say the new Pope was the son of an itinerant shoemaker, although others deny this and place his birth higher. Whatever the status of John XXII, there was no uncertainty about the man.

He was old, seventy-two, when he succeeded Clement V on the papal throne, which he has been accused of taking by storm after nominating himself. He had learned the law at Montpellier, added medicine at the University of Paris, taught later on at Cahors and Toulouse. Here he made friends with the Bishop, who was also son of the King of Naples, and this connection led to the vacant Episcopal See in Fréjus, a pleasant post on the French Riviera. From there he became a counselor to Robert the Wise, and from Naples news of his ability reached Avignon. Clement V summoned him to advise on the case of Boniface VIII and that of the Knights Templars, made him a Cardinal and transferred him to the Episcopal See of Avignon. He was less than five feet tall, of deceptively frail build and excellent health.

John was going to need that health. At seventy-two he would find himself the chosen victim of a murder plot hatched by his Cardinals — the Italians, that is — who wanted a Pope that would take them back to Rome. He would during his reign start a fortress-palace at Avignon, refill to bursting the Church's coffers that had been gutted by Bertrand de Goth, deal with his enemy Louis of Bavaria (the Emperor), face the heresy charges of William of Ockham, subdue an antipope in Rome. He would fight the whole band of Spirituals who stood for poverty while he stood for wealth. He would radically change Catholic dogma. He would amass a mountain of gold. All this lay before him at an age when many fold their hands and sit waiting to be dead, as they look backward over the dead past.

※ ※ ※

King Philip asked John to delay his coronation, wishing to attend in person; John waited a month, then went ahead with the ceremony anyhow, being crowned at Lyons the first week in September. He had faithfully promised Cardinal Napoleone Orsini of the Italian party that he would take the Holy See back to Rome. The story is that he swore on the consecrated Host that, except to carry out this promise, he would never again mount horse or mule.

Now, in order not to break his word, he traveled from Lyons to Avignon by boat. On October 1, 1316, barges bedecked with flaming banners passed rapidly down the Rhône.

Under a turquoise sky, the neighboring populations crowded the riverbanks to see the new Pope sail along. John XXII was deep in conversation with his nephew, Jacques de Via, and Cardinal Orsini.

"My brother!" said he to the Cardinal, "see how beautiful is the sky of France! And you want me to leave my own country forever, and go and die in that ruined city you call Rome! . . . Oh, no! My brother, the God who gave Peter the power to bind and loose is everywhere. I am determined to remain at Avignon. For me your Italy, smiling to you, would be nothing but a land of exile."

"But," replied the Cardinal, "Rome should be the capital of the Christian world. If you wish to prove faithful to your promise, you will live in no other palace than the Vatican."

"I know very well what the glory of God and of Christianity requires of me," answered John. "The Cardinal forgets that he is Italian and I French. The votes of the Conclave have put the Pontifical crown on my head. I am now the Vicar of Jesus Christ on earth, and from you I expect complete obedience."

The astonished Italian, bowing low, withdrew to a group of Cardinals from his own country.

"My dear nephew and son in Jesus Christ," continued John to Jacques de Via, "it is not without reason that I dread the burden imposed on my weakness by the Conclave of Lyons. I am resolved never to move the Holy See to Rome, and the Italian faction will never leave off raising up enemies against me."

"God will not abandon the successor of Peter," said his nephew.

"May it be so," answered John.

Then he walked to the end of the barge and sat down alone. While the river hurried them along, Orsini whispered his despair to the Italian Cardinals. They had chosen a Pope who loved France. They would never see Rome again.

※ ※ ※

As the boats came in sight of the Rock of the Lords, shouts of welcome rose from the river side. The Avignonese, who feared they had lost the Papacy, now jubilantly watched it floating back again. Had they known that their former Bishop already planned to build a papal palace here, their cries could hardly have been louder.

Once on land, John should have mounted a white mare, in contrast to the Cardinals on their black palfreys, for the ceremony of the *cavalcata*. Instead he proceeded on foot through the flower-strewn streets to the Episcopal Palace, his lawyer's mind insisting on strict observance of the letter of his vow. It is reported that during the eighteen years he ruled, he never once mounted mule or horse.

To show that he had come to stay, John laid out the foundations for the Fortress-Palace of the Popes, and built himself a summer palace at Sorgues, below the Fountain of Vaucluse. He also appointed ten new Cardinals, nine of them French, three of them his nephews. From Avignon, Paris and Naples, French influence streamed out.

The Pope further took time to admonish Philip the Long about his behavior: "Very dear Son," he wrote the King of France, "we learn with pain that when you attend Divine Service, you speak now to this one, now to that, and you think on these occasions of matters which distract the attention you ought to be paying to the prayers which are being sent Godward for you and your people. You should, too, since your coronation, present a more decorous appearance . . ."

Not long after John arrived in Avignon an attempt was made to introduce something lethal into his food. No doubt the jeweled "serpent tongues" which he collected were responsible for his escape. The Pope set great store by these poison detectors, which were objects of precious metal lavishly studded with emeralds, rubies and pearls. The King of France once sent him eleven of these remarkable tongues. Unfortunately we are not told exactly what happened when the poison came within their range; whether they would dart out, hiss, change color, or light up, is not reported.

From then on, John distrusted brews. Small wonder that he came out against the alchemists. "Those wretched alchemists," he wrote, excommunicating them. "Always promising riches that they never demonstrate. Have they themselves discovered a fortune in their ovens?"

The conspirators next tried magic. A letter from John describes the situation: "The magicians . . . have prepared brews to poison us and some of the Cardinals, our brothers, and not having managed to induce us to take them, they made images of wax under our names to attack our lives by piercing them. But God has preserved us and caused three of the images to fall into our hands."

That magic was fearsome is shown by the police dossier on Bernard Délicieux, arrested in Avignon in 1317. Bernard had, the file said, "possessed, read in all its parts, and learned the contents of a book of witchcraft, which he had annotated on the margins and divided according to subjects. This book contains certain characters, many names of demons, the manner of summoning them and offering sacrifices to them, the means of causing to collapse, through them and their mediation, houses and fortresses, to sink ships in the sea, to win the confidence, credit and affection of the great and others, to enjoy the charms of women; to bring on blindness,

the breaking of limbs, other infirmities and even death itself
to persons absent or present, by means of certain images and
certain superstitious acts, and to engender many another
calamity more or less horrible."

Some of the tiny wax figures were fashioned to look like
John. The plotters drew circles around them, passed them
through rings, placed them in front of mirrors, and then
pierced them through. Getting them ready was complicated
enough: an effigy of the victim would be modeled in clay or
virgin wax, after which a swallow was killed. Its heart and
liver were torn out and placed respectively under the effigy's
right and left arm. The figure was then jabbed with sharp
needles, to the accompaniment of appropriate expressions of
distaste. Sometimes the image was made of graveyard earth
mixed with bones. A magical inscription completed the spell
and helped to hasten the desired result.

John, spare and frugal, escaped the brews; it was nephew
Jacques de Via who fell dead at the Pontiff's feet. Lacking
modern crime-detection methods, there still had to be a cul-
prit, and Hugues Géraud, Bishop of Cahors, was selected, although others may have been likelier. Hugues was at first
only imprisoned for life, but was later "turned over to the
secular arm," a polite way of saying that he was subjected to
unspeakable tortures. He was skinned alive to remove his
sacerdotal and episcopal character; then he was drawn
through the streets of Avignon on a sledlike hurdle and given
over to the mob, who tore him apart with red-hot tongs;
after that his quivering fragments were thrown on a bonfire
in front of the Papal Palace.

John's Constitution *Super illius specula* (1326), which
tarred magicians with the brush of heresy, inveighs against all
such members of his flock as should enter into a Hell-pact,
fashion images, rings, mirrors, phials, and the like "to hold

the demons," and obtain information from demons for pur-
poses of their own.

※ ※ ※

The scoundrelly Bertrand de Goth, after routing the Conclave at Carpentras, had improved the hour by running off
with the enormous sums of money in Pope Clement's treasury
and also the sumptuous furnishings from his Château of Monteux — these perhaps including the table service of pure gold
which Edward of England had sent him to Lyons at his crowning.

When John XXII became Pope, he tried to discipline Bertrand. In November, 1320, he issued a summons to the
wicked Baron, but Bertrand had withdrawn with all his loot
to a remote and heavily guarded stronghold, and no one
seemed to want to deliver the summons. A second decree
was issued, then a third, *Cum Venerabiles*, describing the
Baron's guilt in all its details, listing every stolen object and
excommunicating him unless he should appear within forty
days. There was good reason for drastic action:

> Not only [wrote John] has our rebellious son carried off all
> the money-treasure, but the vessels of gold and silver, the
> books, the rich carpets, the precious stones, the ornaments,
> the titles, the privileges, the acts in the archives, the minutes
> of trials and many things more, as if he were all the heirs to-
> gether.

Bertrand meanwhile was enjoying his spoils. When the
forty days were up he set out toward Avignon, marched for a
few hours, and shouting with laughter, turned home. He
wrote the Pope he was sorry, that he wanted to come but was
not able. His agents then made certain appropriate overtures

to some of the late Clement's Cardinals, thus managing to obtain a prorogation, and this John professed to regard as a victory.

To regularize the whole matter, Clement's Cardinals succeeded in getting Bertrand to Avignon, where he appeared with a big escort, explaining that he was only a rude soldier and had acted in good faith. He confessed that the late Pope had left him 300,000 gold florins for a pious purpose; regretted the delays that had taken place; and said he would now consecrate this money to the currently proposed Crusade. The Clementine Cardinals wept, the fire and sacking of Carpentras and the rape of the Monteux treasure — amounting to 1,704,800 gold florins — were forgotten, the case boiled down to the 300,000 florins "for a pious use." It was agreed that this sum should be divided between the Holy See and Bertrand, who also swore on the Bible to equip a thousand armed men for the Crusade, and for good measure pledged his heirs as well. The Crusade never took place; the Holy See never got the 150,000 gold florins; the excommunication was lifted; and the Baron lived joyfully on.

※ ※ ※

This was perhaps the only time that John was bested in a financial transaction. Early on it had become clear that he possessed one talent to an incredible degree: he knew how to collect funds. In his hands, everything turned to gold for the papal treasury, so that history has named him the Midas of Avignon. Having that unappeasable concern for money, he put down with remarkable cruelty the excesses of religious orders whose very existence was a personal criticism. For he firmly believed that Christ and the Apostles were owners of property, and demonstrated his conviction by becoming one of the richest of Popes.

Among those who attacked him for this were the Franciscan "Spirituals." Some aspects of the problem that plagued the Spirituals seem ludicrous now. Beginning with the precept of Berengarius that neither Christ nor His Apostles owned anything, either individually or in common, the matter of ownership was fervently discussed: In the act of eating, did the friars' soup belong to them? This question was referred to the Pope, but the Franciscans, impatient for an answer, went ahead on their own and decided after long debate that, at the moment of eating, the soup was not the property of the eater. The "Carnals" disagreed with the "Spirituals" on this and were forcibly ejected from some monasteries; they left, protesting their soup was theirs. Meanwhile John pronounced as follows: "One can separate the use from the ownership, of things which are used without their substance being destroyed, such as a horse, a book or an article of furniture. But it is impossible to separate the two with reference to things which one cannot use without destroying them."

This further inflamed the Spirituals. Theologians and great Universities debated the question. In 1323 John finally made an irrevocable decision in his bull *Cum inter nonnullos:* he stated that Jesus and the Apostles not only owned what they used, but also had the money to supply their needs. "Heresy!" cried the Spirituals. And they went over to the Pope's enemy, Louis of Bavaria.

An earlier Pontiff, Nicholas III, in his bull *Exiit qui seminat* had already established the doctrine of the poverty of Christ. Anyone denying it was, this Pope said, heretical.

Small wonder that Dante called the florin "the cursed flower."

William of Ockham, the Franciscan "Prince of the Nominalists," in Avignon on charges of heresy and confined to quarters for four years, in 1328 also fled to Louis. So far as

William, champion of the secular power, was concerned, Pope John was a heretic, and neither pure nor simple.

All Europe was busy with the controversy. Outer symbols began to represent the inner clash of ideas. The Dominicans, against the Franciscans and for the Pope, painted and sculptured Jesus not in a crown of thorns and nude as did their adversaries, but wearing a King's crown, a purple toga with gold fringes, a girdle with gold tassels, and on His feet, rich buskins. The crucifixes of certain other zealots on the Pope's side showed Christ with only one hand nailed to the Cross, while the other dipped into a purse suspended from His belt, to indicate that He authorized money for necessary use.

Later John did something else: it is apparently he who added a third crown to the papal tiara. Hildebrand, who died in 1085, had worn a King's crown with the legend *Corona regni de manu Dei*. Boniface VIII added another, that said *Diadema imperii de manu Petri*. John's three crowns purportedly combined the ideas of spiritual, temporal, and ecclesiastical power. (The tiara by now is over a foot and a quarter high; of cloth-of-silver, jewel-studded, it bears three crowns and has three lappets or hanging *infulae* in the back. The Pope owes his diadem to the Persians of the olden time: tiara is *tajvar*, possessor of the crown.)

There were other questions which agitated the Franciscans. Desiring to imitate Saint Francis even to wearing exact copies of his clothes, they produced as many different and violent opinions on this subject as there were brothers. What material should their robe be made of? Should it be short or drag on the ground? Was the proper color white, black, gray or brown? What about the cord at the waist? Some held for a pointed hood, others demanded that it be round. An area of argument existed as to whether the skirt should fit closely or bell out.

Inner violence was soon reflected in acts. The Spirituals, under Bernard Délicieux, raised an army and attacked their enemies, the Dominicans. Monasteries were besieged, fields laid waste. The principle of poverty was inculcated by denuding the monks of all their possessions before driving them away.

Only the Spirituals would be saved, and Pope John was the Anti-Christ. For this viewpoint, four of the bravest were burned to death in Marseilles. These particular four were priests, Jean Barran, Guillaume Santon, and Adéodat Michel, together with a deacon, Pons Roque. Among others arrested were twenty-one who recanted, were jailed and escaped, leaving behind them this written message:

> We leave, not the Order, but the walls; we quit, not the Faith, but the husk; we come out, not from Church, but a blind synagogue; we flee, not a herdsman, but a headsman. Awesome against our oppressors, one day we will return. One day we will gain the victory and build on earth the reign of Christ.

In all, the Pope accounted for a good many of the Spirituals. He named the ruthless Brother Michael, himself a Franciscan, as Grand Inquisitor for meridional France, writing him: "It is our intention that you should proceed forthwith to uproot by any and every means these pestilential men."

And not only men. A document informs us that under this Pope "a great number of sisters of the Order of Saint Francis were burned alive in various localities for having stubbornly maintained that Jesus Christ and the Apostles possessed nothing."

Evidently, when it came to burning heretics, John believed in sex equality.

· THE LAUREL

ETRARCH'S memory, many times, would turn backward to a certain spring dawn in the Church of Saint Claire at Avignon. It was during Holy Week. It was about six o'clock — at the first hour — when he first set eyes on Laura, saw her emerging fatefully, swan-white in the early shadows. She was so very young then; almost a little girl. (Juliet herself would be almost grown beside her.) Without warning in that moment he committed the next twenty-one years of his life; entered into and lost himself in "that labyrinth from which I think there is no way out."

That was the morning when he saw for the first time the thick-spreading gold hair, the luminous eyes, the slight young body, then all unsung, and now familiar to the ages.

He was twenty-three years old. "Love spurs me on but

reins me in," he wrote. "Comforts and terrifies, burns me
and turns me to ice, flatters and spurns me, summons and
drives me off . . ." "I see, yet have no eyes. Tongueless, I
still cry out. On fire to perish, still I beg for help . . . With
empty arms, still I embrace the world."

※ ※ ※

She was; but who was she? Petrarch immortalized her,
but what was her name? No one is even sure of the color of
her eyes, only that her lashes were black. She probably had
blue eyes, because he compared her to a palace with alabaster
walls: the gate of the palace was ivory, its roof massy gold,
and its windows were sapphires.

Exactly where did she live, and what did she do? She produced eleven children in twenty years, triumphantly answers
the Abbé de Sadists, an assumption which will only please
masochists. Meanwhile, surrounded by her maidens, she still
walks the countryside around Avignon, wrapped in a delicate
Puvis de Chavannes mist. Her anonymous immortality curiously becomes her.

It is better not to know. The mind must not go everywhere. The days when the earth softens, presaging spring;
the velvet fall of blossoms, unidentified perfumes, the early
moving of love in the heart, are best not examined too closely.
Let Laura walk, and no one lay the ghost.

Walking is what she was usually engaged in, no matter what
the Abbé de Sade maintains. Petrarch's Sonnets prove this.
But it has been definitively remarked by a member of the
French Academy that one cannot see her walking through
Avignon, the children, arranged according to size, parading
two by two ahead of her, she herself bringing up the rear
with the baby, and suddenly coming upon Petrarch. The impossible theory predicates that he, stirred to passion at the

sight, would hurry home lovesick as ever to reimmortalize her in another sonnet.

Many a paper war has been waged over Laura and Petrarch. The Devil quotes Scripture and the Petrarchists justify their divergent opinions on the basis of the poet's own writings. Their love has generated considerable acrimony among scholars erroneously thought impartial. For example, Brisset says of the Abbé de Sade: "Refractory to that reasoning which even the most superficial reflection inspires in everybody, he mires himself down in even the clearest questions, he persists, he draggles along in them with a really infantile simplicity." And again, "For this quibbler, just as two negations equal an affirmation, so two absences of proof add up to one certainty." The Abbé's great sin was that he claimed Laura for his ancestress. She was, he said, Laura de Noves, daughter of Audibert de Noves, who became the wife of Hugues de Sade in January, 1325, and produced with him, while Petrarch worshiped from afar, the celebrated eleven.

The annoying thing is that this Laura de Noves died on or about April 6, 1348, a fateful day, as we shall show. At least, she fell ill of *something* on April 3 and duly made her will, and her widower, the tireless Hugues, married one Verlaine de Trentelivre that September. But there were many Lauras around Avignon then, and besides, the plague was raging there and deaths were rising to a thousand a day. This dark-eyed, prolific Laura was buried in the Church of the Franciscans, in the second chapel as you entered, where the de Sades' sepulcher was. But we are not concerned with this at all, and can pass it by; Laura de Noves was the wrong age anyhow. Such at least was Alexander Vellutello's light on the subject, he having left Italy early in the sixteenth century and gone to Avignon for the specific purpose of discovering the true Laura. Alas, by then he could not even find her tomb. In his

life of Petrarch written in 1535 he claimed that Petrarch's
Laura was the daughter of the local Lord at Cabrières, Henri
Chiabau. This Laura was baptized on the 4th of June, 1314,
and she never married. We know from Petrarch himself the
exact day when he first set eyes on whoever she was: April 6,
1327. This particular Laura would have been thirteen, which
jibes with the sonnet that describes her as a little girl when he
first saw her, virtually a child. By this date Laura de Noves
had been married well over two years, and was, it is reason-
able to conclude in the circumstances, pregnant.

There is, however, a whole bouquet of other Lauras to
choose from. As Carias, who fairly recently wrote of Laura
not to claim her as a forbear but almost as a mistress, well suggests, some believe in no Laura at all, others in too many
Lauras. There is Laura des Baux, and Laura of the island village of Thor, and Laura Isnardi, and Laura of Caumont, and
Laura of Lagnes, and Caria's addition, Laura of Châteauneuf,
or of St.-Saturnin, or Jonquerettes. There is no shortage of
Lauras. The reader is put off by the glut. A kind of inverse
bafflement sets in, somewhat like that experienced by the good
people of Salzburg over the authenticated bones of Saint Ru-
pert: when they got them assembled, they found they had a
saint and a half.

Disgusted, Brisset writes that although the originals of the
de Sade family documents have never turned up, some de Sade
has always claimed her: it was Gabriel in the sixteenth century, and Richard in the seventeenth, and the Abbé in the
eighteenth. He tells, leaving the reader to judge, of one
Tomassini who, in 1650, had first believed in Laura of Chiabau and then shifted over to Laura de Sade simply because a
de Sade had laid claim to her. This particular Tomassini left,
at least, a useful comment for posterity on the whole matter:
"Let," he concluded, "each one think what he pleases."

A number of scholars describe how Laura soon lost her beauty, because she was worn out with her unremitting *accouchements*. But her trouble, it now appears, was not sexual at all, but purely textual, being due to a misreading of Petrarch's "Dialogues with Saint Augustine" (his *Secretum*, begun about 1342) where he says: *"corpus illud egregium crebris partubus exhaustum."* The five manuscripts (none autograph copies) which Brisset examined showed different readings of the key word: *patubs, ptibus, ptubs, partubus;* while the first edition of Petrarch's Latin works (Joannem de Amerbach, 1496) reads: *pturbationib. (perturbationibus).* Brisset therefore concludes that Laura's travail was not parturition.

As for whether Laura, with or without problems, existed at all, there were people even in Petrarch's time who did not believe in her. One of his most intimate friends, Giacomo Colonna, the Bishop of Lombez, wrote to him in 1335: ". . . your Laura is only a ghost built up out of your imagination so as to have a subject to exercise your Muse with and make a name for yourself . . . If there is any reality in all this, it is your passion, not for your fictitious Laura, but for the Laurel that is the crown of poets and that, as your works and studies demonstrate, you are hastening after."

And Petrarch answered: "Would to God that my Laura was an imaginary person and that my passion for her was only a game! Alas! It is a frenzy! . . . One can, certainly, imitate illness in action, voice, gesture; but one cannot take on the look, the color of a sick person. How many times have you noted my pallor, and my torments?"

His wonderful Letter to Posterity confides: "I fell prey in my youth to a most violent love, but one unique and good, and I would have suffered from it longer if a death, cruel but useful, had not put out the flame that was beginning to cool."

By the time she died he had loved her twenty-one years, and he did not stop at the grave.

Then there is the note about her passing, which he wrote on the flyleaf of his Virgil and which appeared in the edition of 1472, the third, of the Sonnets: "It is with a kind of bitter sweetness that I have found it good to set down a memorial of this sad happening, here in a place that falls so often under my gaze, so that I shall remember there can be nothing further to charm me in this life; and that, now this great bond is broken, I shall well know the time has come to flee from Babylon [Avignon], as I continue to look at these words and think of how swiftly life flies on. This, thank God, will be easy enough for one who examines, bravely and like a man, the useless sorrows of the past, the empty hopes, the unexpected outcomes."

Petrarch says that Laura was buried after Vespers on the same day of her terrible death, in the Monastery of the Franciscans (where, to complicate matters, Laura de Noves was also buried). This was outside the city on the bank of the river Sorgue.

※ ※ ※

Somewhere in the vineyards, among the swelling hills, in meadows where streams pass and in spring the willows pour out their delicate green rain, is Laura's country.

Her setting was the countryside around the town: trees, flower-spangled meadows, rippling water — not city walls. But she was no peasant, bound to a farm; she went elegantly dressed, like a lady of the Court. Petrarch first saw her in Avignon; Augustine in the *Secretum* mocks at him for escaping from her into solitary places and then sighing and turning his eyes backward toward the city. She was no country girl, but a town girl in a country frame.

Life goes on ageless here, outside the city; only the observer is new, but not the scene. Men in blue and purplish clothing stoop and tend the earth, in their hands tools, their shape eternal. White blossoming trees step out, like white peacocks spreading their tails in courting. Children run, the road winds softly. A gray village passes, under mild sky, and the air smells of honey. What was her name and address? No one knows. But Provence has kept her place exactly as she left it.

⚜ ⚜ ⚜

In 1533, in the Church of the Franciscan Monastery, three men either made what they thought was a discovery, or else perpetrated a hoax. One of them, Maurice de Sève of Lyons, claimed the chief credit for finding, in what he took for the de Sade chapel, an uninscribed slab bearing two worn, escutcheonlike symbols and a laurel. Causing the tomb to be opened, they saw within it some delicate bones and a little lead box. They opened the box and found a parchment inside, folded up and sealed with green sealing wax. This document proved to contain a sonnet. There was also a bronze medal, one of the sides blank, the other showing a woman opening her garment at the breast, and the letters: M L M J. De Sève at once assigned the sonnet to Petrarch, and interpreted the letters on the medal as follows: *Madonna Laura Mortua Jacet.* The dead Laura rests here.

Columbus' fairly recent discovery may have made slightly less noise. Even King Francis the First came by to see these wonders, and being a poet too, he wrote out a tribute to the departed lady and her lover, ending it thus:

> *Who shall praise thee, except by sitting mute,*
> *O gentle soul, held in so high esteem!*

For silence evermore doth speech confute
When who would speak is lower than his theme.

He also commanded that a suitable mausoleum should be erected to honor the illustrious dead.

For a long time after that, streams of pilgrims used to visit the monastery on the riverbank, to look at the medal and the sonnet. In the eighteenth century, an Englishman purchased the one, and the de Sades got the other. Then the French Revolution swept down like the Mistral and tore everything away; the monastery was sold and the chapel destroyed, and the bones, whoever their owner was, vanished into the public domain.

One thing is sure: the skeleton was not then and never had been Laura's. Experts found that the sonnet was inferior to anything Petrarch would have been able to write. And the bronze medal was judged not possibly anterior to the end of the fifteenth century; it was identified as an amulet worn for protection against the plague, the letters being the initials of four very well-known personages: Matheus, Lucas, Marcus, Johannes —

As for the mausoleum ordered by Francis the First, an early nineteenth century writer, d'Arnavon, Gallically adds: "Many historians have praised Francis the First for this mausoleum, which did not cost him anything but the command to build it, since it is still to be erected."

· WHERE THEY DANCE

ALL THESE people came and went over Avignon's magical bridge. Most of the ones who passed there never doubted that it had come into being as their ancestors related:

Once upon a time, in the French Savoy, a widow sent out her boy named Bénézet to watch her sheep. Suddenly the sun began to melt and everything went dark. Bénézet trembled in the yellow darkness, splattered with tiny half-moons. And then, three times, a voice called to him out of the murk:

"Bénézet, My son . . ."

"I hear Your voice, but see no one," cried Bénézet.

"I am Jesus Christ," the voice said. "Leave these sheep and go; build a Bridge across the Rhône."

"I never heard of the Rhône," cried the boy, "and I dare not leave my mother's sheep."

"Trust in Me," the voice answered. "I will gather the sheep."

"But, Lord," cried Bénézet, "how can I build a Bridge? I have nothing but fourpence in all the world."

"I will furnish the means," said the Lord Christ.

The boy set out, and soon a pilgrim joined him who was really an angel but looked like anyone.

"I will show you the place," said the pilgrim.

When they came there and stood in the wind on the banks of the vast, plunging river, the boy was terrified.

"One cannot build a Bridge across such a wide river!" he said.

But the angel sent Bénézet to the ferryman, to bring him across so he could stand before the Bishop of Avignon. And the ferryman took as his hire the boy's threepence, all that was left of the four.

Bénézet went up to the Cathedral, where multitudes had gathered to hear the Bishop preach. And he spoke out in a loud voice, "Jesus Christ has sent me hither to build a Bridge across the Rhône!"

The Bishop turned to his Provost. The unforgivable had happened: his sermon had been broken into. "Take the yokel out!" he commanded. The Provost took Bénézet out, by the ear.

"Jesus has sent me," the boy wept. "I have come to build a Bridge!"

The Provost laughed. "Not even King Charlemagne dared try it," he said. "Even the Romans failed."

"But *He* sent me!" the boy cried again.

The Provost's eyes narrowed. His brief patience was at an end. "If you speak truth," he mocked, "then carry off that stone."

Bénézet looked at the stone. It was thirty feet long and seventeen broad. He walked over to it and he made the sign of the Cross. And suddenly, feather-light, the stone leaped to his shoulders, he hardly helping at all, and he carried it down to the river, to the place where the Bridge would begin.

Then the Bishop and the Provost and all the people were amazed at the twelve-year-old boy, and they brought money and aid to him from all sides and the Bridge was built.

When Bénézet was only nineteen, he died, and they buried him on the Bridge. The account says that in 1669, a flood swept off eighteen out of the twenty-two arches and a part of the structure fell, disclosing the boy's body, which was found entire, "even the bowels being sound." Again in 1674 he was taken up again, and carried with royal honors to the Church of the Celestines, his final place of rest.

Jesus had called out to Bénézet on September 13, 1177, on a day when the sun was eclipsed. From 1307 until now, Philip's Tower has watched the Bridge from France, while Avignon's walls have looked on from the other side, and in time of war, the Bridge was cut.

Because of an old song, people around the world have heard of this bridge. They think of the Avignonese as still dancing and circling out there on the broken-off span, and perhaps they are. The words of the song are like this:

> *On the Bridge at Avignon,*
> *That's where they dance,*
> *That's where they dance.*
> *On the Bridge at Avignon,*
> *That's where they dance*
> *As around they fly.*
>
> *From now on, without boat or ferry,*
> *From now on, without boat or ferry,*
> *Cross the water, easy and merry.*

Our Lord Abbots go like this,
Once again, they go like this,
As to speechify and preachify.

All together, stop and sway,
All together, stop and sway,
Each salutes in his own way.
The soldiers they all go like this,
Once again they go like this,
Hand and forehead lifting high.

The fine gentlemen go like that,
Then again, they go like that,
Put on a hat, take off a hat.
The good farmers go like this,
Once again, they go like this,
Scrape one foot back as they pass by.

The fair ladies go like this,
Once again, they go like this,
Their dresses circling like a pie.
Once the Bridge was dedicated,
Opened up and celebrated,
Everybody home did hie.

If, as some contend, the Roman for priest (Pontifex) really came from "bridge-maker," the structure's holy overtones are plain; but effective engineering principles in such a period were, perhaps, just as supernatural as a Voice out of the sky. In the house of Bonpas, situated on the Durance River near Avignon, there was a chapter of bridge-building monks. These particular monks — in effect a construction company — had taken vows to build and maintain bridges. One of the Order's chief engineers was Bénézet, who designed and supervised the building of the nearly impossible Avignon span. After eight years, or it may have been eleven, of continual trouble, he completed the Bridge in 1185, and it managed to weather almost five centuries.

As for the tolls, it cost a horse and rider two deniers to cross over, a donkey one, a wagon four; a pedestrian paid two oboles, but the rate for pigs was cheaper, one obole per pig. An obole was half a denier; a denier was the twelfth part of a sou of Tours; and a *livre* (pound) of Tours was worth twenty of these sous.

· DOGMEAT FOR TIGERS

he necessity of burning nuns was only one of many problems that confronted John during his long reign. Four years after his coronation the masses suddenly welled up. Blindly as lemmings the poor poured out of their hovels. Coming as this phenomenon did without apparent means of communication, and as if because of some influence in the air, some psychic epidemic, it took on the nature of a miracle. Thousands from all over France gathered in the valley of the Garonne. They had vague notions of a crusade and they marched two by two behind the Cross on the way to the Mediterranean and perhaps the Holy Land.

These runaway masses, the so-called "Pastoureaux" (Little Shepherds) soon degenerated from crusaders into brigands, out of their need for food, and lacking positive motivation, they turned against the Jews. These were easy to identify since the Lateran Council of 1215 (the Twelfth Ecumenical) had decreed that Jews should wear a special round hat with a kind of spike; for this and other reasons, they were different from the rest and difference was guilt. Furthermore, rumors of a strange treaty between the King of Granada, the Jews and the lepers may already have been on the roads. One year later, in 1321, a conspiracy was supposedly uncovered whereby the Jews had contracted with the lepers to poison all the wells and fountains of France. Many Jews were burned alive because of this and others banished; the very rich escaped by paying a mountainous fine.

A rage of destruction now shook the Little Shepherds and they began to spread ruin and death without stopping to discriminate. Even Bernard Guido, Grand Inquisitor of Toulouse and vicious anti-Semite, feared their attacks on the Jews. "Watch out!" he warned. "When you throw dogmeat to tigers, you give them an appetite for human flesh!"

The Jews of Avignon would have been likely victims with the rest, but the Governor of Languedoc blocked the murderous Shepherds as they marched on Provence. Thus Avignon's Jews were saved, and the Pope's protection monies as well.

A more fundamental threat to John XXII grew out of the Battle of Wethwis in 1322, when Louis of Bavaria defeated Frederick of Austria and ended in his own favor the struggle for the title of Holy Roman Emperor. John, however, refused to crown Louis, who finally named his own Pope in Rome, thus creating the initial schism of the fourteenth century. It too was rooted in the move to Avignon. It was one of those strange, prophetic events, a rehearsal for the Great Schism of the West. Summoned by the Pope to Avignon, Louis replied: "No one shall ever get me to Avignon; for the

See of Peter is not in Avignon, but in Rome, and in Rome must the Emperor be crowned!"

Threatened by John, Louis appealed to a General Council, and there the rights of the secular power against papal absolutism were so ably championed that John excommunicated Louis on March 21, 1324. Excommunicating a man was like stripping a medieval town of its walls. The excommunicated had no rights; anyone could injure him, in his person or in his possessions, without sin.

Louis went to Rome and had a makeshift coronation. In full regalia, he enthroned himself in Saint Peter's square, and after a herald at arms had obtained silence, a monk with a loud voice cried out three times: "Is there anyone here who wishes to defend the priest Jack of Cahors, calling himself Pope John XXII?" The Pope was then branded as a heretic: partly because he said Jesus and the Apostles owned property; partly for getting the King of France to send against the Sicilians troops who had been mobilized for a Crusade against the Saracens; again because he "desired to unite in his person the spiritual and temporal powers, in spite of this declaration of the Savior: 'My Kingdom is not of this world' " — and finally for other heresies lumped together.

Then Louis rose from his throne, and announced that as Emperor and in the name of the Senate and the people of Rome, he was deposing Jack of Cahors from the papal dignity, and was handing him over to the secular arm to be burned alive.

Having disposed of John, the Emperor decided to name his own Pontiff, and settled on one Peter Rainalucci of Corbario, a Franciscan, the son of poor peasants. Early in May, 1328, the yellow-eyed Louis, dressed in his splendor, preceded by the Lords Banneret of the Roman people and followed by his numerous suite, summoned this Peter Rainalucci and publicly, before the multitudes, sat him down on a throne to be Pope.

At a sign from the Emperor, the usual leather-lunged crier lifted up his voice with: "Romans, will you take for Pope Brother Peter of Corbario?" And the shout came back: "We want him!" Whereupon the Emperor placed the tiara on Peter of Corbario's head, the ring on his finger, the cope about his shoulders, and named him Nicholas V. Duly then, in his turn, Nicholas crowned Louis.

Two Catholics were burned to death for saying that Nicholas V was a false Pope.

The new Emperor symbolized in his person all those who were against the rising power of France, to which John was committed. The Pope tried to get another Emperor elected in Germany, but was less successful than Louis: the people of Basel murdered the Legate John sent them and threw his corpse into the Rhine.

Meanwhile there were difficulties with Nicholas V. As Peter of Corbario, the anti-Pope had been a loud critic of luxury, but now things were different; where money was concerned he became as heretical as John, and required so much that Louis found he could no longer afford him. Peter, however, learned rapidly, and was soon raising large sums from the sale of Church titles and benefices. Those who had already contributed to Pope John for this purpose, now faced the alternative of paying a second time or losing their investment. Nicholas also issued two bulls against "Jack of Cahors," and after a sumptuous reception in Pisa, had the effigy of John, clothed in pontifical garb, burned there in the public square.

The troubles piled up. Peter, when young, had married Giovanna, a girl of his village, and five years later retired from matrimony to join the Franciscans. During all his years of monkish poverty, Giovanna never came near him. Now that he was successful and Pope, she remembered that she was a deserted wife; she brought suit and won, although there were certain obstacles to her being wife-in-residence at the See of Rome.

The masses of Rome, like a woman, are changeable. Emperor Louis made a disastrous attack on Naples and retreated to a capital in full mutiny. Through clouds of flying stones, he left for Todi, where Nicholas had prudently preceded him, and John's Legate, Cardinal Orsini, entered Rome in triumph. By the spring of 1329 Louis gave up his Italian adventure and returned to Germany, while Pope Nicholas hid.

One day a messenger arrived at Avignon with a letter for John XXII. It began: "To the Most Holy Father and Lord, Pope John, Brother Peter of Corbario, prostrate at the feet of Your Holiness, and recognizing himself worthy of every punishment. They charged you in my presence with crimes so atrocious that I had the audacity to mount the Apostolic Chair. But . . . I have given up my sacrilegious pretension. I stand ready to renounce it in public, be it at Pisa, be it at Rome, or wherever else Your Holiness shall command."

John sent for him. On the morning after he reached Avignon, sounds of hammering rose from the great hall of the Consistory; carpenters were hastily knocking together a platform so that all might witness Peter of Corbario as he humbled himself before the Pope. Crowds gathered early; many an individual claimed to know someone in the Pope's confidence: the sentence was already decided, they whispered. Burned as a heretic; that, of course; but for a crime so monstrous as opposing the true Pope? Surely a new torture . . .

In a sudden stillness, Peter of Corbario stood before them on the wooden platform. Facing John, he spoke. Bible words poured from his lips, Luke's account of the return of the prodigal son. He confessed all, he renounced all. "I have sinned against Heaven and against yourself." He came down from his platform and waited before the Pope and there was a halter around his neck. He collapsed and threw himself, weeping, at John's feet.

John lifted him from the floor and removed the halter. He let Peter kiss his feet and his hands. As a wave of surprise rippled through the hall, the two men kissed on the mouth.

They say that Peter was, thereafter, treated as a friend and guarded as an enemy. He was assigned a place to live in John's palace; it was under the treasury. The same dishes were served him as appeared at the Pope's table. Although he had access to books, he was forbidden to speak. After three years of this, he died, and was buried at Avignon in the Church of the Franciscans.

· PETER'S PENCE

EANWHILE John was turning everything to gold.

It is difficult to obtain the facts on papal financing. We do know that Robert Grosseteste, who was Bishop of Lincoln and a friend of Roger Bacon, conducted a mid-thirteenth century investigation of the amount received by foreign clergy in England, and found it to be three times the King's income. Also, just before the return to Rome of Gregory XI — that is, in 1376 — the "Good Parliament" was to declare the Pope's taxes on the English people five times those of the King's.

The Avignon Popes had many sources of revenue, deriving from their temporal and religious powers. Dispensations and simoniacal activities (simony is, technically, buying or selling ecclesiastical preferment or spiritual gifts), the sale of papal offices, administrative and other, appointments to livings, and the right to try cases, were always profitable. Heinrich von Langenstein stated in his *Letter on Behalf of a Council of Peace* (1381) that one individual might hold up to three hundred Church livings. And there were always people who wanted to buy *something*, if only the legitimization of a child.

Besides these resources, the Pope had lands which included, in what is now France, Avignon (after 1348), the Comtat Venaissin, and in Italy the Papal States, with suzerainty over Ferrara, the Kingdom of Naples and Sicily, Provence, Sardinia and Corsica. Naturally, when Italy was in a state of anarchy, nothing much would come in from there. Again, the Great Schism was to split all revenues two and sometimes three ways. The influx of gold was constant but not uniform.

The Pope would obtain revenue by granting a franchise to a city seeking democratic privileges, or by yielding it as a "reversible fief" to some Baron. Clement VI received 10,000 gold florins a year from the d'Este family in exchange for the Duchy of Ferrara. The Malatestas paid in an annual fee for the March of Ancona. The overall estimate of Clement's receipts from Italy is above a million gold florins. Under Gregory XI the total was estimated at four million gold florins from Italy alone. This quadrupling of income occurred within a space of thirty-odd years, one more proof of the increasing power and avidity of the Avignon Papal Court. No financial stone was left unturned. In addition to the other papal exactions the Kings of England were expected to pay the Pope a thousand pounds sterling a year for Ireland.

Then there was Peter's penny, a personal tax levied by the Pope on all Europe. A letter from Benedict XII to the King of Poland informs him that this was to be paid per capita, not by towns. Although lacking population figures, we still know that it brought in enormous sums.

Then there was Holy Year, which attracted to Rome, for plenary indulgences, pilgrims variously estimated at from two hundred thousand to two million. On one such occasion, two priests provided with rakes were kept busy indiscriminately raking in gold and silver night and day.

The greatest revenues, however, came in from Expectatives, Reserves and Annates, and these John is credited with inventing. An Expectative was the Pope's somewhat lugubrious mandate appointing a successor to a not-yet-vacant living. When a churchman died, John would order that the post vacated by his new appointee should be filled by the man next below, that one's now-vacant post by the man below him, and so on down a long line. Of course each had to pay for his promotion. Although this ecclesiastical escalator must have led to the automatic advance of many who were not suited to higher office, it was certainly a practical device for multiplying the revenues.

As for the Pontifical Reserve, it was of two types: (1) a general Reserve, having to do with no fixed time or place, as when John reserved for himself all appointments in all the cathedrals of Christendom; and (2) a specific Reserve, as when Benedict XII reserved the nomination of all offices whose holders died at the Avignon Court. The Annate was a duty payable to the Pope by anyone receiving a benefice; it is said to have amounted to one year's revenue.

Funds of course poured in from many other sources, including such taxes as the *servitia communia* and *servitia minuta*, the *visitationes ad limina*, the *pallium* duty, fines, monies paid in as commuted vows, and the payment of mintage rights, besides legacies and gifts. And there was many a lesser tax, such as the "procurations," which grew out of the right of an ecclesiastic visiting his benefice to receive hospitality for himself and his suite — and the interesting "right of pillage," which was, originally, the right to despoil the house of a dead Bishop.

A good deal of banking and exchange obviously went on at Avignon, where money from all over Europe converged. Apostolic Mandates issued there also served as a sort of bank draft on specified Bishoprics. Describing how some prelates had hundreds of benefices, the Abbé André says these could be scattered through different provinces of Europe, just as a modern investor might own shares in various foreign companies: "An insatiable hunger for benefices gnawed at the clergy." The "capitalists" of the fourteenth century used their funds, he says, "to exploit ecclesiastical benefices. People speculated on the age or infirmity of an incumbent, on the influence of this or that Cardinal, on the possibility of the Pope's changing his mind, on projected reforms; out of it grew dangerous games with a rising and falling exchange on this fourteenth century Stock Market . . . We even find courtiers and brokers licensed to sell benefices and effect their actual or fictitious transfer . . . No more than they do today on the Stock Exchange, did anyone dream of asking where you came from, or who you were, once you had paid out the desired sum of money. From all over Europe, people flocked to Avignon, now become the leading business center of the world."

An eyewitness from the days of John XXII wrote: "Everytime I went to the apartment of the Lord Pope's chamberlain, I inevitably found bankers, money changers, tables loaded with gold, and clerks weighing and counting out florins."

※ ※ ※

John's energy was ill-starred. Although he used his political wisdom to contain and annul the schism of Nicholas V, mediate between France and England, England and Ireland,

England and Scotland, to push the Turks back to Asia and create Mongol enemies behind them, and interfere successfully in the Italian power struggle, he will not be remembered for these things. He endures, aside from his theology, for the insatiable ingenuity with which he mined ecclesiastical offices for gold.

The problem was, how to keep track of all these fines, taxes and charges. A strange Constitution listing the wages of various sins has been attributed to John. The historian Joudou affirms in his *Histoire des Souverains Pontifes à Avignon* that the text of this Constitution will appear at the end of his first volume, and recommends it as an aid to understanding the mores of the fourteenth century. Unfortunately, something happened between the printing of this volume and the binding, so that copies of Joudou's history which actually contain the document are quite rare.

This elusive Constitution, selections from which follow, is entitled: *Taxae sacrae cancellariae apostolicae, et taxae sacrae poenitentiarae, itidem apostolicae.* Textual alterations may well have occurred here in the course of centuries, some of them intentional perhaps, possibly the work of Reformation propagandists; and the list shows odd discrepancies (for example, a priest had to pay the same fine for fornication with a nun, a close relative, or any woman whatever); but at the very least, this inventory has the dreadful truth of caricature. Mincing no words, it demonstrates how the purely spiritual penances of early Christianity, such as fasting, sackcloth and ashes, and abstinence from the marriage bed, had gradually become replaced by the more convenient payment of a fine:

If an ecclesiastic commits the sin of the flesh, be it with nuns, be it with his cousins, his nieces or his goddaughters, or finally with any other woman, the guilty one shall be absolved for the sum of 67 pounds (*livres*), 12 sous.

If, outside the sins of fornication, he asks absolution of the sin against nature or of bestiality, he shall pay 219 pounds, 15 sous; however, if he has committed this sin only with young boys or with animals and not with women, the fine shall be reduced to 131 pounds, 15 sous . . .

A nun who has given herself up to several men, either at one time or on successive occasions, in her convent or outside it, and who would wish to obtain the rank of Abbess, shall pay 131 pounds, 15 sous.

Priests who would obtain authorization to live in concubinage with their female relatives shall pay 76 pounds, 1 sou.

For every sin of lust committed by a layman, the absolution shall cost 27 pounds, 1 sou; for incest one shall add in conscience 4 pounds.

The adulterous wife who asks absolution to be sheltered from all proceedings and to have wide license to continue sinful relations, shall pay the Pope 87 pounds, 5 sous. In a similar case, the husband shall submit to the same tax; if they have committed incest with their children, they shall add in conscience 6 pounds . . .

A husband who has struck his wife roughly shall pay into the treasury of the Chancellery 3 pounds, 4 sous; if he has killed her, he shall pay 17 pounds, 15 sous; if he has committed this crime in order to marry another, he shall pay in addition 52 pounds, 9 sous. Those who shall have assisted the husband in the murder shall be absolved at 2 pounds per person . . .

The wife who shall destroy the child in her womb, and the father who shall have aided in accomplishing this crime, shall each pay 17 pounds, 15 sous. The person who shall procure the abortion of a child of which he is not the father, shall give a pound less . . .

Whoever has killed a Bishop or a high Church official shall pay 131 pounds, 14 sous, 6 deniers . . .

Whoever would wish to buy in advance absolution for any accidental murder that he might commit in the future shall pay 178 pounds, 15 sous.

A heretic who is converted shall pay for his absolution 269 pounds. The son of a heretic burned, or killed by any other torture, shall be rehabilitated only by paying 218 pounds, 16 sous, 9 deniers.

An ecclesiastic who is not able to pay his debts and would like to escape prosecution by his creditors shall give to the Pope 17 pounds, 8 sous, 6 deniers, and his credit shall be re-established.

The permission to set up merchandise shops and to sell different commodities under the portico of a church shall be granted at a price of 45 pounds, 19 sous, 3 deniers.

For the making of contraband and for defrauding the Prince of his rights [smuggling] one shall pay 87 pounds, 3 deniers . . .

A virtuous monk desiring to pass his life in a hermitage shall pay into the treasury of the Pope 45 pounds, 19 sous.

A wandering apostate desiring to re-enter the fold shall pay the same sum to be absolved.

Monks and priests desiring to travel in lay clothing shall have the same tax imposed on them.

The illegitimate child of a priest desiring to serve in his father's parish shall pay 27 pounds, 1 sou.

An illegitimate child desiring to enter Holy Orders and possess benefices shall pay 15 pounds, 18 sous, 6 deniers.

Laymen who are crippled or deformed and who desire to enter Holy Orders and possess benefices shall pay to the Chancellery 38 pounds, 2 sous.

One who is blind in the right eye shall pay the same sum; if he is deprived of the left eye, he shall give to the Pope 106 pounds, 7 sous; those who squint shall pay 43 pounds, 3 sous.

Those who are eunuchs shall pay to the Pope to enter Orders the sum of 300 pounds, 15 sous.

If a man desires to obtain by simony one or several benefices, he shall address himself to the treasurers of the Pope who shall sell to him at a moderate price.

Whoever may wish to break his oath and still be guaranteed against all prosecution and all ignominy shall pay to the Pope 131 pounds, 15 sous . . .

Whether or not this *pièce justificative* is as important as Joudou believes, something like this list undoubtedly existed. In Avignon "everything was for sale," and a price scale — in that era of the "just price" — was an obvious necessity. Meanwhile it is clear that sin was a major economic resource of the Church.

※ ※ ※

John's epitaph might be read in this one fact: when he became Pope, the treasury held 70,000 gold florins; when he died, 17,000,000. Jewels, gold and silver plate, miters, crowns and other precious objects added another 7,000,000.

Some attempts have been made in recent times to modify the severe criticism of Gregorovius and others, criticism based on the accounts of John's contemporaries, and a remarkable reduction of the above figures has been achieved. Samaran and Mollat jointly studied this Pope's fiscal policies in *La Fiscalité en France au XIVe Siècle*, with results that are recommended to all who wish to apologize for John and his money.

· THE BEATIFIC VISION

BESIDES John the financier, there was also John the lawyer; in him the temptation to pontificate on dogma was very strong. By this, a Pope could gain an immortality on earth. There were so many Leos, Gregories, Benedicts, Innocents, Bonifaces. Old men when they came to the Holy See, and their time short. John had reigned longer than most, but all he had accomplished could be swept away. Events recede, organization can die with the organizer, money is wasted by the succeeding spendthrift, even his work on the Palace could be altered or undone. And he was the twenty-second John. Yet if one's name were associated with Church doctrine, one would be remembered. So may his thoughts have run.

On All Saints Day, 1331, in the Church of Our Lady of the

Lords at Avignon, John arose and preached a new and star-
tling belief: he said the righteous would not see God before
the Day of Judgment. He based his announcement on a long
study of Revelations, Chapter 6, verse 9: "And when he had
opened the fifth seal, I saw under the altar the souls of them
that were slain for the word of God, and for the testimony
which they held."

Only after the Last Judgment would the souls of the
martyrs be placed on the altar and enjoy the Beatific Vision of
God. Only then would the Saints see God's essence. Prior to
that, they would behold only the humanity of Jesus.

John XXII went further. On the 15th of December, he
stated to his congregation that "before the Resurrection, the
souls separated from the body possess neither eternal life, nor
beatitude proper, nor the beatific vision."

He continued to unfold his theme, and on January 8 he
made the deduction that neither the devils nor the damned
dwelt in Hell. In other words, Hell itself would not be open
for occupancy before the end of the world.

The body of the Church was shocked by this doctrine, so
contrary to the accepted opinion, both of theologians and
rank and file believers. For if even the Saints were not to
come into the presence of God until the Last Judgment, how
then could they intercede for man with the Father? Of what
use to man here on earth was the invocation of Saints? Yet
this invocation was one of the most powerful attractions of
the Church. The vast majority of believers found in this
process a necessary personal relationship, an attachment. To
have this reasoned away meant a serious distortion of their
whole religious pattern. The doctrine of indulgences also
suffered extensive damage by it; a soul granted an indulgence
would still have to await the end of the world before behold-
ing the Glory of God. Did John, who had so concerned

himself with increasing the revenues of the Church, not see that he was clogging one of the channels through which money was sluiced most freely into the treasury?

We must conclude from the descriptions of John's able mind, his university training in law, his agile administration of a complicated institution, his competent maneuverings in the involved European politics of his time, and his lifelong studies, that he was aware of the theological conclusions that could be drawn from his doctrine. He simply believed that he was right.

John's enemies rushed to the attack. In Germany, the Fraticelli argued for a council which would condemn the Pope as a heretic. In France, even his friends were concerned. This news so disturbed him that he spent three days shut up in prayer and meditation, at the end of which he ordered an open Consistory.

"If in our sermons and our lectures," he told the Consistory, ". . . we have in the public presence advanced something relating to the happiness of the Saints in the other world which is contrary to Scripture and to the orthodox Faith, we expressly revoke it."

This appeared to satisfy everyone, including two bitter enemies, Bonnegrazia of Bergamo and England's "Invincible Doctor," William of Ockham.

Almost a year passed and then the Pope was close to death. On the 3rd of December, 1334, in front of his Cardinals, in a public Consistory, he made his final doctrinal revision.

By now John had shrunk still smaller, mummified by age; his face was oyster-pale, he trembled under the weight of ninety years and strong emotion, yet he walked bravely, and sat down on the great papal throne with its miter-shaped back, its winged, half-human, half-animal figures carved in relief at either side; and he made his confession of faith; made it not to his Cardinals but to his God. As he came to the last words, we hear him speaking with increasing emphasis and care.

"We confess and believe that the souls separated from the body and completely purified are in Heaven, are in Paradise with the angels, and with Jesus Christ, and they see God in His Divine Essence, clearly, face to face" — did he pause here, did he speak his final restrictive phrase even slower? — "as much as the state and condition of the separated soul permits."

At the end, facing eternity, he did not abandon his position. He had sought the advice of the learned, he had subjected his own nearly inflexible will to the will of the Church, but he affirmed to the last the possibility that souls separated from the body by death might not see God as would those reunited with the body at the Resurrection.

This statement of John's has been called a retraction; if so, it is a retraction divided by two.

According to Benedict XII, John's immediate successor, John made a full retraction in a bull which he was prevented from sealing by death. This, Benedict said, was incorporated in his own bull of January 29, 1336, *Benedictus Dominus Deus*. Perhaps. But then comes the cornada from the other horn of the dilemma: if John did not contradict himself, he was contradicted by the succeeding Pope.

December 4, the day after his partial retraction, fell on a Sunday. Early that morning John, visibly failing, having suffered a violent flux during the night, asked to be placed in an armchair where he could look out over the plains of Provence, beautiful even then, stripped bare by the wintry wind. To each of his Cardinals, one following the next, he gave his trembling hands to be kissed goodbye. At nine o'clock, holding the Cross to his breast, he died.

And now great crowds of people flocked to look upon

the man who had been their Bishop and for eighteen years, their Pope. He lay in the Church of Our Lady of the Lords, crowned with his tiara, wrapped in his cope of gold.

No one saw John again for four hundred and twenty-five years. At that time his body, being removed from the basilica into a chapel, and exposed to the light, was still intact: not quite five feet tall, it was found wearing white silk gloves, a big gold ring with a blue stone, a tunic of violet silk, and the cope studded with gems. On the head was a little miter of white silk matching the gloves, and with red silk lappets hanging from the back.

In 1793, as happened to many dead during the Revolution, John's body was molested and robbed and the violators played ball with the skull. Today at Avignon, the figure that lies in John's place, on the slab in his tall Gothic tomb, is not John: a Bishop does duty there for the small-boned, white-faced little nonagenarian who once shook the world.

※ ※ ※

· THE ROSE-STREWN DRESS

T is strange that Petrarch, that classicist, orator and poet; that Papal Ambassador, Canon, Prior, Archdeacon, Archbishop's and Prince's envoy, honored guest of such cities as Venice and Rome; that man courted by Popes and Kings, Queens, nobles and the creative great — should be remembered primarily because of his unknown Laura. For she was unknown: "She lived hidden; the inattentive world saw her not." As she lives through him, he has lived through her.

We know from Petrarch that she was of noble blood, of a life humble and tranquil (not, then, at the Papal Court), had a sweet singing voice, a high intelligence, was mature for all her youth, and gay for all her pensive air. We hear repeatedly that — besides being unknown — she was famed for her virtue, knowledge and all-around perfection, but we are never told what she was good and wise and perfect about.

Laura must have been married, since he calls her a woman, not a girl; she probably had a child. Gazing from her beautiful eyes of whatever color, walking, talking to her ladies and to Petrarch, suffering from her likewise never-explained *perturbationibus*, these seem to have comprised her occupations.

A glimpse of fourteenth century men and women, including, no doubt, such as Laura, has come down from the contemporary Galvaneo della Fiamma, who says:

"They wear their clothing short and tight, in the Spanish manner, hair close-cut like the French, a thick, long beard like the barbarians, fabulous bristling spurs like the Germans, and they speak in all kinds of unknown tongues, like veritable Tartars. But the women have thrown themselves into even stranger aberrations. They wear immense tunics in layers, covered with fantastic designs. A great quantity of golden buckles holds these draperies in place. The breast is naked, the nose in the air, the hair rippling and curling and the only thing that covers their heads. To see them bearing down upon you in their rich golden belts, spurs on their shoes, to see their horsemanlike stride, to watch their unrestrained passion for dice and other games of chance, for fiery steeds, shining weapons, virile exercises and unchecked freedom, you would say that they want to take over our sex."

Petrarch himself thus describes a group of people approaching his retreat from Avignon: "French luxury . . . has intermingled the clothing of both sexes, and from afar I cannot differentiate between them." Nearer, he makes out "ribbons, necklaces, pearls, coiffures, rings, ornaments for the head, garments edged with purple."

The oldest known portraits of Laura were painted two centuries after she died. It is true that Petrarch called in a famous artist, Simone Martini or Memmi of Siena, to make a painting of her that he could carry about with him "as an eternal source of tears." But this is lost.

We learn a good deal about her appearance from the Sonnets, however, and her hair style and elegant dresses resemble the Fiamma description, although her presence was not tomboyish: she was playful sometimes, but had a kind of young stateliness. For whatever reason we choose to imagine, Petrarch never mentioned her nose; no doubt because it was not Greek, one authority decides. Of her skin, lips and teeth, Petrarch gives us only the traditional snow-roses-and-ivory account. But he was obsessed with her eyes, even if he only once saw fit to hint at their color; again and again, we hear of the brilliance of her eyes. He was forever stirred as well by her rich, finespun blond hair, her hands, her feet, her smiles and sighs, the grace of her gestures, her whiteness, her gait, the sound of her voice, and he was unusually responsive to her dresses and jewels:

"A garment of purple," he tells us, "edged with azure and strewn with a design of roses, veils her fair shoulders, a wondrous garment . . ." "Look, with what art it is covered with gold, with pearls and purple, this dress she has chosen . . ." "O lovely hand, squeezing my heart, pressing my whole life into its small compass — O white glove, modish and sweet, masking fair ivory, and fresh roses . . ." "That gait which is no mortal's, but some heavenly being's!" "That hair, now bound with pearls and precious stones, now loose in tresses blonder than fine gold, she spread it out with such grace, she gathered it back with motions so charming that my heart still leaps at the thought of it . . ."

The landscape of their passion was barren as the moon. She would pass him by, on foot; or, with her ladies, she would drift down the Rhône in a small boat. Once, he picked up her white glove. Once, as he sat dreaming, she put her hand over his eyes. At a gathering of nobles, he saw some now unidentified visiting Prince single her out from the crowd of beautiful women and kiss her forehead and her eyes.

Since it was not then the custom for virtuous women to receive men in their homes, the two must have met outdoors, or in a friend's garden; at least they met somewhere with a measure of solitude, since Laura had to defend herself from him for twenty years, and self-defense requires privacy.

Probably she was the power behind him, the woman without whom, it is often said, almost no man is great. "The little I am," he wrote, "I am because of her; if I have a measure of fame and glory, I never would have achieved it unless this noble love had cultivated the few tenuous seeds of virtue that nature planted in my heart . . . She separated me from the society of the vulgar, she became my guide in all my ways, she spurred my lagging genius and roused my torpid soul." We are prepared to accept her perfection on faith, believing that a man of Petrarch's stature could only have loved the best. On more cynical days we wonder if her main claim to fame is not that she resisted Petrarch. In any case it is lucky for history, lucky for the memory of knightly love, that she never yielded; that he finally won for himself the laurel crown, never the laurel.

Sometimes she would offer him hope, and then withdraw it again. She sought out and spurned him. She advanced and retreated, her mood and appearance varied; cloudlike, she would take different forms. All this held him a long time. When she grew older and, though still distant, kinder, we can retroactively prophesy the result: her increasing acquiescence induced in him the coolness he later describes; she had lessened the pain which by now had become a necessity to him; hence, luckily, the intervention of what he calls her "useful" death.

Petrarch, forever in demand and sought after, was in love with her indifference, her "tranquil disdain" of him. Like many overly loved people he wanted the one individual he could not have. "No prayer moved her, no caress subdued her; she guarded her womanly honor and, in spite of her age and mine, in spite of many circumstances which would have softened even a heart as unyielding as diamond, she remained unassailable." He was, as the French would say, much chaster than he wanted to be, but somehow he almost crows as he writes: "even to this day, your eyes have shed never a single tear for me, never but anger and disdain."

Carefully, he hugged and hoarded his pain. "If, O my Lady, I can only hold out long enough to see the powerful years subdue the brightness of your lovely eyes, and your hair of finespun gold change into silver; if I can see you put aside your ribbons and your furbelows, and lose this beauty which makes me hesitate to tell you the story of my sorrow — perhaps then love will give me the courage to count out for you the years, the days, the hours, of this too long martyrdom . . ."

Past she went, cool and remote, decked out in gold and pearls, carrying her white and vermilion flowers. The reader too, even after six hundred years, begins to be obsessed with her, especially with her eyes, jewellike and full of strange fire, looking down the centuries. That Petrarch suffered from her the torments of the damned in Hell no one will question; nor that he fed on his suffering. "Oh! blessed be the first adorable torture that love engendered when it usurped me, and this bow, and this arrow that pierced me, and this wound made in the deeps of my heart!"

He wrote to the Bishop of Lombez how for ten years "I have dragged my heavy chain . . . indignant with myself that a woman's yoke should for so long have bowed me down."

In 1341 he wrote that in this fifteenth year of his love, her eyes disturbed him more than on the first day he saw her. Then the sixteenth year of his sighs came and passed. In 1344 he said that seventeen years of his love had gone by; and he was still wishing that he "could light up a thousand burning desires in that icy being . . . see her eyes fill with tears when they turn toward me."

Meanwhile, he took to endless travels, affirming that the "object of all his peregrinations was to win his freedom." "But she follows me," he says elsewhere, "she exacts her due." In the Ardennes forest: "I think I hear her, when I hear the branches, the winds, the leaves and the birds lamenting, and the water as it runs murmuring away over the grass. I go along singing the praises — O, far from wise thoughts! — of her whom Heaven can never take far away from me, because I have her in my eyes. I seem to see with her ladies and young girls, and then they prove to be only beech trees and pines." At Lyons in the waving green summer he stood by the Rhône, and sent it along with a message: "Before paying thy tribute to the sea, pause thou attentive where the grass is greenest, the air most tranquil. There dwells our sweet and living sun who decks and blooms on thy left bank . . . Kiss thou her foot, or her fair white hand."

Always his love, his "shameful and unfair enslavement," went along with him, like an old man of the sea. On the Italian coast, he was shaken at the sight of a laurel branch.

His journeys would always end in Avignon; he would come home to "certain death." "I had hardly reached the confines of that well-loved city when the old load of my troubles fell back upon my vacant heart, and the contagion of my hideous sickness reappeared."

Sometimes he thought he had broken free: "It would take a long time to tell you, my Ladies, how heavy this new freedom is, now that I have escaped from the prison where love held me so many years, and did with me whatever he pleased . . . Often I say, as I sigh after what has vanished: 'Alas for the yoke, alas for the chains and the irons! Far sweeter were they than this walking about in freedom.' "

※ ※ ※

Petrarch was his own prison. But since in any case he hated Avignon for spiritual reasons, because what was going on there affronted the best that was in him, he withdrew to the solitudes of Vaucluse. "From ungodly Babylon where shame is King, from whence by now every virtue is banished away, hearth of anguish, mother of all the vices — I have escaped here to prolong my life . . ."

As much as possible thereafter, he shunned the city, of which he said, "I will not call it the cause, but the laboratory of all my sufferings." More than once, forcing himself back there, he found he could not stay the night, and he would hurry out of town and get back to his refuge, the "Closed Valley."

He had chosen a place where the high bony mountain forms an amphitheater of gray rock. The sheer cliffs tower there, with caves near the top, like huge flute holes gouged out. From the valley below them a path reaches up, and along it the slanting water hurries, in many colors of purple and green; quiet part of the year, but in the rainy season the river booms and drums.

This path ends at the foot of the cliffs, where there is a great, round pool hollowed into the rock; a strange bluish-green, tourmaline circle that they call The Fountain. Here the river Sorgue is born. The drama was in the contrast between the dark, silent pool and the white torrent suddenly leaping from its edge, down and away through the rocks; between the clangor of Avignon and this eternal peace.

Petrarch had only a peasant to serve him here, "an aquatic animal, raised amidst the springs and the waters . . . to call him loyal would be to take something away from him; he was loyalty itself." The peasant had a wife burnt dry and wrinkled by the sun. "If Helen had looked like her," said Petrarch, "Troy would be standing now." He spent hours and days here alone, without speaking, without music except the drum beat of the Sorgue hurrying down over the boulders. His books, too cumbersome to take on his travels, were here in his rustic hut (later enlarged and beautified), on the water's edge. His food was country bread, figs, almonds, a fish out of the river. Over a small bridge, he had an island garden, and he also planted things up nearer the Tourmaline Pool.

Did he see as he toiled up here, "where only birds could be," or further down as he fought the stream to defend his bit of earth, the pilgrims arriving long after he would die? The common strangers being shown around "his" house, crowding the small, shadowy rooms with red-tiled floors, staring at a wooden table "where he used to write"; at a picture of the wrong Laura, the dark Laura de Noves; at a bunch of blackened laurels on the wall "because he always went around crowned with laurel." Could he guess that men, gossiping still, would say that *she* had been here — here in his inviolable sanctuary where only longing and memory could ever come, and presence would have spoiled the dream?

"In this valley closed about on all sides . . . pensive and with slow steps, I walk with my love." Laura was not at Vaucluse, but everywhere. "Many a time, in the clear water, and on the green grasses, in the trunk of a beech tree and again in a white cloud, I have seen her living . . . The wilder the place where I am, the lonelier the shore, the more my thoughts bring her before me." Looking back in after years, he was to write in a letter of how he burned more hopelessly than ever in his retreat, and the fire would escape from his lips and fill the sky and the valley with lamentation. "From there have come those songs in the vulgar tongue about my youthful anguish, songs on account of which I blush today, that I am sorry to have written, but which as we see, pleasurably affect all those who suffer from the same disease."

As two decades went by, his love began to wear itself out, like a storm used up: "I have never wearied of loving you, and I never shall weary of it, O my Lady, but I come now to the time when I find myself too weak to bear my pain any longer, and to go on weeping forever." Again he says to her, "For a long time I have been tired of thinking how I am never tired of thinking about you." His dire prophecies of his own imminent death, made for example in 1340, are somewhat mitigated for us who know what he did not, that his death date would be thirty-four years beyond. He still wrote that his sore was "resistant to the power of essences and magic, and of stones brought from over the sea." But later he said, "It can warm me, the terrible ray, but burn me no longer; her memory can trouble my slumber, not interrupt it." This, however, was before the ultimate wound, of Laura's death.

· THE WHITE CARDINAL

ETRARCH endured the climate of love, John slept in his tomb, and Jacques Fournier, at the news that he had been chosen Avignon's third Pope, looked about him and exclaimed: "Illustrious Lords, what have you done? You have elected an ass!"

Actually they had offered the Papacy to Jean de Comminges, but only if he would promise never to take the Holy See back to Rome. He refused. For a full week thereafter the Italian and French parties among the Cardinals had stubbornly checked each other's moves until the only way out was to find a candidate who was above the battle. Their choice fell on Jacques, the baker's son.

This man, who took the name of Benedict XII, was no fool, whatever he may have cried out. They called him the

White Cardinal, because before he was Pope, and even after, he went on wearing the white robe of the Cistercian monks. He had entered this branch of the Benedictine Order early, applied himself to its rules, studied hard. His father was the baker of Saverdun, but his uncle was John XXII. Understandably, he did not stay on in the cloisters. Supported by a generous stipend he read canon law and theology at the University of Paris, moved on to become the Abbot of Fontfroide, then Bishop of Pamiers, and in 1327 of Mirepoix. That year his uncle promoted him to Cardinal.

Benedict had made a name for himself with the Inquisition. In the seven years during which he sat in judgment at Pamiers on those accused of heresy, his court of inquisition was in session an average of more than one day each week. Relentless, unforgiving, he bore down upon his victims, so that people began to speak about him in whispers throughout Languedoc.

"A demon infests the countryside!" they told one another. "If he lives much longer, it will be death for us all." Their general opinion was summed up in the wish: "May he fall over a cliff!"

A Prince held the bridle of the baker's son's white ambler, when they took Benedict to Avignon's great Church of the Dominicans to be crowned. Afterward he was escorted away, flanked by his Cardinals in wide red hats, astride their black palfreys. The Princes of the Church next proceeded to "adore" him — *adoratio* being the term used for the genuflections, the foot-and-hand kissings of Cardinals to the newly crowned Pope: *adorare purpuram*, in Imperial Rome, was the morning-kissing by Court officers of the Prince's robe; and the Popes had given over Rome's purple to the Cardinals for their color.

Benedict was tall and red-faced, and had a resonant voice.

Paul of Siena's statue, a cast of which is in the Avignon Palace, shows a tiaraed man with a broad, well-fleshed face, wide eyes, firm chin and a plump old right hand raised in an Apostolic gesture while the left hugs to his breast two enormous keys.

He lacked the polite manners that John XXII had acquired at the Court of Naples, and retained to the end the behavior of a monk. A story widely spread in Provence has it that one day the white-haired baker of Saverdun, wearing his work clothes and carrying his cakes and jam, came to Avignon for a glimpse of his magnificent son. The scandalized courtiers stripped the old man, reclothed him in silks and velvets and took him to the Pontiff. At sight of him Benedict lashed out: "That is no father of mine! My father was a baker, and you have brought me a Lord!"

Whereupon they hustled the old man away, undressed him again, put his old clothes back on him and returned him to Benedict for a filial embrace.

※ ※ ※

Although some maintain that Benedict planned to take the Holy See back to Rome or even to Bologna, the work he did on the Palace of the Popes was, as usual with the Pontiffs of the Avignon period, an accurate barometer of his true intentions. Three months after being elected, he brought in a man called Pierre Poisson from Mirepoix, to plan and supervise the new construction. The conceptions of John XXII for the papal residence seemed to the new Pope not sufficiently expansive, and nearly all John's work was torn down to make way for Benedict's. New foundations were laid, that would support more massive walls and higher towers.

Of these towers, the *Tour des Anges* was the first to be

erected, and since Benedict intended to live there himself it
went up with exemplary speed, considering the solidity of its
fortresslike walls and the building methods of the time. Two
years after the first stone was laid the roof was covered
with lead and Benedict moved in. During his entire reign
he stayed on here in the noise and dust of tearing down
and building up. Like all those who live in towers, his days
were filled with steps. To reach his library, he had to go up
dozens of steps, to get to his study, down dozens, and to
bathe, down a hundred. His tower is variously called the
Tower of Angels or the Tower of Lead, depending perhaps on
whether it is being viewed from the bottom or the top.

Speaking of the steps, one notes that a man could not
climb them without wheezing, and remembers the age of
most Popes. Each step must have brought Benedict that
much closer to Heaven. Yet, from the standpoint of defense,
these towers with their cramped stair wells could hardly have
been improved on. A step barely accommodated one person;
walls bumped the elbows. There might be space here to
carry a weapon, but not much to wield it. Only a single
enemy could advance at a time. Once he was toppled, the
way would be blocked. However, domestic obstacles arranged to ward off dangers from the outside, themselves beset the resident every day.

We do not know at what point the Pope discovered, like
many another builder of a new home, that a finished structure
may hold surprises. The records, however, show that the
architect of Benedict's tower became an ex-architect shortly
after its completion. A new man, Bernard Canelle, replaced
him.

Besides pulling down his uncle's concrete structures, Benedict set about undoing John's abstract works as well. He
would issue a bull on the Beatific Vision denying what John

had promulgated. He would cancel the Expectatives (offsetting, however, the resulting loss of revenue by increasing the number of benefices reserved for papal dispensation). And he began to act quite friendlily toward Louis of Bavaria, the same who had independently set himself up as Holy Roman Emperor and created his own Pope in opposition to John.

Benedict would have done better to stay out of politics. He had no talent for it. This move to rehabilitate Louis and strengthen him in his imperial position could only antagonize Benedict's French ally, Philip the Long. The Pope knew this, for he complained to Louis's Bavarian Ambassadors shortly after they arrived in Avignon on April 28, 1335: "I am well disposed toward your master; but the King of France has written me that if I absolve the Emperor without his consent, he will treat me worse than Boniface was treated." His voice choked and his eyes filled with tears before he added ineptly, "Besides, how do I know your master won't return me evil for good?"

One might have thought Benedict the suppliant rather than Louis.

To combat this move of the Pope, Philip secured the support of Robert the Wise, King of Naples, and the Kings of Hungary, Bohemia and Poland, and they threatened to elect a new Emperor in Louis's place. Upon which Benedict weakly assured Philip he had made the terms of Louis's rehabilitation so stiff that they would never be accepted, and for this reason had kept them secret from the King.

As for his uncle's venture into dogma, Benedict felt — whatever he publicly announced — that John had never surrendered his true opinion; that to him the souls of the holy were to remain under the altar until such time as they should rejoin their bodies at the Resurrection, and only then behold the Glory of God. Neither, apparently, was the purported

bull which John left unsigned at his death, a satisfactory re-
cantation in Benedict's view. Something drastic had to be
done.

As arcane controversies flared and flickered, the Pope
withdrew to John's château at Pont de Sorgues, with a bat-
tery of Cardinals and leading theologians. The whole party
stayed there four months. The very length of this retirement
shows how vital seemed the necessity of repairing John's near
débâcle. Just what went on behind those thick, forbidding
walls nobody knew, but on January 29, 1336, Benedict
issued his bull *Benedictus Dominus Deus in donis suis*, in
which he declared that anyone would be punished as a heretic
who should dare to teach otherwise than this: immediately
after leaving their bodies, the holy do see God face to face.

They also say, but this comment recurs monotonously
about Pontiff after Pontiff, that the new Pope was a reformer. No sooner was he crowned than he issued an order
to Bishops and all others who had the charge of souls to
leave the licentiousness of Avignon and return to their duties
at once. He himself spoke of "innumerable abuses" in the
Church. He set forth a long list of regulations to restore
discipline and suitable behavior to a clergy whose corruption
is thoroughly attested by eyewitnesses — adherents, not op-
ponents, of the Catholic Church. To quote Benedict:

> The worship for which the clergy was established, is neg-
> lected; holders of benefices and canonicates, having loosed
> the reins of reason and modesty, have flung themselves into
> fields of license, pursuing their untamable passions. But, still
> more dangerous and disastrous, a great number of ecclesi-
> astics, having shamefully cast off the yoke of continence to
> which they had subjected themselves, have followed, even as
> the horse and mule devoid of intelligence, their animal in-
> stincts, rather than the rule of reason; and they wallow in the

slough of lust, and they keep concubines, under the wing of her who should be the mother and guardian of good morals, that is, of the Church of God, that they have changed into a disorderly place, without stopping to consider the incalculable harm they are doing to their own selves.

In the papal household, too, he saw the need for change. Two hundred and forty people, some clergy, some laymen, had clustered around John XXII by the end of his life. Not all, of course, were venal, but at best the contribution of most was dubious. They fed upon visitors to the Holy See, charging money for such services as the presentation of petitions, their palms always up.

Wandering monks were another of Benedict's difficulties. Large numbers of rebellious inmates had been driven out of the monasteries for various acts, and their conduct was not improved by freedom. They roamed everywhere, looking for adventure, exploiting the populace with pretensions of piety. Benedict ordered them back behind monastery walls.

Aiming at a top-to-bottom reform of the monastic orders, he selected his own, the Cistercian, as the first to be overhauled. He managed to establish new rules among his white-clad brothers, and is also remembered by the Benedictines for curbing luxurious living, debauchery, and a casual tendency to regard as common property any articles belonging to laymen. But among the Dominicans he struck an adamant resistance that lasted till his death, and may even have contributed to it, for we learn that he sometimes ran a fever after his conferences with the Grand Master of this Order.

Forgetting his own uncle, Benedict was most successful in ridding the Papacy of nepotism, at least for the duration of his reign. He is credited with the statement: "The Pope should be like Melchizedek, who had neither father, mother, nor genealogy." A nephew who thought of coming to Avignon to seek his fortune was told by a Cardinal that he would be wasting the trip. "Nature does not speak to him," the Cardinal warned. A niece had a chance to marry into the nobility but had to make do with a plain merchant when Benedict refused to provide her with an adequate dowry. He did, however, helpfully pay the traveling expenses of the newlyweds back to their shop in Toulouse.

The Fourth Council of Avignon in 1337 went along with Benedict's attempts to reform the clergy. Priests were forbidden to eat meat on Saturday, unless Christmas fell on that day. Clerics must forego secular moonlighting, they must not engage in commerce or carry weapons, and they must shave off their beards. They should be somewhat less severe on the excommunicated, who in those days suffered such additional penalties as having their houses stoned and a coffin placed in front of their door. The Council also expressed its anti-Semitism: Jews were, as so often, required to wear a distinctive emblem; Christians were strictly forbidden to call in a Jewish physician.

In Austria and Germany, anti-Semitism was also a disease, even then. In the diocese of Passau, a consecrated Host smeared with blood, had, it was claimed, been found before the door of a Jewish house. Waves of persecution followed. Benedict's investigators, however, reported that a priest had taken an unconsecrated Host, smeared it with blood and planted it in the straw in front of the house.

Again, a hotelkeeper in Alsace revealed that, to protect the rest of humanity, all Jews must be put to death. God had commanded it. Farmers, shopkeepers and laborers left their work to follow this man, whom they called Armileder. Their bloody crusade turned on Colmar, where they demanded that all the Jews who had taken refuge there be handed over to them. The timely arrival of Louis of Bavaria broke up the murderous band, whose leader fled to Lorraine, where this early-day Führer was caught and killed.

These peoples were not the only anti-Semites: England required the Jews to wear on their breasts a label of colored wool, and in 1290 expelled them altogether. After all, the rise of Christian usurers, such as the "Caorsins" or money lenders of Cahors, was making them expendable.

Benedict's later political attempts proved that he had not learned from earlier mistakes. His eyes were wide, but his vision narrow. When he shipped over Cardinal-envoys to arbitrate the chronic War, Edward III of England did not even permit them to land. The Pope showed to advantage, however, in his insistence that Europe's rulers should stand by the contracts they made with him. This insistence was equaled by his concern for the inviolability of papal territory, as is vividly illustrated by the Fieschi Affair, which came about in this way:

The most corrupt of all papal officials was apt to be the Marshal of the Court, a sort of Chief of Police in Avignon. He was so high-placed that his womenfolk called themselves

"Ladies of the Pope's family." In fact, a City Hall archive under the austere Gregory XI would preserve a sumptuary law forbidding all women of any class whatever, except for relatives of the Pope, wives and daughters of the Marshal, and other great ladies, to wear furs, gold, silver, silk or pearls.

Here also, Benedict tried his reforming hand, and improvment indeed occurred if only because a great number of officials suddenly disappeared rather than face trial. The Pope then decided to send over to Toulouse for a new man, a friend — one Marshal Jean.

The Marshal's office carried with it certain perquisites. There is on record a compact between the crusading Jean and the City of Avignon, giving him the right to make collections from the local prostitutes, their pimps and associates. In exchange, these women, who had been restricted to specified quarters, or permitted (as in modern Nice) to patrol one side of a street but not the other, could solicit freely anywhere in Avignon. This treaty-making and keeping everything legal and shipshape greatly facilitated the taking of direct bribes.

Of course the receiving of money from prostitutes by a papal official was not generally considered corrupt practice, as is proved by the reforming efforts of Guillaume Durandi at the Council of Vienne, where he recommended that the Pope's Marshal should not have the right to levy tribute on streetwalkers. Durandi also wanted the ladies restricted to distant parts of town; he did not like to see them looking for customers at the gates of Church dignitaries, at the doors of churches, or in front of the Papal Palace.

It may have been through contacts with the underworld of Avignon that agents of the King of France approached Marshal Jean. What they wanted was Nicolini Fieschi, a gentleman from Genoa who lived in Avignon on the rue Curaterie. He was, they thought, a secret envoy of the King of England lobbying against French interests at the Papal Court.

One shadowy morning before dawn, the darker shadows of armed men slipped Indian file through a door that someone opened to them. Guided by whispers they broke into a bedroom. They seized Fieschi in his sleep, gagged and bound him, and hurried him out through the black streets to the Rhône. Once across the river on French soil, the kidnapers threw their victim into the prison at Villeneuve.

Benedict raged. He sent off a stiff protest to France, pointing out that the city where the Pope lived should be open to everyone, that it was international, that no one should fear for his safety while he was in Avignon.

Nicolini was set free, but this was not enough for Benedict. The guilty must pay. It would be a warning for all. Obtaining proof that certain individuals had been involved in the affair, he hanged them in front of the house in the rue Curaterie. He let them swing there, to show how he felt about papal land. For others of the plotters he reserved a less easy death.

Benedict knew that someone close to him was at the root of it all; and how could he reform the whole Catholic world if he could not trust his own household? The axe had inevitably to cut down Marshal Jean, chosen by the Pope for his excellent record at Toulouse. Even though the prisoner had been a friend of the onetime Inquisitor, it could only go all the harder with him now. The Marshal, it is said, resorted to a hunger strike, as a sort of trial by ordeal; more likely, what he knew of unbearable tortures ahead made eating impossible. Then he took poison, forfeiting "the Question" as well as Catholic burial. His body, untortured, was thrown out to the rats and dogs.

It was under Benedict that Avignon, open-mouthed, saw in its streets a fifteen-man embassy from the Great Khan of the Tartars, bringing furs and silks and a letter which read:

> We are sending our Ambassador André Franc with fifteen companions, to the Pope, omnipotent Lord of the Christians, he who is in France, past the seven seas, where the sun goes down. We wish these to open the way to other ministers, those whom we plan to depute ever and again to the great Pontiff of God the Supreme, as well as those whom we ask him to send us. We beg him to bestow upon us his fatherly blessing, and call us to mind in his powerful prayers, and direct his favoring gaze toward the Christian Alaits, his servants and his children. Given at Combala, on the 3rd day of the moon of the 6th month.

In October, 1338, the Pope sent off several officially accredited Franciscans to the Far East by way of Constantinople and Jaffa. Marco Polo was then only fourteen years gone, and although the people had laughed at his tales and a priest had urged him to abjure them on his deathbed, the Popes took notice and the "Time of the Missions" set in. Leaving under Benedict, the Tuscan John of Marignolli crossed all of Asia from the Volga to Peking, and all of China from Peking to Canton, and returned to Avignon under Innocent VI, thus missing Clement VI altogether. In 1340 a new embassy was sent off to Uzbeg, Mongol Khan of the Golden Horde, whom the Pope felicitated on his tolerance to the Christians; simultaneously Benedict was causing a crusade to be preached in Hungary, Poland and Bohemia "against the Tartars and other infidels." Islam, however, had gotten control of the Mongols, that strong new blood; the Muslims considered Asia their domain, and a divided Christianity could not withstand them there.

Under Benedict again, the Muslims were crushed at Spain's southernmost point, the port city of Tarifa, across from Tangiers. Knights of many countries had been sent into Spain by the Pope for the long fight with the Muhammadans, and there gained remission for their sins, exactly as if they had fought in the Holy Land. Now from this battle the victors crowded into Avignon bringing Moorish spoils. Against the noise of bells and trumpets the populace exclaimed over shields and harness set with precious stones, scabbards of wrought gold, the silken banners of Islam — and a special gift for Benedict, the war horse of the winner, Alfonso XI of Castile.

Andronicus, Emperor of the East, sent an envoy to Benedict too. Pressed by Asian hordes, he had to look somewhere for help, and he dispatched the monk Barlaam to Avignon, offering in exchange for being rescued vague promises of reuniting the Eastern Church with Rome. The only result of this embassy was that Petrarch picked up a little Greek. Many a time, the Greeks would talk unity with Rome, contingent on receiving aid; and the Pope would withhold the aid, waiting for fulfillment of the promise.

※ ※ ※

Like most reformers, Benedict had a bad press. For whatever reasons, Petrarch condemned him as a man without character and without strength, always in tears. It is certain that Benedict knew nothing of Italy and cared less, and that he had no interest in taking the Holy See back to Rome. To Petrarch's implorations he had returned a definite answer: the Papal Palace. Here is Petrarch's comment: "While in New Babylon we build towers both useless and absurd, so that our pride may mount skyward, whence it is sure to fall in ruins, there is no one left to guard and avenge the most lowly dwelling of Christ. The capital of all the cities under Heaven is fallen down; the houses of the Apostles crumble . . . as *they* [the Popes and Cardinals] raise up their palaces of massy gold."

Evidently he was not placated by Benedict's sending 50,000 florins to Rome for the repair of Saint Peter's and the Lateran. Did this, it had been asked by some, mean that the Pope was turning back? Not so, judging by all the hammering going on in Avignon.

Since Petrarch was an Italian we are asked not to believe him when he describes Benedict as an old man weighed down by age and wine. This Pope has reached us as many-faceted, to say the least: an austere reformer, a mystic, a man of secret tears; and at the same time one of whom the Italians made their proverb: *bibere papaliter*. A Dominican, in fact, called him *potator egregius*, which might be rendered as first-class drunk. It is Petrarch, still Italian, who gives us the story of the eels.

They had sent His Holiness a gift of eels from Lake Bolsena, the same kind that Pope Martin IV (Simon of Tours) was, according to Dante, purging away by abstinence in the Beyond. Martin used to have his eels killed by dunking them in the wine called vernaccia, to enhance their flavor; and that Pope's love of them was reportedly so marked that it found its way into his epitaph, his sepulcher affirming: *Gaudent anguillae* . . .

Benedict shared the eels most liberally with his Cardinals, keeping only a trifling portion for himself; but once he had a piece in his mouth he discovered his mistake. Ruefully, the Pontiff said: "I didn't know Italy could produce anything so good."

Whereupon Cardinal Colonna answered: "I didn't know

that a man so well-informed as Your Holiness didn't know that Italy produces nothing but good."

※ ※ ※

The White Cardinal grew fat and old. His body betrayed him, and the great dropsical legs would no longer bear him up. He died April 25, 1342, toward the hour of Vespers, leaving behind him a noble monument: the Palace of the Popes. In seven years he built more than half the present edifice; the walls were roughly from six to thirteen feet thick, averaging sixty-five feet in height and in some cases rising above 165, and altogether they enclosed about 54,000 square feet. A prime example of fourteenth century military architecture, a place that would never be taken by force.

※ ※ ※

· THE LAUREL CROWN

O N APRIL 26, 1336, Petrarch came to a remarkable decision: he would climb Windy Mountain. This exploit of his lived on in history as a significant event, because he went up to look at the view. Ventoux is the highest mountain in that part of the world, rising 6300 feet above the plain, and he knew he could see both France and Italy from the top. In fact, what finally spurred him upwards was the spirit of revived antiquity: he reread Livy on the mountain climbing of Philip of Macedon, and Philip's viewing at one and the same time of the Adriatic and the Black Sea.

After long cogitation, it was Gherardo that Petrarch chose as his companion for the ascent. Although both brothers had enjoyed the same material advantages, the second one was "poor in sense and knowledge," with no taste for books, given to huge meals and interminable dancing, in the early days shared in by Petrarch too but referred to by him as laborious pleasures. Like Petrarch, Gherardo wrote poetry to an unknown woman. When his lady died he was desolate enough to utter blasphemy; more constant than Petrarch, however, he took his grief to the Carthusians at Montrieux, and his main preoccupation thereafter was to save Petrarch's soul.

Petrarch tells how he weighed and rejected each friend before the climb: "This one was too apathetic, that one overanxious; this one too slow, that one too hasty; one was too sad, another overcheerful; one more simple, another more sagacious, than I desired. I feared this one's taciturnity and that one's loquacity." And since on a journey "every weakness becomes much more serious," in the end he settled on "my only brother."

They left early one morning, traveled northeasterly from Avignon, got to Malaucène and rested a day. The next dawn they were up, and accompanied by two servants began the difficult ascent. It was "a long day, the air fine."

So singular was their undertaking that an old shepherd whom they met in the valley tried to talk them out of it. The man expatiated on what he himself had gone through, half a century earlier, on the same journey: clothes torn to shreds, body the same, exhaustion, disappointment. He said that so far as anyone thereabouts knew, nobody had tried to go up since. They left their impedimenta in his care and went on, with him still shouting admonitions.

Gherardo took the steep path. "I weakly took the easier one . . . just an excuse for my laziness." Several times, Petrarch repeated this maneuver, ignoring the calls of Gherardo, only to catch up at last, tired and irritated, and find his brother sitting placidly at rest. Finally Petrarch sat down too and addressed a lecture to himself: "What you have repeatedly been through today . . . happens to you, as to many another, on the journey toward the blessed life . . . What is it holds you back? Nothing at all . . . except that you prefer a path that looks easier . . . that leads on through low and worldly pleasures. And yet at long last, and after many an easier turning, you must either climb up by the steeper way . . . or else choose to lie down in the valley of your sins . . ."

The highest peak was known as "Sonny," although, comments Petrarch, "it is the father of all the surrounding ones." The climbers eventually struggled up to it, found a level place, and rested.

Petrarch saw the clouds under him, and was dazzled. He saw Italy too, but "rather in my mind." He forgot the outer for the inner panorama. He told himself that it was exactly ten years now since he had left the University of Bologna, "and I am not yet in a safe harbor." He asked himself if, provided he lived as virtuously as possible until that time, he would be prepared to face death eight years hence at forty. "I rejoiced in my progress, mourned my weaknesses, and commiserated the universal instability of human conduct."

He forgot where he was, and why. Then the lowering sun warned him it was time to climb down. But he dwelt again on the wide view. He could see the mountains around Lyons, "and to the left the Bay of Marseilles and the waters that whip the shores of Aigues-Mortes." As usual he had with him a copy of Augustine's *Confessions*, and he produced it now to get a special message for himself, by letting its pages fall open and reading whatever his eye first glanced at. The leaves opened to this, in the tenth book: "And men go abroad to admire the heights of mountains, the mighty billows of the sea, the broad tides of rivers, the compass of the ocean, and the circuits of the stars; but themselves they consider not."

Gherardo clamored for more, but Petrarch closed the book. "I was satisfied that I had seen enough of the mountain." Ashamed, he scrambled down from his pinnacle, and until they reached the foot he did not speak again.

That night at Malaucène, Petrarch reported the experience hot off the griddle in a letter to Dionisio da Borgo San Sepolcro, who had given him the copy of Augustine, and in closing told him: "The time during which the servants have been occupied in preparing our supper, I have spent in a secluded part of the house, hurriedly jotting down these experiences on the spur of the moment, lest . . . my mood should change . . . and so my interest in writing flag."

※ ※ ※

Five years later, Petrarch received tangible evidence that his worldly fame was growing, whatever the condition of his soul: two great cities offered him the laurel crown of poets; specifically, the University of Paris and the Roman Senate made him this offer, which he received from each on the same day, and which neither had in his time accorded to anyone. It goes without saying that he chose Rome.

Before assuming the crown he paid his respects to another crowned head, Robert the Wise, King of Naples, a ruler who, whatever his own great accomplishments, enters the Avignon story primarily because of a woman: his granddaughter, the beautiful Joanna, who was either a murderess or not, as we shall later see. Petrarch was only five when the scholarly Robert had sat down on Naples' throne. To Dante he was "the fluent phraseman." To Petrarch, "a second Plato in intellect." To Boccaccio, the most learned King since Solomon.

To G. Villani, the wisest monarch in Christendom for five hundred years.

After that blood bath known as the Sicilian Vespers (1282) which drove the dynasty of Anjou off the island, the Kingdom of the Two Sicilies was split, and all through the fourteenth century, war was normal between the two halves. During Petrarch's lifetime, three Angevin rulers succeeded one another on Naples' throne: Charles the Lame until 1309, Robert the Wise his son, now reigning, and Joanna. At Avignon, Robert had been crowned by Pope Clement V "King of Naples and Jerusalem," the latter only an empty title acquired long before from a descendant of one of the Latin Kings of Jerusalem for an annual payment of 4000 pounds of Tours.

※ ※ ※

Man expects almost as many virtues of his rulers as he does of his servants, but erudition has seldom been one of them. Robert was, Petrarch affirmed, the only Prince of his time who "patronized science and virtue . . ." As a student at Bologna, the poet had already determined to seek him out for a patron. He could also, at the Court of Naples, frequent Philippe de Cabassole, Bishop of Cavaillon, appointed later on in Robert's testament as a Regent of the Kingdom. Philippe is still of nostalgic interest because he owned that once elaborate château at Vaucluse, whose few crumbling walls are slowly passing back into the rocky hill above the Sorgue River.

Robert was a tall man, well-knit, with majestic features and an expression of philosophic serenity. A devotee of physical exercise, he was especially fond of competitions with the crossbow. There was an open space in his castle grounds, walled on three sides and sloping to the harbor, where, watched some of the time by Petrarch, he won many such contests.

This most powerful of Italy's Princes had not hesitated to take issue with the Papacy. He was articulate, and he wrote a treatise against Pope John's idea of making a dogmatic decision as to the poverty of Christ. He himself sided with the Spirituals on this, and they and their like lived and taught safely in his Kingdom. Even after the publication of John's bull *Cum inter nonnullos*, Robert was of the same opinion still. He received at his Court the violently anti-John and pro-poverty Philip of Majorca, his brother-in-law. And Queen Sancie, Robert's consort, carefully safeguarded in a Naples vestry certain written attacks on the Pope.

When a boy, according to Boccaccio, Robert had been sluggish until his enthusiasm was sparked by Aesop's *Fables*. As he grew up, he applied the teachings of the philosophers to theology. He wrote sermons as well as treatises, and collected a vast library, besides hiring copyists of Arabic and Greek manuscripts and causing works of Aristotle and Galen to be put into Latin. He was a pillar of the University at Naples, at a time when Naples was a focal center of Muslim philosophy (from his day the University at Salerno, the earliest in Europe, founded by the Muslims thirty miles away, had begun to decline, although it survived to be closed by Napoleon in 1811). He made this University of Naples the one place in his realm where the civil law could be taught, and attended lectures there himself, standing up to hear them.

Robert was one of many sources through which Muhammadan learning came through into Christendom. He was a lesser version of Emperor Frederick II, a century before, who had spent his early days among the Muslims of Sicily and spoke Arabic like a Saracen. Robert — and Naples — were much influenced by the Muslim philosopher Averroës of Cordova (Ibn-Rushd), known as the greatest medieval commentator on Aristotle, whose works he spread. (As Browne and Dieterici have shown, Arabian philosophy, teaching that "perfection was to be reached by a combination of the Greek philosophy with the Arabian Religious Law," passed to the Moors, was further developed by Averroës, and "gave rise to the Christian Scholastic Philosophy," rendering it "the greatest service in restoring the Aristotelian element.")

Robert's very championing of poverty against the Pope is Muslim. That poverty was a Muhammadan ideal no one who has studied the life of the Prophet and of the Imám 'Alí will deny; to this day a Muslim is not unlikely to boast that his father died poor, and to quote Muhammad's statement: "Poverty is My pride."

Now Petrarch selected Robert to judge, symbolically no doubt, his qualifications for the laurel crown. And when they parted, after long and pleasurable dialogues, the King bestowed on the poet — in the well-known Muslim fashion — his own mantle as a robe of honor.

※ ※ ※

Petrarch was crowned in Rome at Easter time, on the 8th of April, 1341. A curious account, supposedly by an eyewitness, actually a burlesque, exists of the somewhat grandiose event, which did not fail to arouse its measure of jealousy.

On the great morning, says this account, Petrarch first heard a solemn Mass at Saint Peter's. He was then "appropriately" dressed: a purple leather sandal was placed on his bare right foot, to symbolize the tragic poets, and a violet shoe on his left, shaped like a buskin, to symbolize the comic, with a blue band wound around the leg. Violet, the supposed witness says, is the color of love, and blue the color of that jealousy which is inseparable from it. Over his doublet of gray taffeta a long violet velvet robe was put on him. This was lined with green taffeta to indicate that a poet must always produce new, fresh ideas; and they fastened a belt of diamonds around his waist, to mean that a poet must keep his ideas secret. Over the velvet robe came another, a white one, opened at the sides, as worn by Emperors at their triumphs, since there are relationships between poets and kings, and white is the purity one must find in their virtues. He wore a sort of Bishop's miter made of gold cloth on his head, with pendants behind. Around his neck hung a lyre, the poet's symbol, and he had a chain made of dragons' figures, to show that like the dragon he must renew himself every year. A girl, barefoot, with floating hair, carried his train; she also held a lighted candle, and wore a bearskin scarf; she symbolized folly, which thinks it sees better by candlelight than by the sun. Thus ornamented, Petrarch mounted a triumphal car hung with gold cloth, and liberally decked with laurel, ivy and myrtle. He held a great ivory lyre in his hand, and placed near him were pens, paper, ink and books. Various Olympian deities were represented beside him; a naked Venus, the three Graces, a flock of cupids; Patience drove the four horses, and Bacchus, surrounded by vases of wine, rode the shafts. In the parade a peasant, all in brown and bearing a switch, chased after a languid, perfumed man on a litter, to symbolize toil chasing away idleness. There were also two choirs, one of voices, one of instruments, and sundry fauns, nymphs and satyrs dancing. The streets were strewn with flowers, the gates of palaces and temples were open, and there were great crowds everywhere, even on the roofs. From their windows, the ladies of Rome threw down roses, jasmine, and lilies, also pouring out rose water, orange water and other perfumes — a whole year's store, according to the supposed witness. One young woman accidentally emptied a vase of aqua fortis on Petrarch, instead of perfume; it happened at a moment when he had just removed his miter, and he got the full force of it. The "witness" says that it turned him bald, probably for life, but adds comfortably, "I think he is too wise to worry about it much."

Arriving at the Capitol, Petrarch gave a discourse, and received three crowns: an ivy one, because Bacchus crowned the first poet with ivy; a laurel one for victors, and for victorious poets in the ancient contests; and a myrtle one, because this is the tree of Venus.

The day ended with a banquet at the Colonnas', and "when the supper was finished, in order to amuse the great company of most distinguished ladies, he danced, in his doublet, a beautiful and vigorous Morris [i.e., a Moorish dance] with little bells on his arms and legs: which was regarded as a gesture of politeness, and of greatness of soul, worthy of a poet who had just triumphed."

※ ※ ※

More sober descriptions indicate that this crowning was mild enough, and not unlike the Nobel Prize–giving ceremonies of modern times. The event took place in the Senatorial audience-chamber of the Capitoline, overlooking the Piazza on one side and the Forum on the other. There were many nobles present and clerics too and also a trumpeter to quiet the buzz of conversation and summon the populace, and Petrarch's discourse, unearthed about 1874, was some three thousand words long. The poet wore, of course, his robe of honor from Robert the Wise, and we can visualize him on that day from a description in another connection by Boccaccio, who writes of his gentle manner and his graceful gestures, of the fact that he "never bursts into loud and sense-less laughter," of his placid and humorous way of speaking, his engaging smile and modest gait.

The coronation was, says Gibbon:

> performed in the Capitol, by his friend and patron the su-preme magistrate of the republic. Twelve patrician youths were arrayed in scarlet; six representatives of the most illus-trious families, in green robes, with garlands of flowers, ac-companied the procession . . . at the voice of a herald Pe-trarch arose. After discoursing on a text of Virgil . . . he knelt before the throne and received from the senator a laurel crown . . . The people shouted, "Long life to the Capitol and the poet!" . . . In the act or diploma which was pre-sented to Petrarch, the title and prerogatives of poet-laureate are revived in the Capitol after the lapse of thirteen hundred years . . . They did him honour, but they did him justice.

☙ ☙ ☙

·CLEMENT AND CAESAR

Bah!'' exclaimed Avignon's new Pontiff, Clement VI. "My predecessors didn't know how to be Popes!"

Proceeding to set the example of how a Pope should be, he also prevented his successors from following it; he used up all that fabulous treasure that John XXII and Benedict XII had so patiently hoarded.

Clement, the noble who followed the baker's son on Avignon's throne, had the habit of success and wealth, the easy assurance often inherited with birth. At ten he was handed over by his father to the Benedictines, and began to display a love of books if not of cloisters. Still very young, he was made Bishop of Arras, which helps to explain why he later chose as Cardinal a boy of eighteen.

Benedict had left a solid but unbeautiful Palace behind him.

Clement would doubtless have enjoyed tearing it down; since this was almost impossible he disguised it with a new structure placed well ahead and to the right of the old. The L-shape of Clement's Palace joined with Benedict's to make a large courtyard, and the ensemble thus became, architecturally, more symmetrical and satisfying, although in those days the inside was, of course, the main aesthetic attraction.

Benedict's "enormous, frowning cloister" was now changed into a dream palace, with gilded walls, frescoes by pupils of Giotto or Memmi, blue archways spangled with painted stars, high airy terraces embellished with rare flowers, stables full of pawing white thoroughbreds in gold harnesses, great halls hung with tapestries from the East. It already was provided with huge kitchens, pantries, places to store wine; now were added rare foods, delicate vintages, and armies of servitors, down or up to the official whose duty it was to taste whatever the Pope was about to eat. The Palace had become in effect a town; it had chapels, towers, baths, wells, gardens, and hundreds more of winding steps.

Clement's nonarchitectural changes could hardly be classed as improvements. John's practice of dealing in Expectatives had been abolished by Benedict, but such opportunity for raising more money was not to be neglected now; Clement sold them hand over fist. A hundred thousand shoppers for benefices flocked into Avignon. Austerities evaporated, even recluses could have meats, sweets and fruits. All that came in was lavishly flung out; there was something for everyone. More would always be forthcoming. Nepotism, rooted out by Benedict, was tenderly fostered. Nephews sprang up like dandelions in spring and spread as carelessly, their dubious morals equaling their incapacity. Experience did not matter at all; blood was enough.

Either out of his enormous liking for women, or because

he had run out of nephews, Clement made a niece *rectrice* of the Comtat Venaissin, a remarkable advance for feminism in the fourteenth century. Villani's testimony is that women entered the apartments of this Pope as freely as Cardinals. Meanwhile he did not escape the charge of homosexuality.

That Clement the Magnificent had no calling for the religious life is unassailable. Here was a Pontiff who enjoyed worldly and sensuous pleasures, who hankered after satin and ermine and soft, fair skin, paintings and poems and pleasing sounds, rare animals and birds, courtly behavior and the gallantries of love.

This man was not a Pope but a King. When he said his predecessors had not known how to be Popes, he meant they had not known how to be Kings. His precept that "no one should leave the presence of a Prince unhappy, none should leave with empty hands," embodies his conception of what the Pontiff ought to be: like Julius Caesar, all to all. Superficially, indeed, he reminds one of Caesar; it can do no harm to list some of the similarities:

Both were Chief Priests, both Lords of Rome and enriched by Gaul; both were of noble birth (Caesar said he came down from Venus, through Aeneas); both were fearless spenders, lavish bestowers of favors; both were builders, both bookish; both were talented at the law, and could be strict judges in a morals case: Caesar annulled an ex-praetor's marriage because it took place the day after the bride's divorce; Clement excommunicated Casimir of Poland for marital infidelity. Both, too, could be clement. Both were orators; one reformed the calendar and the other appointed a commission to revise the reform; both needed money and took it, and used alliances and thrones and offices as media of exchange. Both were fond of elegance: Clement would not live in Benedict's Palace; Caesar tore down the country house he had just built because it did not suit him in every least particular, and went on his campaigns carrying tesselated and mosaic floors, and collected pearls, statues and pictures. Both were givers of banquets; both put on combats for festivities (gladiatorial combats — jousts); both were bald (Caesar was privileged by the Senate and the people to wear his laurel wreath at all times; Clement had his tiara). Both, as well as being loved by noble ladies, were sexually equivocal. They lived about the same length of time, Caesar dying at fifty-six, Clement at sixty. We may, if we wish to carry on the parallel beyond death, remember that Shakespeare imagined Caesar's clay as stopping up a hole to shut out the wind, and we read that Clement's head was turned into a wine cup.

When we see Clement as a King and dispense with too many moral judgments, his stature emerges. Clement was one of the most civilized men of the fourteenth century. His court blazed with talent. Here he gathered the best of the nobility, painters, poets, architects, men of medicine and other learned professions. Astronomers and sculptors mingled here with such as Petrarch and Boccaccio. Along with activities of the mind, there were the continual great banquets, balls and tournaments. Women of high birth, intelligence and beauty, participants in Courts of Love, were present here.

Clement's personal library further illustrates his intellectual interests: Homer, Plato, Terence, Virgil, Horace, Seneca, Apuleius, as well as Rufus Quintus Curtius the historian of Alexander, and Prudentius, the first celebrated Christian poet (born in Spain in 348) are said to have been included.

While minds were whetted on debates within the Palace, hearts were further excited at tilts and tourneys on the flat alluvial ground of the nearby island of Barthelasse. The most brilliant of these tournaments was doubtless the one held in 1351 when the King of France had come to Villeneuve and the bravest of his entourage wheeled and galloped and struck lance against lance before the ardent, dark-eyed ladies of Provence and Languedoc.

It was January at the time. Visitors from up north would perhaps not have found it cold, but furs could hardly keep the Mistral from stabbing icy fingers down the backs of southern women when they rode swiftly along the Alp-fed river, listening to the sharp snap of banners as wind and water buffeted their boats. Returning, the ladies, limp from vicarious dangers, weary of the wind and powdered with dust from the field of honor, would have to come home on their amblers or jouncing together in carts, for the rapid strength of the river discouraged its ascent.

One of the banquetings to honor Clement has been described by an Italian who was there. The great hall that day was covered from ceiling to floor with precious hangings, the dais decked with crimson velvet lined with ermine, and with silks and cloth of gold. A soft-piled rug hid the vast floor. The banquet was served by four knights of the Pope assisted by fifty squires of the Cardinals. The banquet itself comprised twenty-seven separate main dishes. These included a pastry shaped like a fortress — which held an enormous stag, a wild boar, some small deer and a rich scattering of hares and rabbits. After the fourth course the Cardinal's gifts were presented to His Holiness: a white horse worth 400 gold florins, two rings, one set with an immense sapphire, the other with an equally gigantic topaz, each being worth 150 florins (one gathers from these financial particulars that as regards gifts, it was not the sentiment that counted, but the price) besides a drinking cup worth 100. Lavish favors were also presented to various other guests. After the fifth course they brought in a fountain surmounted by a tower and a column, out of which spouted five varieties of wine — from Provence, La Rochelle, St. Pourçain, the Rhine, and of course, Beaune. Around the edge of the fountain were piled such birds as pheasants and partridges, peacocks and herons. After the seventh course, when appetites seemed to be slowing down, a battle between knights was staged in the banquet hall to revive them, and a concert followed.

Dessert was simple: two trees appeared, one seemingly of silver, bearing pears, figs, peaches, grapes and apples of gold; the other one green as a laurel tree, and jeweled with colored, candied fruits. Following this, the chief cook and his thirty helpers were able to execute a dance. The Pope then temporarily withdrew to his apartments, and on his return came the high point of it all: A wooden bridge had been specially constructed over the Sorgue River and apparently led across to the festivities. This was now unbarred and the rabble crowded on to it, eager for a closer view. They had no sooner jammed on to the bridge than, to the huge enjoyment of the watching guests, it gave way as prearranged, plunging them into the river.

※ ※ ※

· THE PRINCE IN
THE WEB

T WAS in this Clement's time that his
vassal, Robert the Wise, died, and
Robert's granddaughter, Joanna, succeeded to the throne of Naples. She
was about sixteen that year, and married to Prince Andrew
of Hungary, who has come down to us as handsome, but with
a squint. Two years later, handsome or not, the young
Prince was dead, leaving Clement with a *cause célèbre* on
his hands that to our day has never been unraveled. When he
had cut through the knots of this affair, the Pope owned Avignon.

☙ ☙ ☙

It happened when Naples was still hot, with that September
heat that carries over from summer. The Neapolitan Court

had gone to Aversa for a breath of air, but it would soon return to Naples for the coronation. Then there would be two thrones here instead of one: Queen Joanna's — and Andrew's. During the long days Joanna pondered this, and her pretty mouth tightened. Murmuring of weariness she went to sit apart. Her ladies nodded in sympathy, not surprised, because she was six months gone with child. They left her alone.

Joanna was nineteen now, and she was a ward of the Pope; Queen of Naples, but not, as she had confided to Petrarch when he in 1343 came as Papal Ambassador to her Court, its ruler. Now the thing which she so much distrusted would happen after all.

In memory she went back to her grandfather's last years. Robert had a number of losses to mourn at the end. Her brother Charles had died of a fever, and that left only Joanna and Mary to inherit the throne. The Pope agreeing to it, Joanna had been married off to Andrew of Hungary. In August, that had been — 1342. Then Robert made out his testament and appointed her, Joanna, the Duchess of Calabria, as his successor, adding that a regency should assist herself and Andrew and Mary until all three were twenty-five. Andrew was to get the principality of Salerno in case she died without a child. Well, it looked as if he wouldn't have that now. Forcalquier and Provence were to be united in perpetuity to Naples "as one inseparable domain."

Her grandfather had seemed frightened when he died. He had called his nobles around the bed and made them promise to recognize Joanna as their Queen. Whatever their thoughts, they had promised.

Then in the beginning Pope Clement put off her coronation, since besides her queening it also meant that Andrew, brother of King Louis of Hungary, would be King, or almost King. But Clement had at last succumbed to the pressure of the Hungarians — perhaps the gift of 100,000 gold florins had something to do with it — and had ordered the event for September 18. The Queen stirred heavily in her chair. She knew the ambition of the northerners too well to think that Andrew would really be no more than a Prince Consort. And as a woman, a girl, what power had she? Men seldom wanted a woman's rule. But the will of her grandfather, Robert the Wise, had placed her on the throne, and there she intended to stay.

Joanna struggled with the enormous problem, her round young face for once darkened. Her hands drew some material from a sewing basket and she began, absentmindedly, to plait the strands of silk and gold, hardly noticing as she worked that she was fashioning a cord. This was a dark strand — her marriage; this was Andrew, twenty months younger than she, desirable enough (except for the squint); and this gold strand here, this was Luigi. Surely there must be some better way to form political alliances than to marry two opposite people when they were children; but that had been her grandfather's wish.

The gold and silken threads wove in and out, somber and bright, one upon the other, then covered in its turn. This cord had been her life. This strand was Philippina, her governess, if that was the word. Philippina had brought her up: taught her to bow gravely in acknowledgment, to wear a royal smile except when queenly annoyance suited her purpose better. Policy, dancing, protocol, the sifting of compliments for their meaning; all these, besides delight in her slim, beautiful body, Philippina had taught her. Strange that Philippina knew so much about Court ways; she would never reveal where she came from, but plenty of others did it for her: from the dregs, they said; her first husband was a fisherman, and she arrived at the Court as a wet nurse in the time of Robert the Wise. Wherever she came from, Philippina was clever, she had known how to rise at the Court of the Two Sicilies. She recognized ability, too, and when she took a second husband he was a Muslim slave who had pulled himself out of the kitchen. The slave had become Grand Seneschal when his master died. They had a son. But here even in her mind Joanna stopped. She knew what the gossips whispered, that she herself had learned of love from the son.

Love. Love was her cousin Luigi. She sighed, an unaccustomed sound from her pale rose lips. At nineteen, she suddenly felt old. Why couldn't she have married Luigi instead? Andrew thought of nothing, except riding and food, and dancing with the village girls, along with his Hungarians.

As a dark strand slipped between her fingers she heard a vague drunken shout. The Hungarians again. She lifted her head to listen. They always kept apart, drinking, bellowing at their own jokes. Out of hand, now that the crowning of their Andrew was so near. Only a few days now, and he would be King; already, he was trying to act like one.

It was Friar Robert's doing; he had worked hard for this, the fat little monk who never washed. Even his robe stank. He was always padding around in his bare feet, showing his pretended poverty whenever she had a new dress or a new ring. She hated that red face and shaven head.

And Andrew? Did she hate Andrew too? When she lay wearily awake, these hot nights, remembering Luigi, listening to Andrew snoring beside her, she would ball her fists and shout silently: I hate him! I hate him! And yet there were times when, in a way, she pitied him. If only he were at home in Buda; then she could forget. But he was here, and always would be, because at nineteen the future is forever, and there was no way out.

Just lately they, the Neapolitans, had come and whispered

to her that there *was* a way out. She had almost fainted dead away. What they spoke was unspeakable. Unthinkable. But her mind turned traitor; again and again — she drew on the plaited cord and smoothed it out — it set arguments before her: the good of the Kingdom; in war, men had to be destroyed; a Queen is not as others are.

The shadow struck across her hands.

"What are you making?" It was Andrew. She moved, impatiently. No matter what he did or said, it was never right. She continued to weave her colors in and out.

"Is it to be a belt?"

She touched her swollen belly and felt the flush rising in her cheeks. Did he mock her pregnancy?

"Or perhaps a sword knot for the coronation?" He leaned closer.

She looked up at him; she watched the heavy jaw and squinting, bloodshot eyes, and smelled the warm, winy breath. Something made her say: "Why — it's a cord to strangle you!"

And then she smiled.

※ ※ ※

To his friend Cardinal Colonna, Petrarch wrote:

My God! How Naples is to be pitied! What a change the death of one man has brought about. You wouldn't know the place: religion, good faith, truth, all banished away. I could be in Memphis, or Babylon, or Mecca. Instead of Robert, so thoroughly good, so pious, so just — an overstuffed little monk, red faced, barefoot, his skull shaved, half-covered by a dirty robe, bowed over less by age than deceit, sunk down in debauchery, flaunting his poverty and still more his hoard of gold, holding the reins of this tottering state . . . This monster, not to be gazed at without horror, oppresses the weak, disdains the great, tramples justice under foot, and shows the extreme of insolence to the two Queens. Court and city tremble at his feet. In every gathering, a dismal silence is the rule. Even inside their houses, people whisper. The slightest gesture is punished like a crime and you hardly dare to think.

What a grief for me, to have to negotiate with a man of this kind about freeing Count de Minorbino . . . The only one who stems the torrent is Philip de Cabassole, but even his voice can hardly be heard above the din of this corrupted Court. He would not have stayed on here, either, except that he is held here by pity and the last instructions of the dying King, who committed the realm to him.

※ ※ ※

The days went heavily by; they were pregnant too. Word came from Naples that there must be no more delay. The servants, packing for the coronation, hummed to the dim sound of minstrels playing. One day more and Andrew would be crowned. The Hungarians were boisterous. Some of their noise reached the Celestine monks in their part of the castle, and they had to pray all the louder to shut out the world and perhaps their own envy. The Neapolitan party at the Court were much subdued, for them, and they drifted away to their rooms.

No moon that last night, and no breeze. The air stood in layers, chill and warm, as the stones released heat stored up during the day. Joanna had been long in bed, alone. Andrew was out, about his pleasures. Quite late, he came to their room. Joanna dozed. Andrew came over toward the bed, shedding his clothes.

Later in the night, muffled footsteps ran along the gallery outside, and there was a low, insistent knocking at the door. "A message from Friar Robert," mumbled a voice. And as

Andrew delayed, it continued, "Bad trouble in Naples."
Grumpily, Andrew rose and opened the door. It was the last
mistake of his young life.

In the blackness, a hand closed over his mouth as others
grasped his arms and legs. The door of the bedroom was
hastily fastened from the outside, shutting in the sleeping
Queen.

Six hundred years have gone by, without revealing just
what happened next. We only know a King was killed that
night, and regicide is no small thing; it brings the deaths of
other men, and even invading armies in its wake. The most
credible witness to reach us is Andrew's obscenely handled
corpse.

There was a contemporary, Bouzano, who wrote that Joanna wakened and begged Andrew not to leave their room.
Perhaps she was weary of having waited so long for him, or
suspected he was being called to other revels. When the King
was seized, Bouzano says, a shadow slipped over to her bed,
waving its sword, swearing to cut out her life if she should
cry for help. And then the door was fastened, and she
screamed, "Let me out! Let me out!"

But the Queen's own account says nothing of this.

The brutality that followed is as incomprehensible to most
observers as the gang killings and the torturings — in themselves a throwback — of our own times. Andrew was a boy
of about seventeen, sleepy, and spoiled with high living. Surprised as he was, expecting a familiar, and unarmed, he could
not have fought back.

Who hated this boy enough to kill him? He was disliked
as a foreigner, it is true, but who hated him? It must have
been someone very close. The factions around the throne
could easily have dealt with him by conventional means:
poison, a quick knife. But Andrew was not killed by pro-

fessionals; he was killed by amateurs, bunglers. It was a personal murder, homemade.

He was held and gagged. Later, his mouth was found to have been battered with an iron glove. Purple marks from the cord they used to strangle him were seen in the folds of the dead neck. Under oath, witnesses affirmed that he was dragged along the gallery by the genital organs, that he was then hanged by the cord with which he had been strangled, from a balcony overlooking the park, blood seeping from his scalp where the hair had been ripped out. Some, noting convulsive life still in the body, climbed from below and caught hold of the knees, pulling with their full weight till the cord parted and the corpse slumped to the ground. It was then dragged along in the darkness and hanged again. The murderers were looking for a well to drop it in when Andrew's old nurse, who had suckled him, came running out with a candle, and they vanished, leaving their work to history.

These were the facts which Clement had before him at the trial of Queen Joanna.

‧‧‧

On the second day after the murder they destroyed Tomasso Hambriccio, personal chamberlain of the dead Prince. Carried to his execution on a cart, he was tortured along the way with hot pincers. He did not address the people who had come to watch; the fourteenth century had a simple method of preventing loose talk: they had torn out his tongue by the roots.

Except for Charles of Durazzo, the chief suspects were Joanna's Neapolitans, who knew the palace routine and stood to benefit if she remained as sole ruler. There was Philippina and her faction. Catherine, Princess of Taranto (by title Empress of Constantinople) was another.

King Louis of Hungary, Andrew's brother, had no doubts. He wrote to Clement: "The assassins are Joanna, the murderer of her husband, the widow of my brother; Maria, the sister of Joanna; Robert, Prince of Taranto, and his brothers . . ." He had convictions, but no proofs, and he wanted the crown for himself.

The idea of a Queen killing her husband was not new; there were still plenty of people who could remember Isabella of France, she who with Roger Mortimer conspired to destroy Edward II of England some twenty years before this. The French, who should know, say that she had a tube made of horn stuck into Edward's intestines, and that through this a red hot iron implement was passed. It was still fresh in people's minds, undoubtedly affording an example of how memory affects judgment.

The dead man's son was born to Joanna at Christmas time. Terrible months went by. Then the rabble howled for Philippina, and she slumped to the floor and clawed at the young Queen's knees, begging to live. But the Queen heard only the shrieking of the mob outside. She let them take Philippina and her kin, including Roberto, whom people said was Joanna's first love. Philippina cheated the crowds of her burning, because she died under torture. They had to be content with the sight of her head, fixed to one of the city gates.

Within a month of these orgies Joanna married her cousin Luigi of Taranto — less than a year after the murder of Andrew. She did not wait for a dispensation from the Pope. Clement had been reluctant to grant one, although the King of France argued the need for a man to strengthen the young Queen's rule. She had a man now, but a weak one.

King Louis of Hungary did not limit himself to accusations — he marched on Naples. As he approached, Joanna bade her people a queenly farewell.

"Having decided to destroy . . . a monstrous calumny, I am going to kneel before the Vicar of God on earth that he may know my innocence as God in Heaven knows it. One regret torments me . . . that of having been until now your Queen only in name . . ."

※ ※ ※

Who killed Prince Andrew? There are too many suspects by now. It is certain that Joanna did not cry out much for vengeance or look around with diligence for any murderers; that she did not interfere with the delivering over to mobs for frightful extermination, of suspected men and women who were her friends. But then, she was only the Queen, not the ruler.

She was there; she had the motive, she had the chance. The crime prevented the double coronation, it allowed her to marry the man of her current choice, her grief real or not did not forestall a new, illegitimate pregnancy. Accusation, however, has never been guilt. And two such observers as Petrarch and Boccaccio, both of whom had been at Joanna's Court, believed her innocent.

※ ※ ※

· THE JUDGMENTS
OF LOVE

OANNA, now on her way to Clement
VI, has the right to be judged within
the context of her time.

A central difference between the life
of our own day and the fourteenth century was this: Europe
— there was no America — was almost entirely Catholic.
Even when the Great Schism of the West developed, it was
to be a division between Catholics; there was no split over
dogma, only over which Pontiff was the true Head of the
Church. If Oxford's learned John Wycliffe would confront
the Pope with his English Bible and denounce not only
Rome's corruption but its doctrine too, still he, like Huss and
Luther, belongs in effect beyond the Schism. In the 1340's
the Catholic Church had no formidable opposition except the
Muslims, who were paying no attention and against whom

most Christians were traditionally united, and Catholic writers of the times felt free to criticize, among themselves, the actions of the Church. This was, of course, before Coster and Gutenberg and a large public readership. These writers could be bitter; they could exaggerate, as Petrarch is charged with doing; but they were all part of the one family of believers, outsiders were not listening in, and they have left to the ages a vivid composite picture of lamentable depravity.

Certainly there was plenty to view with alarm. The worst attacks, excepting perhaps for Dante's, Petrarch's and Boccaccio's, would come during the Schism, but the evils were already flourishing many years before. So much corruption had to have a long history: the Augean stables did not fill up overnight. Two centuries earlier, for example, a Spanish Abbott was providing bed, board and perquisites for his seventy concubines. The Bishop of Liège had, by the time of his deposition in 1274, fathered sixty-five bastards. Witnesses at the posthumous trial of Pope Boniface VIII swore that he said: "There is no more harm in adultery than in rubbing one's hands together."

As for those of lesser note and station, fourteenth century critics condemn the convents in wholesale lots as being no better than brothels, and expose the infanticide practised so frequently within their walls. The laws themselves bear witness against the times: to prevent incest, stringent rules were repeatedly laid down forbidding priests to live with their mothers and sisters. We know that monasteries, shutting out the world, could become hotbeds of homosexuality.

Among laymen there existed, besides the usual immorality, the resident adulterer, the lover who lived with the family; what the French have termed *cigisbéisme* was widely practised in the higher ranks of society, the word deriving from *cicisbeo* or the *cavaliere servente*, being related in sense at least to the modern German *Hausfreund*.

Wandering minstrels satirized all this in their songs, sparing neither monk nor Prince of the Church; while the theatrical shows — often put on in the open space next to the church — were as explicit in gesture as in word.

At Avignon the multitude of prostitutes who gathered to collect their share of gold pouring in from all over the Christian world may imply the relative propriety of the convents though no credit to the Papal Court. Before blaming these gentlemen of the Court too much, however, one should remember the private lives of their exemplars. History has kept Petrarch's repeated cries about the wicked city:

> Woe to Your people, Jesus Christ! Woe to Your people, Christ! All that they say about the two Babylons, that of Assyria and Egypt; of the four labyrinths, of Avernus and Tartarus, is as nothing compared with this Inferno . . .
> This sink of all the vices, these fishermen not of men but of money . . .
> . . . Nimrod . . . who undertakes to climb the sky by raising haughty towers . . . Cerberus the all-devouring; Pasiphaë, taken with a bull; the Minotaur, fruit of a love most foul . . .
> I see with what tiara Semiramis, giving herself the appearance of a man, covers her forehead; how she dazzles with her wit the eyes of those around her and how, soiled with incestuous embraces, she treads men underfoot.
> He has, too, his Alcibiades, and none is more swift to follow evil counsel . . . I know not, I confess it, which is more disgraceful, his brazenness, or our forebearance . . .
> The waters of the Rhône, the blasts of the Mistral and the North Wind are less violent than the passion and instability of their minds. You could not call them a people, but a dust whirled around by the gale.

[And, of Christ] Whose name they celebrate night and day with exalted praise, Whom they clothe in purple and gold, Whom they load with diamonds — this same Christ they buy, they sell, they traffic in; they tie a bandage over His eyes as if to keep Him from seeing, they crown Him with the thorns of their impious wealth, they soil Him with the spittle of their impure mouths, they follow Him with their viper's hissing . . .

In all these places you behold, wielding the scepter, the successors of a band of poor fishermen who have forgotten their beginnings. They walk abroad in their purple, proud with the spoils of Princes and peoples. Instead of those little boats in which they used to set out, looking for a living on the Sea of Galilee, they live in high palaces. They have parchments at the tip of which there hangs a leaden seal, which are nets to catch poor dupes with, whom they then proceed to scale and lay on the grill to appease their gluttony . . .

Instead of the bare feet of the Apostles, we see the thieves' swift horses . . . covered with gold, stabled in gold, *nibbling on gold* . . .

The most evil is the one who prospers most; the righteous, if poor, is trodden under foot; simplicity passes for madness . . . God is mocked . . . the good are laughed at, and things have come to such a pass that soon, they will laugh at none . . .

I will not speak of adultery, seduction, rape, incest; these are only the prelude to their orgies. I will not count the number of wives stolen or of young girls deflowered. I will not tell of the means employed to force into silence the outraged husbands and fathers, nor of the dastardliness of those who sell their womenfolk for gold . . .

Give us back Nero . . . give us back Domitian . . . we could, at the price of a little blood, buy Heaven and come to glory in our martyrdom. We are devoured by a secret ill: it is not life they are taking from us, it is goodness; we can neither live in virtue nor die with honor . . .

The question arises whether the Courts of Love had a moderating effect on these licentious days, for some view them as a counter force to the prevailing bawdiness. Certainly they contributed a refining influence, but refinement did not eliminate their chief ingredient.

There were three strong elements in the medieval relationship between men and women: sex raw and crude, by no means restricted to the "lower classes"; sex love, disguised in allegory and bathed in sensuality as in the completed version of the *Roman de la Rose*, where the rose is not a rose; and counteracting both of these, the idea of chivalrous love with its dramatization of purity and chastity (an idea that our own coarse times, in which the complaint is often made that virtue is uninteresting, would do well to reinstate).

This chivalrous love, besides representing, perhaps, a spontaneous reaction to excess, owed much to the Crusades. Muhammad had improved the status of women. "Reverence the wombs that bore you," the Prophet had said (Qur'án 4:1). And again: "Paradise is at the foot of the mother." He secured rights for women which in our day have had to be forced out of Western governments by embattled Christian feminists. He had restrained polygamy at a time when it was widely practised, improved the position of women in divorce, given them property rights, made them separate individuals — persons — even if married, so that they could even sue their own debtors in the courts. We must remember that to the Church Fathers, woman was in Tertullian's phrase the "Devil's gateway," while until quite recently a married woman's status in the Occident was expressed in the sentence: "My wife and I are one and I am he."

Chivalry is a child of the Arabian desert, says Ameer Ali. Choosing from among hundreds of instances of Muslim chivalry, he tells how the Emperor Humáyún was escaping from his enemies when the bracelet of an alien Queen was brought to him; at the summons he at once turned back and defeated her foes before resuming his own march. This author continues: "Oelsner calls 'Antar 'the father of chivalry.' 'Alí was its beau-ideal . . . The wars of the Crusades brought barbarian Europe into contact with the civilisation of the Islamic East, and opened its eyes to the magnificence and refinement of the Moslems; but it was especially the influences of Mohammedan Andalusia on the neighbouring Christian provinces which led to the introduction of chivalry into Europe. The troubadours . . . were the immediate disciples of the *romanceurs* of Cordova, Granada, and Malaga. Petrarch and Boccaccio, even Tasso and Chaucer, derived their inspiration from the Islamic fountain-head."

The Courts of Love were probably more influential on art than on life. In this or that château, noble ladies sat as judges of these Love Games, and decided according to a rather elaborate Code of Love and a detailed knowledge of troubadour poetry, general questions about love or specific cases between rival nobles; the "Court" might end with the winner crowned, a banquet and a ball. Less elaborate was, among both the Arabs and the troubadours, the *tenson*, a word from the Provençal *tenso* meaning contention, which denoted a lyric usually featuring a debate on love. To pass judgment on his *tenson*, a troubadour (often a noble) would select a particular Court.

A famous Court case, decided in 1174 with the Countess of Champagne in the chair, was as to whether love can exist between husband and wife. It was settled in the negative:

> We pronounce and decree . . . that love cannot extend its powers over two married persons; for lovers must grant everything, mutually and gratuitously, the one to the other without being constrained thereunto by any motive of neces-

sity; while husband and wife are bound by duty to agree the one with the other and deny each other nothing. Let this judgment, which we have passed with extreme caution and with the advice of a great number of other ladies, be held by you as the truth, unquestionable and unalterable.

Marriages, be it noted, were then what is illogically referred to as of convenience; they were political or business alliances; and although the Church ruled that a girl could not be given in marriage before the age of twelve, brides of five were common. Grooms had to be fifteen at least, the Church said.

Among the thirty-one articles of the Code of Love were:

Whoever cannot conceal a thing, cannot love. Love must always grow greater or grow less. Love is always exiled from its dwelling by avarice. Love that is known publicly rarely lasts. An easy conquest renders love despised, a difficult makes it desired.

About 1276 Jean Chopinel of Meung had finished the controversial *Romaunt of the Rose*, adding eighteen thousand verses to the original four thousand of Guillaume de Lorris. The poem was a best seller. Two hundred manuscripts are still extant. France's "first woman writer," Christine de

Pisan, would come out against it, defending womanhood in her *Epistle to the God of Love*. Back and forth, France debated the question of knightly love, pure and self-sacrificing, versus seduction as glorified in the *Roman de la Rose*. The most serious and dignified minds were involved; for example Jean Gerson, Chancellor of the University of Paris, was violently anti-*Rose*. Petrarch himself was not convinced of the *Rose*'s merit. He said its author was like a dreamer who never wakes up. He sent a copy to one of his friends, however, telling him this book was the best-known work of the times.

The famous *Romaunt* is crowded with allegorical personages, only the hero being as is. An illustrated manuscript in the British Museum shows such villainous *Rose* characters as Dangier and Malebouche dressed like Muhammadans. A sort of early-day "How to Win Friends," the text admonished the would-be lover to wash his hands, use his toothpick, and, provided he has the voice for it, sing if asked to.

The two authors were as dissimilar as the Bunker twins. The first wrote for Lords and Ladies, was courtly, graceful, devoted to women. He stated that his object was to set forth all the laws of courtly love:

> *Here is the Romaunt of the Rose;*
> *It doth the art of love enclose . . .*

The second was tough, a hater of Kings, priests and virgins, as much a champion of "nature" as a psychoanalyst. Exalting the man of science (including the alchemist) quite as a modern would, he addressed himself to the rank and file. Of Princes he wrote:

> *Their body is not worth an apple*
> *More than a carter's body,*
> *Or a clerk's, or a squire's.*

Worst of all, he gave seduction a Christian cast, reserving
Hell for the chaste, carrying the rest up to the flowered fields
of Heaven.

※ ※ ※

Many have shown how the sensuous hand was hidden then
in the churchly glove. Churches were, in fact, places of ren-
dezvous: Guillaume de Machaut and Toute-belle embraced
between two pillars of a church; Petrarch first saw Laura in
a church. Even two long centuries later, Romeo's first encounter with Juliet is the occasion for a love debate (a *tenson*) which is ecclesiastical as well as legalistic:

ROMEO: If I profane with my unworthiest hand
    This holy shrine, the gentle fine is this:
    My lips, two blushing pilgrims, ready stand
    To smooth that rough touch with a tender kiss.
JULIET: Good pilgrim, you do wrong your hand too much,
    Which mannerly devotion shows in this;
    For saints have hands that pilgrims' hands do touch,
    And palm to palm is holy palmers' kiss.

※ ※ ※

Generally speaking, the Courts of Love were by the fourteenth century pale copies of earlier models that flourished
when knighthood did. By now the Albigensian wars had
ruined the South. The "finders" or troubadours (trouvères
in the North of France, minnesingers or "love-singers" in
Germany) had gone their ways. The "last troubadour,"
Guiraut of Narbonne, had died in 1294. But earlier the Arab
influence had been strong at Avignon, and the wandering,
singing noblemen had passed here; this place, and Carcassonne,
and other French towns had been in Muslim hands, which had
its civilizing effect. Wishful thinking might also have exerted

a pull toward chastity: departing knights certainly favored it for the ladies they left behind.

The Courts of Love then — and they existed — mitigated the grosser aspects of sex. Verbally at least the participants rose above animal behavior. Of courtly love and chastity, they seem to have thought: a pretty conceit, a nice literary convention, so useful in poetry, and, thank Heaven, there's still the alcove.

These Courts provided expression for an emerging Western feminism which was also being helped along by the husbands' frequent absences. They foreshadowed Portia. They were heralds of the literary salon, and also, in spite of their coeducational attendance, they may be considered an early form of that equivocal blessing, the woman's club. They constituted a forum where women (only first ladies, of course) were important, even dominant, where current trends in literature, art — if only that of love — and morals were discussed. Writers performed here for the ladies as they still do today. And other games were played here too: we learn that Obizzo, Marquis of Ferrara, presented the Dauphine de Viennois with a chess set in silver-gilt.

The *Arrêts d'Amour* (Judgments of Love) of Martial d'Auvergne need not be taken too literally; they are, however, indications of attitudes then prevailing. The fiftieth *Arrêt* condemns two men for having betrayed the secrets of Love, and sentences them to be whipped with the thorny branches of a rose bush. Again, a woman is banished forever from the Empire of Love for having sold her favors; she is henceforth to be the property of all, available to anyone. In another, a woman who has died in a state of rebellion against the officials of the Court of Love is forbidden burial — an obvious parody on a Church procedure against rebels. The *Arrêt* immediately following deals with the annulment of vows in the case of a monk who has entered the Franciscan Order after having sworn perpetual faithfulness to a woman.

There were two Love Parliaments in Provence: one at Aix, shifting in the autumn to Signe and Pierrefeu; the other at Avignon during the winter, at Romanil in fair weather. According to Nostradamus the Courts of Love began in 1162 and closed in 1382. In any case, they passed; but the names of those dead ladies live on in the mind: Phanette, Mascarose, Amphélisie; Doucette, Hugonne; Miramonde, Rixende, Alaète, Almodie.

Not all fair women, drifted now to some far country with Villon's snowfall of lost years, spent their days at Courts of Love. There was, for example, the Bavarian Isabeau, the greedy, flighty Regent of France, who in later decades gave France to England by the treaty of Troyes. Or there was Philip's daughter Isabella, with her tube made of horn. And at some point in all this hierarchy of beauty, there was Joanna of Naples.

※ ※ ※

It was a spring day in 1348 when the Queen rode into her beautiful city of Avignon, which by then had grown larger than Rome. Welcoming young Cardinals and nobles galloped and wheeled about her, bright rugs and tapestries swung from crowded windows along her route, flowers carpeted the road. Still, death from the Far East had recently slipped into these houses. She came to a place of mourning, although the increasing loads of dead were bundled out of her sight.

Part of the way, going to the palace set aside for her use, she passed along the streets on foot, with a canopy of cloth of gold held over her, eight Cardinals walking behind her, and about them an honor guard of Clement's soldiers.

The Queen savored all this the more for having just been

let out of jail. When she had gotten to Nice by galley from Naples, she found herself imprisoned by her own nobles because of their fear that, to save herself, she would give up Provence. Three weeks had been spent at Castello Arnaldo, until Clement learned of her plight and had her freed.

All Europe seems to have sat in, through its Ambassadors, at Joanna's trial before the Pope. In the great hall of the Papal Palace, centrally placed on a dais and the focus of every eye, Clement waited for her on a throne of red and gold. Around him on lower seats sat his Cardinals and further away prelates, nobles and foreign envoys crowded to watch. But even Clement in his triple tiara and jeweled, embroidered robes lost the attention of the audience when the young Queen paced into the hall. She wore a long blue mantle edged with fur and strewn with flowers, and on her head was the open crown of Naples. A bright curl fell to either side of her round, childish face. As the notables stood back to let the Queen, her flanking Cardinals and suite come through, they saw that her confiding eyes were full of tears. When she got to Clement she kneeled on a scarlet cushion at his feet and bowed her head and kissed the golden cross embroidered on his shoe.

Clement took Joanna in his arms. He raised her up and set his mouth against her warm, young lips, then placed her on a chair at his right hand. He offered a prayer, after which the proceedings began. There was much Latin on behalf of King Louis of Hungary, brother of the deceased, a long detailing of the charges against Joanna, and Prince Andrew's ghost was made to walk once more. Things had never gone well between Joanna and her Prince, the prosecution said. Her nobles had thwarted him at every turn; his people were not welcome in Naples; from month to month his coronation was deferred. On that last night, was the Queen not there in bed, wakeful and hearing it all, when they killed him virtually beside her door? Did she cry out? Did she move a finger to help? Did she take any noticeable action afterward, to hunt down the murderers and bring them to book?

In the silence, accusing eyes turned on Joanna. But now the Queen rose and spoke out with some Latin of her own. She and Andrew had looked forward to the coronation as the answer to their problems, she said. She described her horror at the odious crime, and how sick she had been, carrying her and Andrew's child. Gesturing toward the Hungarians, she told how, without a trial, Louis had accused Charles of Durazzo and put him to death, and how he had stolen her little boy. The Hungarians stopped their murmuring. Many who were present wiped their eyes.

The upshot was that Joanna stepped out of the Palace a free woman. Clement pronounced her his own beloved daughter, unspotted of guilt. In true Clementine fashion, he also bestowed on the vague Luigi of Taranto his mark of high papal appreciation for distinguished service, the Golden Rose. Andrew was buried again. Present beauty is better than corruption, and there are not many who remember the dead.

※ ※ ※

Before she received her absolution and her permission to marry Luigi — what could the Pontiff do? She was five months gone with child — Joanna sold Avignon to Clement for 80,000 florins, and there are those who claim that even this amount never changed hands.

As to whether pressure was exerted upon the young Queen, how can one doubt that Clement would have seized the opportunity? Judicial ethics was a luxury the fourteenth century could seldom afford. One can, nevertheless, make no case that would stand up in court to prove that the sale (on June 12,

1348) was forced; the statement signed by Joanna and her husband, Luigi of Taranto, says that she received the money. But if she was paid, why was she obliged to go borrowing from her Lords in Provence, and pawning her jewels directly after the sale?

Gregorovius comments in a footnote:

On December 21, 1334, Robert [the Wise] had declared that Provence was inalienable property, and on February 19, 1348, Joanna had sworn before the parliament at Aix never to sell the smallest fraction of it. In 1350, 1365, and 1368 she protested against all her sales. Her successors did likewise, and after 1481 the French kings repeatedly claimed Avignon.

❊ ❊ ❊

6 · THE STILLBORN
APOCALYPSE

CLEMENT had no thought of leaving
Avignon for Rome, but neither did
he want to lose the former capital of
Christendom. In 1343 an embassy ap-
proached him from Rome to plead for the return of the
Papacy to Italian walls. At its head was the disquieting Cola
di Rienzi who would four years later ride so high on a wave
of popular acclaim as to threaten the temporal possessions of
the Pope. Of even greater moment would be the widely held
belief that Rienzi was inaugurating that new era of the Holy
Spirit in which under the guidance of the third Person of the
Trinity all the old forms would be swept away, the Church
with the rest.

※ ※ ※

Back at the end of the twelfth century, word of a book called *The Everlasting Gospel* was passing swiftly from one Mendicant Friar to another. It was believed that an angel had presented this book to a priest named Cyril who turned over the Heavenly gift to the Abbot Joachim. The book was engraved on copper plates, being not quite so de luxe an edition as the later Book of Mormon. No magic spectacles were required to read it, although it was, understandably, somewhat hard to understand. John of Parma interpreted it thus:

The Old Testament period was under the direct influence of God the Father. With the advent of Christ came the age of God the Son. The time was now ripe for the reign of God the Holy Ghost. A new era was being introduced, a culmination; in the new day man would not have to rely on faith, for everything would be founded on knowledge and reason. Among the Spirituals the *Everlasting Gospel* replaced the Scriptures.

Its author clearly regarded the Old Testament prophecies as being then due for fulfillment, much as the Muslims did. The ninth century 'Alí Tabarí, for example, explained in his *Book of Religion and Empire* how the Old Testament prophecies refer to Muhammad. Isaiah 9:6, "the government shall be upon His shoulder," ought to read "the sign of prophecy is on His shoulder," said Tabarí, and would thus plainly designate the mole or "seal of prophecy" on the Prophet Muhammad's shoulder: the Millennium, they thought, had already begun.

Some fifty years after John of Parma, a man arose who began to see himself as the embodiment of these messianic hopes. This man was Cola di Rienzi. He was the son of a tavern keeper and a washerwoman and was born about 1313. He had studied fervently the glory that had been Rome, and convinced himself that he was destined to restore it.

Petrarch was then working on his *Africa* — its hero being Scipio Africanus, the conqueror of Hannibal, Rome's greatest foe. This admired but unpublished, unpolished work, which in later years embarrassed him to the point where he threatened to burn it, was intended as a new *Aeneid*, a "national epic of Italy." He was dazzled by the young Rienzi's vision of a fatherland, single, "harmonious, peaceful, holy, indissoluble." Scipio, too, had been young, able, dreaming, and scholarly. Rienzi was Petrarch's hero come to life.

They met somewhere, outside the Palace, as a letter shows. "I seem to have been hearkening to a god, not a man," wrote Petrarch afterward. Thinking over what Rienzi told him of Rome, he wept. As for Rienzi's plans, so far as Rienzi himself or anyone knew them, Petrarch yearned to "share in so noble, so glorious an enterprise!"

Clement was gracious to Rienzi. He did not dream of leaving Avignon for Rome, but he liked handsome, intelligent young men, particularly those who could express themselves fluently. He was himself an admirable speaker. He may have smiled indulgently over passages from Rienzi's oration such as this one:

"I have seen Rome, the prostitute of the Caesars, the beloved wife of the Popes, who today reject her like an adulteress; the capital of the Christian world weltering in blood, the great lords disputing over her remains."

He did feel it necessary to put the envoy in his place, and neatly told him, "You offer me the offices of your city, but do you not realize that this city belongs to me, and that you offer me what is already mine?"

Guessing at Rienzi's ambitions, the Colonnas managed to turn Clement against him; he was banished from the Palace and had to idle away several months in Avignon, without funds and ill. Petrarch, however, won the Pope back, and

Clement gave the young man an appointment carrying five florins per month.

In April, 1344, Rienzi, aflame with a vision, his head full of plans, left Avignon and made for Rome. For three years he worked day and night. He had frescoes painted on the walls, showing Rome to his illiterate public as a widow in her weeds, in a boat going down in the sea. The nobles were there as wolves and lions, the lawyers as foxes; as for the adulterers, murderers and thieves who made up so much of the population, these were depicted as apes, goats and hogs. People gathered to watch and listen, and he worked upon them with oratorical skill, explaining the pictures and painting new ones in the air, of a brave new world full of democracy and peace, showing them the contrast between their present and their past. Once when he addressed a huge crowd at the Lateran Church, he wore a dazzling white robe falling from his shoulders, and on his head a hat with three crowns from which a sword hung down.

He knew by now that he was inaugurating that new era of the Holy Spirit, in which under the guidance of the Third Person of the Trinity all the old forms, the Church included, would be swept away. He was the Knight of the Holy Ghost.

By May, 1347, the Revolution was ready. Rienzi had won not only a popular following but a tight inner circle of like-minded men who had sworn him allegiance. He prepared himself for the big moment by hearing thirty Masses at the Church of San Angelo. The next morning, the Sunday of Pentecost, crowds of Romans streamed toward the Capitoline Hill. The day was well chosen. Rienzi's chief enemy, Stefano Colonna, was out of town: he had gone to Corneto, taking his troops with him.

This time Rienzi's address, though strong, was brief. He said he was ready to die for the Pope and the welfare of the people of Rome. He read out a list of laws by which he proposed to free them. Power, he told them, was to reside in the people. This, it later developed, meant they would have the power to choose Rienzi.

Nominally, he was to rule jointly with the Pope's other vicar, the Bishop of Ostia; but since Rienzi claimed to be visited by a dove which would settle on his head and provide inspiration, and the Bishop had no such visitor, it was only natural that Rienzi should assume more and more authority. If not the Holy Ghost itself, surely the fowl was a messenger from that mystical Entity. He began to sign his decrees: "Nicola, by the grace of the Lord Jesus, stern and merciful Tribune of liberty, of peace and of justice, illustrious Liberator of the Holy Roman Republic."

☙ ☙ ☙

It is certain that Petrarch was among those who supported the new master of Rome. Apparently the poet wrote him "daily." He addressed eulogies to him and exhortations, and through him sent word to the Roman people (who had seen Petrarch crowned with laurel not so long before and had made him a Roman citizen) that Rienzi was sent to them from on high. He lamented that "neither my calling nor my lot permit me to assist you in deed."

Aglow with triumph, Rienzi on July 28, 1347, "in the first year of the City's freedom," wrote Petrarch and invited him to Rome. "Liberty," he wrote, "is now the very life and breath of the Romans. Its sweetness is tasted anew after the lapse of ages . . . wherefore the Romans, snatched from the noose . . . make a joyful noise unto the Lord . . ."

For a time there actually was a moral revival in Rome. Laws were based on the Mosaic eye for an eye, criminals were punished, citizens began to feel secure in their lives and

property — this in a city where it had been said that a woman
was not safe in her own home. Christian virtues began to appear. Eighteen hundred lawsuits were said to have been settled amiably by agreement between the litigants. Another remarkable phenomenon was that for a while intellectuals were
respected.

Rienzi was a creature out of time, a kind of coelacanth in
reverse. At a great Festival of the Unity of Italy he "decreed
the existence of the Italian nation" and distributed standards
to the representatives of Italian cities gathered before him.
On this moving occasion he wore a bright red robe trimmed
with ermine. As the Mass of the Holy Ghost (his theme
song) was being chanted, he armed himself as a knight. The
last notes died away. He stood silent before the people. Suddenly his loud voice broke out: "We cite before our tribunal the Pope Clement VI that he may explain the reasons
for his absence. We also cite Louis of Bavaria and Charles
of Moravia that we may judge their claims to the Empire.
We further cite the Princes of Germany . . . to produce
the titles on which they base their pretensions, being certain
that the election of the Emperor belongs to the Roman people." He then quickly drew out his sword, and flashed it
four times, thrusting at the four points of the world. Each
time, as his extended arm pointed the blade to East and West,
to North and South, he shouted: "*That* is mine!"

He began to impose heavy taxes, to mint coins, and in general to replace Clement. His power spread through Italy and
as far as Germany. Joanna of Naples and Louis of Hungary
— as Rienzi proudly informed the Pope — laid their case before him. (Actually, as Clement knew, Rienzi hoped to remove Joanna and secure the Kingdom of the Two Sicilies for
himself.) Crowned as Tribune, he looked forward to being
Holy Roman Emperor with his capital at Rome. He took

upon himself the right to draw up treaties and made such alliances as seemed to him wise; he punished, he pardoned, he decided civil and criminal cases alike. By now he was sending unarmed couriers from city to city, carrying wooden wands plated with silver, which people in their thousands knelt and kissed.

The other vicar, Raymond, lost no time reporting to the Pope all Rienzi's claims and doings, which in any case were not meant to be kept confidential. In Avignon, Petrarch's position as Rienzi's champion began to cost him friends. He consoled himself with Terence: "Homage begets friends; truth, enemies," and continued his correspondence with the Tribune because: "I feel as if I were in the very center of the battle-line." When his situation became untenable he retired to Vaucluse, where he rested in the morning and evening shadows of the hills, in the water-broken stillness.

Clement had no intention of becoming the last Pope. He sent an apostolic letter to the astute Cardinal Bertrand de Deux, then in Sicily, directing him to act. The next courier from Rienzi, bringing a report of his coronation, was beaten up just after he had crossed the Durance River. His silvered wand was broken — over his head — and the letter case hanging at his side was snatched away and smashed. From Vaucluse during the first week in September, Petrarch wrote indignantly to Rienzi:

"O Avignon, named (if we are to believe scholars) from thy vineyards which yield the most bitter grapes and a vintage of blood, is this thy respect for Rome, thy mistress? O remarkable man . . . Thou hast made a glorious beginning . . ." None can doubt, Petrarch said, that Italy may again regain her long-lost power — "Harmony alone is lacking." "Make clear to these men that their pride is far inferior to the lowliness of the poor . . . Crush, trample and

crush . . . this frog which, with its ridiculous puffing, coun-
terfeits the ox's massive bulk . . . The rights of nations have
been outraged in the person of thy envoy — the more significant aspect of this cruelty is that they have wished to do thee
harm . . . liberty and justice, indeed, they hate *per se* . . ."
The poet, like the Tribune, continued to dream of an Italy
united and free, and he hailed Rienzi's elevation as "Prince
of the Romans."

No man ever became a dictator through moderation, but
Rienzi began to commit the wrong excesses. He came under
the influence of bad companions, and as Petrarch later commented, "Would to God that among the bad he had not chosen the worst." His costumes — mistrusted by nineteenth
century historians clothed in decent black — would probably not have set him apart in that magnificently appareled
age. Extravagance, however, was another matter. The citizens looked on their erstwhile savior and found him drunk
with both wine and power, handing out decrees instead of
justice. They felt the heavy burden of new taxes to support
his whims. His relatives emphasized, by imitation, his luxurious living. An uncle, once a barber, now found himself
unable to appear in public without a mounted escort of important citizens. Rienzi's young and beautiful wife went at-

tended by Rome's first ladies, their prettiest daughters plying fans about her.

The Romans rejoiced in the possession of a sacred porphyry bath in which, tradition said, Constantine had bathed and was cured of leprosy. Rienzi bathed in it. Next he "baptized" a pair of hounds under the names of Rinaldo and Giordano Orsini, and drowned them.

On a happier day, Rienzi had assembled the nobles and caused the Holy Sacrament to be brought before him. He had then required the Lords to swear that they would never attack him in person or indirectly, nor attack any citizen of Rome; that they would protect widows and orphans alike, and maintain the new order, and would on every needful occasion appear with or without arms as it should be asked of them.

Whispers may now have reached him of a plot among the Lords and Bannerets to end his life. A would-be murderer had apparently been tortured and had implicated the rest. Rienzi's next move was to invite these leaders to a splendid banquet. They all attended, only to find themselves seized and jailed. A room at the Capitol was hung with red tapestries, and here on the following day, September 15, 1347, after each had made his last confession, the banqueters were to have their heads cut off.

The Capitol bell tolled. Crowds gathered. As the people watched, these men who had ruled Rome four months before came out of their cells. Tears pricked the eyes of waiting citizens, many of whom had served under the victims in the Roman army. Suddenly here and there, to Rienzi's horror, cries for mercy arose; more voices joined in; the noise grew insistent. Rienzi went dumb. He had lost the city overnight, and had not dreamed it.

In that moment he crumbled down. But he made a nimble

decision: he called on the crowds, addressing them as if he were the defender, not the butcher, of these Orsinis and Colonnas. He felt his way along: were there not extenuating circumstances, proofs of the prisoners' good will, of their innocence? Did they not, he asked the people, deserve mercy rather than death? He begged for pity, he demanded pardon. At the end he freed the nobles, returning them to their homes. Later he not only gave them another banquet and a splendid parade with banners, thoroughbreds and trumpets, but went on to place them in high office. (Petrarch never forgave him for this. At the very least, the poet wrote, he should have driven them from their strongholds, deprived them of the means for working further harm. "Fatal and dreadful darkness," was his comment, "which often obscures the sight of men as they struggle over projects of supreme importance!")

On November 20, Petrarch set out for Rome. But as he left Avignon a letter from his friend Laelius was handed to him, enclosing a copy of one from Rienzi, which reported Rienzi's alliance with Louis of Hungary against the Italians, and the increasingly strange goings-on in the Eternal City. Petrarch answered Laelius en route, saying he had not slept for three nights. Of the enclosure he wrote: "I have read it, and have remained aghast . . . I clearly perceive the ruin of my country; whithersoever I turn, I discover causes and fuel for grief. For when Rome is thus . . . mutilated, what will be the condition of Italy? And when Italy has been disfigured, what will be my future life? . . ." It was a death blow to Petrarch; now there would be no united Italy under one great Italian man. (No doubt the fact that Petrarch saw Italy as one, as a single unit, was primarily due to his living far away among the French, to a perspective gained from exile.)

Still hoping, he wrote Rienzi from Genoa, which he

reached November 25: ". . . let not thine own deeds dishonor thy fair name . . . Let not my lyric eulogy finish in satire . . . Where now is that Holy Ghost, the good counselor with whom it was thought thou didst commune? . . . I was hastening to thee, but have abandoned my plans, for I would not behold thee other than thou hast been in the past."

As for Pope Clement, he sent off a Legate to Rome to denounce Rienzi as pagan, criminal and heretic, excommunicate him, depose him, and place the whole city under an interdict. Rienzi, in kingly robes and a crown, turned his back on the envoy, who accordingly encouraged various nobles to revolt. During the early stages of the ensuing battle, Rienzi went into hiding. As couriers arrived with better news, however, he took heart, and once assured that the enemy was safely routed, he had the trumpets blow out victory, and made a splendid entry into Rome at the head of his troops, the scepter in his right hand, olive leaves on his head.

This was almost his last triumph. The people were tired of their Tribune, bowed under their burden of taxes, hungrier day by day from Clement's interdict. In the end, Count Minerbo boasted that he could take the dictator with fifty men. Hunted down, Rienzi made them ring the Capitol bells but no one answered, and weeping, he escaped somehow to the Castle of San Angelo. A month later, wearing another costume change, a woman's dress, he slipped out of Rome. He had reigned seven months, less five days.

He escaped to Naples, which his ally the Hungarian Louis had just conquered. But the plague forced Louis back across the Alps, and the one-time Tribune fled to the Abruzzi mountains where he hid among the Fraticelli, that same people whose Scripture was *The Everlasting Gospel*, and who had found in Rienzi their Man of the New Age. They too

were hiding out. Away from his beloved Rome, without
followers or audience, eating poor man's fare, enduring the
quiet, he stayed over two years. When neither he nor the
little brothers could stand it any longer, they sent him on to
the Emperor Charles IV, saying that perhaps the era of the
Holy Ghost was nigh, for belief dies hard, like hope. In
Prague, he met the cold reception usually accorded the un-
successful. He wrote, however, some remarkable letters from
here, on which Gregorovius comments: "The Tribune in
chains at Prague was more dangerous to the Papacy than he
had been when at the height of his power on the Capitol."

One of them, addressed to the city's Archbishop and dated
August, 1350, says this: "Did I not, contrary to the expecta-
tion of mankind, lead them to a sincere peace? . . . Did I
not decree that all those citizens, who were living in exile
from their native cities on account of party strife, should be
led back, together with their poor wives and children? Had I
not begun to stamp out completely the disuniting names of
Ghibelline and Guelph . . . ?"

There follows here a reference to a great discussion that
had taken place in the Consistory at Avignon, and which
Rienzi had learned of through the indignant Petrarch: the
Consistory had debated whether Roman and Italian unity
would make for happiness in the world at large, and had
decided this point in the negative. Petrarch had written: "The
next time thou addressest the Roman people, O ruler, I beg
of thee . . . to acquaint them with this occurrence, and to do
so in my very words."

Rienzi goes on: ". . . it appears to them [the Cardinals]
that the Church, that is to say that the wealth of the Cardinals,
is increased by the dissensions of cities . . . For, if the cities
be divided by discord and by wars, each visits the Supreme
Pontiff and the Cardinals with gold in its hands, whereby to

curry favor." If they are at peace, he points out, there is no need for such visits. "Hence let there be discord everywhere, that the shepherds of the Church may receive visitations. Let disease come, that convenient recourse may be had to the healer — and would that it were to a healer and not to a leach!"

⚹ ⚹ ⚹

After a year in the fortress of Raudnitz, Rienzi was handed over to Clement by Charles IV, "a dove of the Guelphs," and brought to Avignon for trial. It was August, 1352. In tattered clothing, as he stood between the bailiffs, the prisoner asked for Petrarch. But Petrarch, twelve or fifteen miles away at Vaucluse, did not come.

In a letter to his friend Francesco Nelli written that August, Petrarch described Rienzi's recent arrival in the city, his own reactions, and the then current rumors: how, miserably, Rienzi entered the Curia between his two guards, with the rabble pushing and gawking — he who once was accompanied by the Princes of Italian cities, and all the people of Rome. And how the Pope had now appointed three Cardinals to try his case and find a suitable punishment "for him who desired the freedom of the Republic."

Then came a cry from the heart:

> I had placed in that man my last hope for the liberties of Italy. I had long known him, and cherished him; but when he began to essay that most glorious enterprise, I allowed myself to worship him . . . And therefore . . . the more do I now grieve.
>
> He came, but not in chains. This alone was lacking to his public disgrace; as for the rest, he was so carefully guarded that there was no hope of escape. As soon as he reached

the city gate, the poor unfortunate inquired whether I was in attendance at the Curia, hoping, perhaps, that I might be of some assistance (which, to my knowledge, I cannot be) . . .

Rienzi was being accused of the wrong things, Petrarch pointed out — of what he did at the beginning, "the magnificent beginning," not the end. If condemned for this, then he would be "marked not with infamy but eternal honor."

Unable to leave the painful subject, Petrarch wryly commented that Rienzi had one hope of safety: that he was rumored to be a poet; for anyone "dedicated to so sacred a study" could not be done violence to in Avignon. Everybody was quoting Cicero's *Pro Archia* about it, Petrarch said (Cicero's defense of Archia rested on the latter's merits as a poet). He reminded Nelli that it was he, Petrarch, who had "brought back that speech from far-off Germany" and then sent it to his friends in Florence.

"What greater victory could the muses have scored under Augustus Caesar? . . . never, to my knowledge, has he [Rienzi] managed to write a single line; nor has he devoted to the study of poetry the slightest attention . . . What dangers would Virgil not escape here?"

Petrarch then told of a Cardinal who would continually ask him in wonderment, hearing of this and that one who had strung a few words together for a talk or letter:

"Is this man a *poet?*" And how he himself one day, with difficulty repressing a smile, finally pointed out to the Cardinal how rare a poet is.

Although in great danger over the Rienzi affair, Petrarch wrote still another letter to the Roman people:

"No one dares murmur a syllable, except in a remote corner . . . I, too, remain silent, nor do I affix my name to this letter, supposing the style will be sufficient to reveal the writer." He could, he tells them, "speak convincing words," if the case were being tried "in a safe place, before a just judge . . ." He urged them, not without results later on, to try and set their Tribune free.

Clement took no chances. He put Rienzi in a cell and had him chained to a ring that was fastened into a vaulted ceiling. The Cardinals had sentenced him to death, but the Pope never went through with it; one orator, perhaps, could not bear to see another die of eloquence; besides, Clement was famous for wanting everyone to leave his presence happy. The papal account books show that a bed was purchased for Rienzi on August 14. Tolerably clothed, he ate in his cell from the papal kitchens, and had many books, among them his Bible, his Livy, and his histories of Rome.

Before the whole problem could be settled, another Pontiff would rule in Avignon. Innocent VI disliked the Roman nobles and saw Rienzi as a weapon against them for his own use. Rienzi was pardoned, let off his chain, given the title of Senator, and sent back to Rome and a new countdown to fame.

With a handful of mercenaries, he entered the city. Once more, he was hailed as a savior. In seven years of absence, the people had forgotten all but those triumphant, early months. Again, for him, welcoming arches hung with garlands, houses displaying swinging tapestries and silks, streets paved with flowers. Once more he had, almost within his fingers, the chance to re-establish the Republic and then, who knows, to unite the whole of Italy. Had he managed, he could have changed the history of the human race.

But his magic had worn thin. He plunged his hands into the city's treasure again, getting ready for further luxury and war. The usual enemies reappeared, and would have to be

destroyed. He sent a deputation to Palestrina, to the grand-
sons of Stefano Colonna, his arch foe, bidding them come and
pay homage to the people of Rome. The Colonnas' response
was at least novel: each deputy was laid hold of and had one
tooth torn from his mouth. Rienzi raged, and swore to burn
Palestrina to rubble.

The Tribune then eyed the vast fortune of a popular general, Commander of the Knights of Saint John of Jerusalem.
He jailed him and had him condemned to the scaffold. Going
there, this victim memorably told the crowds: "Romans, my
fate was decided by my riches and your beggary."

There were still other levies, still another death, and then
the people and their leaders the nobles had had enough. In
October, 1354, a mob hemmed Rienzi round again. He tried
to beat them back with the one means he always owned, his
arm of eloquence; but the building from which he cried was
set ablaze, and this fire burned hotter than his speech. He
improvised one more hasty role, and ran off in a final costume
change. Betrayed by the gold bracelets he had forgotten to
remove, he was recognized, he was cut down. But death was
not, after all, unkind. With his dream dying, not to be was the
old question's better answer.

⚜ ⚜ ⚜

Petrarch never quite forgot Rienzi. In the letter to Francesco Nelli he had written these lines, which perhaps are as
fair a commentary on the man as can ever be made:

"His fame rests secure with those who measure the greatness of men by considering the noble qualities they have dis-
played, and not the success which has attended their under-
takings."

· THE SECRET

I F ONE had to sum up human life in a single word, the word would be: goodbye. Clement for all his magnificence was going to catch a mysterious ailment of the body and go his way. Petrarch, however, suffered from an ailment of the soul, known in the Middle Ages as "accidie," from the Greek (ἀκηδία) for noncaring or torpor — a state common to recluses and fasters, and a good many geniuses as well. Now called "acedia," it has also been famed as one of the Seven Deadly Sins.

A typical cycloid, the poet betakes himself to an imaginary analyst, in his case Saint Augustine, and the two carry on incredible, *trompe-l'oeil* dialogues which are set forth in the *Secretum*, begun about 1342.

Augustine says: "You are the victim of a terrible plague of

the soul — melancholy; which the moderns call *accidie*, but which in the old days used to be called *aegritudo*."

Petrarch answers: "The very name of this complaint makes me shudder . . . The way to despair is forever open, and everything goads one's afflicted soul to self-destruction . . . it tortures me for whole nights and days together. At such times I take no pleasure in the light of day . . . I am as one plunged in the darkness of Hell itself . . . I *feed* upon my tears and sufferings with a sick fascination . . ."

"Picture to yourself," the poet continues, "a man beset with innumerable enemies; with no hope of escape or of pity; with no comfort anywhere; with everyone and every thing against him. His foes bring up their batteries, they mine the ground beneath his feet, the towers are already falling, the ladders are at the gates, the grappling-hooks are fastened to the walls, the fire comes crackling through the roofs, and, at sight of those gleaming swords on every side, those fierce faces of his foes, and that total ruin that is upon him, how should he not be utterly dismayed . . . ?"

And Augustine: ". . . your misfortunes all proceed from a single false conception which has in the past claimed and in the future will still claim innumerable victims. You have a bad conceit of yourself."

After this Adlerian remark, Petrarch admits, under the Saint's probing, that almost nothing pleases him.

Augustine advises Petrarch to mark and learn such maxims in his reading as deal with "passions of the soul and especially with this plague of melancholy." It is too bad, the Saint avers, that there should be so much discussion in the schools on the art of living and so little conversion of such reasonings into action. Petrarch is to look around him and count his blessings. Petrarch complains of his anguish at the life of cities and their "tumult." (In all fairness, we must admit the

possibility that some of his tirades against men and things in
Avignon are the product of this "accidie.")

"Who can say enough about the daily nausea of my life in
the heart of this saddest and most chaotic of cities; this
narrow and deepest sink on earth, to which flows all the
garbage of the world? How to describe the sickening look of
it, of these stinking alleys where filthy pigs herd in with
maddened dogs, this rumble of wheels that shake the walls,
these wagons drawn by four horses coming out of the cross
streets, these faces of men so far asunder, the hideous sight of
so many beggars, and then of the follies of so many rich —
some beaten down by grief, others brimful of joy — in short
of so many different kinds, different occupations, and then the
gigantic din compounded of all these confused voices, this
colliding of the headlong mob? . . . Many a time when I
look around me, I think: 'I am going down alive into
Hell.' "

Augustine replies that if Petrarch's inner tumult were
stilled, the noise would not trouble him.

Doctor and patient now pass on to "the deep-seated
wounds." These are in Petrarch's case "love and glory." Another mysterious description of Laura appears, of her "whose
voice and the living expression of whose eyes have nothing
mortal . . . whose very form and motion are not as that
of others." The love affair was by this time sixteen years old.

Augustine reminds Petrarch that some day, Laura may die,
and Petrarch cries out, "May the winds bear away those
words!" As the Saint continues his vivisection, Petrarch insists that Laura leads "a life above that of ordinary lives . . ."
and that "the body of my Lady has been less dear to me than
her soul."

"Are you mocking me?" asks Augustine. He points out that
if the same soul "had been lodged in a body ill-formed and

poor to look upon" things would have been very different. Would the poet have loved it then?

Petrarch talks fast. Since the soul is invisible, he says, ". . . the image of a body like that would have given no indication of such a soul. But were it possible for the soul to be visible . . . I should most certainly have loved its beauty even though its dwelling-place were poor."

Augustine has the last word with: "If you are only able to love that which is visible . . . then what you love is the bodily form."

At one point, where the hard-hitting Augustine-Petrarch advises "external remedies . . . flight or exile," the defensive Petrarch-Petrarch says he has tried it, traveling "across the western regions, and northward, and to the ocean shore. And you see how much good it has done me." He escaped, he says, like Virgil's doe, with the arrow in her side. "I fled, taking my torment with me."

Love is the worst passion, the Saint affirms, because unlike the others, it "asks also a reciprocal passion . . . and thus man's heart is stung and stung again." He reminds Petrarch of the days when he first saw Laura: your "heavy eyes, ever bathed in tears . . . your broken rest and troubled moans, even when you were asleep." And of the insanity of jealousy "which, as one knows too well, is the ruling power in love . . ." He proposes such cures as satiety, shame, reflection and prayer. "This woman you praise, this woman to whom you claim you owe everything — it is she who has killed you!"

But Petrarch answers: "Know only this: that I *can't* love anything else. My soul is used to wondering at her, my eyes are used to watching her, and to me, whatever is not my Lady looks hideous and dark."

※ ※ ※

Like all successful physicians, Augustine exudes confidence. He believes that, contrary to bodily ills, ". . . all the ills of the soul are curable, if only the patient puts up no resistance." He says that Petrarch must make up his mind never to turn back, and go away.

"I prescribe Italy for you . . . Travel there, wherever you please, but beware of solitude." He is to remember Ovid's "Remedy for Love": "O ye who love . . . look out for lonely places. Where are you running to? You would be safer in the midst of a great crowd." Petrarch answers that he has known these verses practically by heart, since childhood. Augustine snaps: "What good has it done you to know so many things, when you haven't managed to make them suit your needs?"

The two men sit there, Augustine of Hippo and Petrarch of Avignon, ten centuries apart, in Petrarch's skull, bandying the classics back and forth: Socrates, Seneca, Terence. Augustine says: ". . . when I advise you to meditate on your white hairs, you come back with a flock of famous men whose hair turned white. What does that prove? Oh! If you could only tell me that those men had lived forever, you wouldn't need to be afraid of old age either. I suppose if I'd brought up baldness you'd have quoted Caesar at me."

Petrarch informs Augustine that he is afraid of thunder, and his *idée fixe* obtrudes even here, for he continues: "One of the main things that has made me love the laurel tree, is that they say it is respected by the thunderbolt." Had Augustine reproached him for this fear, he would indeed have replied that Augustus Caesar was afraid of thunder too. Blindness, he says, would have evoked Appius and Homer; one-eyedness, Hannibal and Philip of Macedon; deafness, Marcus Crassus; inability to stand heat, Alexander . . .

Augustine insists that man ought to meditate about death.

He says we are like the Trojans, sunk in sleep and wine, heedless of the enemy within our gates. He says Petrarch is an old man now (he was thirty-eight) and ought to blush. Petrarch says he is ashamed all right, but can't do anything about it. "Anyway, you know I get a lot of good out of remembering that she's growing old along with me."

By now they are almost at the end of the treatment, but obviously, Petrarch's *idée* remains *fixe*. The Saint orders the poet to reflect on such things as —

Nobility of soul; the fragility and ugliness of the body; the brevity of life, the flight of years; certain death, at an uncertain hour; your shame; the fact that this woman has immeasurably harmed your soul, your body, your chances; the uselessness of it all; the many times you have been mocked, undervalued, disdained; all your tender words, your groans, your tears, that the wind has carried off; her customary haughty air; the lightning-brevity of those moments when she was less unkind; how much you have added to her fame, how much she has subtracted from your life; how jealous you have been of her name, how little she has troubled herself about your interests — and so on and so on.

Leaving his Lady behind, Augustine attacks Petrarch's love of fame. Glory is only "a breath, a variable wind." He reproaches Petrarch for the Roman history he is writing from Romulus to Titus, and for his poem *Africa*. "Writing about others, you have forgotten yourself." The Saint, opposed to all scholarly endeavor, wants him to abandon these projects and meditate about death — as a good medieval Christian should, but as the "first modern man of letters" had no intention of doing.

The Saint admonishes: "Whenever you shall see the blossoms yield to summer's harvest, and autumn's chill replacing summer heat, and winter snows the vintage time, then tell yourself: 'These seasons pass, but to return again, yet I must go my way, and come no more.'"

Petrarch, however, although consoled by the dialogues, remains firm in his own response to the briefness of life: "Mortal man should first have a care for mortal things . . . no door is open for us to pass back again from eternity to time."

· MARY, MOST
BEAUTEOUS

T IS no wonder that Petrarch should
have carried a Heavenly Woman in
his heart, an unreachable Divine Lady,
helping to shape the idea of Laura.
Mary's image was destined to grow in the world, permeating
the consciousness of mankind, even until today's matriarchate,
when the living Son is often reduced to an infant in her arms.

At Ravenna, some of whose mosaics were a thousand years
old when he was born, Petrarch could see another Jesus: a
manly youth, or one garbed as a Roman soldier. Generally
speaking, the Ravenna Mary was not yet an apparent Fourth
Person of a "Holy Quaternity."

The Muslims, who brought in chivalry, elevated (but did
not deify) Mary, who indeed had been worshiped in Mecca
before Muhammad's time; to them she was one of the world's

four perfect women. In the Qur'án there is a whole chapter named after her. Actually, the Virgin's Immaculate Conception, as Gibbon was going to remark, came from Islam. The Qur'ánic passage he refers to is:

". . . And remember when the angels said, 'O Mary! verily hath God chosen thee, and purified thee, and chosen thee above the women of the worlds!'" (30:31–38) A tradition (hadith) from Muhammad states: "Every new-born child is touched by Satan, with the exception of Mary and her Son, between whom and Satan God interposed a veil." This is essentially what the priest still recites, every day at Lourdes.

Christians under the Avignon Popes wrangled over Mary, risking their careers. Was she immaculately conceived or was she not? That is, did her soul, at the very moment of its creation, bear the stain of original sin? Until the twelfth century, the Christian answer had been yes. Saint Bernard called the idea of her being immaculately conceived "a presumptuous novelty." Thomas Aquinas in the thirteenth century (*Summa Theologica* III, 27) said: "If the soul of the blessed Virgin had never incurred the stain of original sin, this would be derogatory to the dignity of Christ . . . she contracted original sin, since she was conceived by way of fleshly concupiscence and the intercourse of man and woman: for Augustine says . . . *All flesh born of carnal intercourse is sinful.*"

The Dominicans always agreed with their "Angelic Doctor" and the Franciscans inevitably took the other side. The Dominicans came to be called *Maculistae* — Spottists; under the last Avignon Pope but one, they would be expelled from all positions in the Sorbonne. But five hundred years would go by before they were finally defeated by the bull *Ineffabilis Deus* which on December 8, 1854, declared the Immaculate Conception of the Blessed Virgin to be an article of faith.

Explain it as one wills, Mary is deep in the life of the world. She is called by Bahá'u'lláh of Persia, in our own times, "that most beauteous Countenance . . . that veiled and immortal Countenance." She will never be expunged.

Toward the end of his life, Petrarch planned to build a chapel for Mary. In his epitaph, it was she he called on to receive his spirit.

༷ ༷ ༷

Across the Rhône from Avignon, over the modern bridge that spans the river now, past a tufted green island, recent and alluvial, are the fruit trees and weathered gray walls of Villeneuve-lès-Avignon (*lès* is the present form of *lèz* — Old French for "beside"), with Philip's tower set up at the edge of France.

The old town of Villeneuve still has an air, for once it boasted many a sumptuous Cardinal's palace or "livery" as the word then was. Along the winding street a bird sings in its square wooden cage and through an open doorway a woman sings too, as often happens in the South.

Here is the bare Hospice of the Sisters of Saint Jean de Matha, housed in what was a mansion three centuries ago and a Cardinal's livery long before that. Up the wide stairs is a door guarded by two life-sized, wooden figures of brown Franciscan monks, and through this door hangs a treasure of France, a vivid portrayal of life in this world and the next, as it looked to men five hundred years ago.

Could that be Laura at last, there in the middle of the picture, palely shimmering, sitting up half asleep? No, the painting, by Enguerrand de Charonton, came into existence a century after Laura was dead; it was commissioned in 1453 — the year Muhammad II took Constantinople. But the colors are fresh as if laid on this morning: sapphire and ruby, frog-green and butter-yellow. Done in gouache on a glossy panel, was Mérimée's judgment when he saw the work in the nineteenth century.

The woman here depicted as being crowned is Mary. She sits in the center of the sky, flanked by two beings in embroidered robes, identical twins, mirror images one of the other: stern and handsome young men with beards and long hair cut to bangs on their foreheads. Their movements are identical, each steadying the Virgin's crown with one of his hands, the raised thumb against the crown's jewels, each lifting his other hand in a vertical gesture full of drama and grace. From beneath the voluminous robe of each, an identical bare foot peeps out.

These two are the Father and Son, while between them above and just behind the crown stretches the Holy Ghost — a great white dove with outspread wings, each wingtip touching the lips of one of the young men, thus joining the mouths.

But the personage who, though lower placed, dominates the scene, the one whom it is all about, is Mary. She sits, drowsily beautiful, sultry and bored with posing, reddish hair, fair skin, long slim hands crossed on her breast, wearing a full blue robe spread widely out to either side, its center flower-strewn. Directly beneath her is a small matchlike crucifix, standing up between two cities: Avignon and Villeneuve — looking about as they did when the Popes were there — doing duty as Rome and Jerusalem. And under both of these, small, but produced with all the relish of a Hieronymus Bosch, the nether world: the people in Purgatory, and the damned. For all the Hell these last are going through, there is a lot of life here — a bat-winged devil enthusiastically working a bellows, a throng of nightmare animals, goatish horns, boarish snouts, besides torture instruments and flames. At a convivial table, cheerfully on fire, another bat-winged devil sits with a naked drinker; under the table, in flames, and come up from still lower depths to watch, are some damned with big eyes, leaning on their elbows. On the Purgatory side is a naked Cardinal in his hat, and by him a naked Pope in his triple crown being received aboveground by an angel. A devil hooks his claw, policemanlike, around another Pope's bare arm.

Above and to either side of the four large central figures — and they are unmistakably four — but reduced in size, stand the hosts of Heaven. (Mérimée believed that the variety of colors here was borrowed from the Paradise of Muhammad.)

Medieval man knew where everything belonged. He lived in Aristotle's finite universe, he had a place for everything and everything in its place. Copernicus' *Revolutions* would not push the world away off center and release the universe for almost a hundred years more, and up to the days of geophysicists and astronauts, to millions upon millions of people the sky and the center of the earth remained convenient holdalls. That the Bible says the Kingdom of God is within you, and that the Paradise of the Qur'án is a symbol (47:15) occurred to very few.

꙳ ꙳ ꙳

· THE TERROR BY DAY

ILL posterity, if there is one, believe,"
wrote Petrarch, "that without anyone's
having seen, either coming down from
the sky or up out of the earth, a de-
vouring fire; without war; without any visible cause of destruction, the world was almost completely depopulated?"

The stealth of this swift and general death, which, they
said, turned the universe into a vast solitude — the mystery of
it, was the worst.

The plague began in China and Tartary, bringing death
across Asia. Rumors flew before it, multiplying its terror. In
some countries, it was said, all the men died and the women
went mad and turned cannibal, devouring one another. From
Asia to Africa to Europe, it came; Genoese merchants
brought it back from India and Syria. The "whole world"

was devastated. The historian Matteo Villani, whose own brother was a victim, affirmed that it began in India in a fire that streamed down out of heaven or else gushed up out of the earth, and spread toward the sunset, swallowing as it went men, animals, trees, even stones. Whoever escaped the fire died of the plague.

Medieval Europeans looked for a moral reason behind all this. Boccaccio says it might have come "because God's just anger with our wicked deeds sent it as a punishment."

According to Maistre Symon Cauvin, grand astrologer and doctor of Paris who wrote a Latin poem about it in 1350, "It is enough to see the faces of these men and women to read therein the baleful writing and the blow that threatens them. That pale complexion foreshadows the approach of death, and death, before the fatal day, appears to sit upon that countenance!"

When the plague started up in a given house, hardly anyone escaped. A touch, a breath, would spread it. And it was so rapid that often the priest died faster than the one he was ministering to. It first came on as a blackish, egg-sized bubo, in the groin or the armpit. Then the victim's voice grew hoarse, his eyes haggard, his tongue dry and cold, while his bowels flamed with an insatiable thirst. He was racked with vomiting and spasms. The buboes multiplied (Boccaccio says) and spread all over the body; then black or purple spots appeared on the arms or thighs or other parts, and these spots were a certain sign of death. The blackened, gluey skin gave off a foul odor, and soon, twisting and screaming, the victim died.

The plague struck Florence in the early spring of 1348. Prayers and processions and instructions to clean the city of all filth and forbid any sick to enter proved of no avail. It generally killed within three days. Nothing stopped it.

Most of the living shunned the sick, and "the authority of

human and Divine laws almost disappeared," for the law-enforcement officers were all dead, sick, or shut away with their families. ". . . brother abandoned brother, and the uncle his nephew, and the sister her brother, and very often the wife her husband . . . fathers and mothers refused to see and tend their children . . ."

Some people formed little separate communities, where they lived temperately, eating, however, only the best food and drinking the best wine, for it had been noted that the undernourished died fastest. "Fewer of those," it was said, "who live a life of ease succumb." This was not always the case, however; one visitation carried off nine Cardinals in Avignon.

Others decided to dance, sing, laugh and get drunk. They made free with anyone's house and possessions, which was not difficult to do, since the doors hung open; for many, feeling doomed in any case, had abandoned their homes and fled. Still others burned cypress logs, or went about carrying flowers and sweet-smelling herbs or perfumes against the blended odors of rotting bodies, the sick and their medicines. Others fled from town "as if God's wrath in punishing men's wickedness with this plague would not follow them but strike only those who remained within the walls . . ."

A few coarse-minded servants, Boccaccio says, were the only procurable attendants, and for high prices would do little more than watch the victims die. He comments, to deplore it, that beautiful and noble women victims, deserted by all, did not scruple to be nursed by menservants as intimately as if by women. But it was his opinion that many more people might have survived if they had had care.

Day and night, people fell down and died in the streets. The fact that others had died in their houses was made known only by the rising smell of decay. The lowest of the population "got themselves called sextons" and hurried the corpses to the nearest church, where the clergy "huddled the bodies away in any grave they could find." Often two or three bodies — of a husband and wife, of three brothers, of a father and son — would be piled on the one bier, and when biers lacked, tables were used instead, for "things had reached such a pass that people cared no more for dead men than we care for dead goats." Yet, such being the custom, it was still desired to bury each one in his brimming family grave. In the villages, the wheat crops stood abandoned, and livestock roamed at will. ". . . such was the cruelty of Heaven, and perhaps in part of men, that between March and July more than one hundred thousand persons died within the walls of Florence . . . How many gallant men and fair ladies and handsome youths, whom Galen, Hippocrates and Aesculapius themselves would have said were in perfect health, at noon dined with their relatives and friends, and at night supped with their ancestors in the next world!" This from Boccaccio in the Richard Aldington translation.

Medieval writers offer these statistics which, exact or not, at least show the shape of the terror: In Siena alone, 70,000 died. In Parma, 40,000. In Trapani, Sicily, no one was left at all. Strasbourg lost 16,000 out of a population of around 30,000. Two-thirds of the population of Iceland vanished. In Paris, which then had 61,000 "hearth fires" — making an estimated population of 274,940 — they were burying 1300 a day. In Avignon during the first days one hundred died per day, the figure climbed to five hundred and ultimately to one thousand per day, and finally, according to one source, "there were not enough living to bury the dead," and in three months 120,000 perished. This obviously exaggerated figure is from d'Arnavon. Marseilles lost all its inhabitants, the last one of whom, it is said, died tolling the bell.

※ ※ ※

It was early in 1348 when Avignon woke up one morning to horror. The strange killer that was to blot out one quarter of the world's population had come across the Alps, and the pleasure-bent people, who numbered something over a hundred thousand then, were all unprepared to look at death. Even today, safely far away in time, their accounts exude panic. They tell of heads still crowned with flowers, bowed in sudden mortal agony; of how one's best-loved would writhe and fall down as one gazed at them; of how doctors shunned the sick, and priests and monks the dying. We know, nonetheless, from the ceremonious welcome for Queen Joanna, who arrived March 15, that life in the city was not disrupted all at once.

The clergy in general did not shine against this darkness. Where they should have been, in sickrooms and churchyards, Begging Friars often filled the gap. Come death to them or not, it was the Friars who prayed with the dying and buried the dead. Later on, as gratitude took tangible form, it was the Friars, not the clergy, who received the people's gifts and were named in their wills. When the danger was over, Cardinals, Bishops and lesser clergy thronged angrily to Avignon, demanding that the Mendicants be suppressed for having invaded their rights, heard confessions, taken alms and burial dues. Clement gave them, in Consistory assembled, a tongue-lashing that history has kept.

The plague turned up its famous heroes too. One of these was Petrarch's brother, and another was the Pope himself. Gherardo, former fop and idler, was in his monastery when the disaster struck. The prior, about to flee, urged him to do as much. Gherardo answered that he would stay at the post where God had placed him. Trying to frighten him into leaving, and perhaps to justify themselves, others told him if he died no one would bury him. He answered that the care of his remains was a problem for his survivors. He stayed, to watch thirty-four monks die one after the other, tending each as best he could, burying each with his own hands. Finally in the whole monastery he and a dog were the only ones left.

Clement, also, tried to help. He placed doctors in the different quarters of Avignon, and caused food and medicines to be distributed. He also bought a tract of land, still called the Flowering Field, at the gate of Saint Roch, where he had the dead buried. Around the Papal Palace and the Rock of the Lords, he was careful to keep great bonfires burning, day and night. But his historic act was on behalf of the Jews.

When the Black Death struck, the people did not look far for someone to blame: for someone who had poisoned the air, and the wells, and whatever was bought and sold. They noted that the Jews were not drinking from the public water supply, and did not seem to be catching the plague. Some said that in retaliation for the decision of the Council of Avignon, which in 1337 under Pope Benedict XII had forbidden Christians to marry Jews or to patronize Jewish physicians, the Jews had gone to India and brought back the pestilence. In streets blocked with the rotting and dying, people shouted, "Down with the poisoners!" Strasbourg, Switzerland, Italy, saw widespread massacres.

But in Avignon, the Jews were safe, for Clement rose to the occasion. He issued two bulls exonerating the Jews, who were not, he affirmed, the cause of the plague and should not be forced into baptism. Clement's greatest claim to glory is this, that he saved the Jews. From this time on they built up quarters which were respected in the papal towns: in Avignon, Ancona, Carpentras, Rome; so that Jews repeated with the rest the popular refrain of Clement's day: "Clement in name! Clement in deed!"

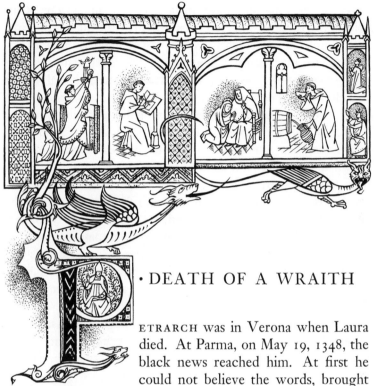

·DEATH OF A WRAITH

PETRARCH was in Verona when Laura died. At Parma, on May 19, 1348, the black news reached him. At first he could not believe the words, brought him in a friend's letter. He did not speak or eat for some days. He had thought "that the Divine was immune to death."

His mind went back to their last goodbye. It had been the autumn before, in November. "She was seated in the midst of the ladies with whom she usually lived, like a fair rose in a bed, encircled by lesser flowers . . . she had put aside all her ornaments, the pearls, the garlands, the bright colors. Although not sad, she lacked her normal gaiety. She was serious, and seemed to ponder. I did not hear her sing, nor speak with that beguiling gentleness . . ." When he left her, "she cast me a glance so sweet, so honest and tender . . ."

As the days passed, he began to sense the dimensions of his grief. "Alas, how our fair-seeming life can so easily, in a single morning, lose what we have won, and only with infinite pains, over many a long year." "Alas, enchanting face, alas, sweet look, alas, that proud and graceful walk, that speech that turned a rebel to a slave, alas, alluring smile . . ." "The pure spirit and the living light" was gone; she who was the laurel tree, and dawn, and the soft breeze; his white rose, his white deer with the golden horns; she had vanished out of life "like a cloud driven by the wind." "Where now are the worth, the merit, the knowledge? Where are the words, affable, chaste and caressing?" Bitterly now he addresses the eyes he had loved: "It is through you that Death, who puts the world in mourning, passed into that bright form." His ship is wrecked in the harbor, his sails and masts are broken, "and this one joy of mine, O Death, you take away; and it is you and the happy earth that cover and keep that beautiful body of a woman."

She had died in the town of their meeting, on the same 6th of April, at the same hour when he first caught sight of her. She had gone as she came, in the blossoming season, the fairest, the days when love is strongest. Many times now, in his mind she appeared before him. "Death made me immortal," she told him. "When they thought my eyes were closed, I had opened them to the eternal light."

Later on, in 1351, the same friend was to give Petrarch a description of this dying. "Pale, no! But whiter than snow that falls, on a windless day, in flakes on some fair hillside, she seemed to rest as if used up . . . Death was lovely on her lovely face." And Petrarch himself wrote of her death scene the way it pleased him; he says that she sat on her bed, calmly awaiting Heaven, while her ladies wept around her. "We see about to disappear," they said to one another, "the marvel of our age, the model of all the perfections. Virtue, beauty, courtesy, will wing their flight with Laura." "She died gently," Petrarch says, "without a struggle, not like a torch that is put out, but like a light with nothing more to feed on, slackening little by little, but shining to the end. Her lustrous eyes were not quenched, they seemed to be shut in sleep. She looked like a tired person, who lays him to rest . . . Thus should die one who lived as Laura lived."

Alas, neither deathbed sounds like the truth, which is that the plague had fastened on Laura and carried her away.

· THE TIARA AND THE DRINKING CUP

LEMENT the Magnificent was still, for better, for worse, on Avignon's throne.

Once in a public Consistory, someone discreetly dropped a letter. Addressed to the Pope, it was picked up and laid before him. It purported to be from the Devil to his "Vicar," the Pontiff, and to the Cardinals as counselors, and read thus:

" 'Continue,' said the Devil, 'to live as you have been doing, and I promise you a place in my kingdom . . . Revise, however, your preachments, because they do not conform to your practice; always despise the life of poverty and the doctrine of the Apostles; fight it and hate it as I myself hate it.' " The letter ended, " 'Your mother, Pride, greets you; your sisters, Trickery, Avarice and Shamelessness; and your brothers, Incest, Robbery and Murder . . . Given in the depths of Hell, to the acclamation of a band of devils . . . who impatiently await your arrival.' "

Authorship of this letter has been attributed to the Archbishop of Milan. Of the charge of incest, at least, it might be well to remember that besides consanguinity, which extended to very distant relatives, there was many another bar to marriage then, including affinity in law, and even the tie between godparents, godchildren, and godchildren's relatives.

Whatever Clement's reaction, his own letter to the Catholics of Armenia incorporates his view of the Papacy as an institution. "Do you believe," he wrote them, "that Saint Peter received from Jesus Christ the exclusive power of jurisdiction over all the earth; that the power of the other Apostles over certain territories was entirely subjected to his, and that all the Popes, successors of Saint Peter, have the same power as he? . . . Do you believe that the Pope can only be judged by God Himself, and that no one can appeal from his judgments to any other judge? Do you believe that he can transfer Bishops, Abbots and other ecclesiastics from one office to another, or degrade and depose them if they merit it? Do you believe that he . . . is not under submission to any secular power, even royal or imperial, respecting institution, correction, and dismissal, and that he alone can make general canons, give plenary indulgence and decide questions of faith?"

Dante commented that the Popes spent too much time on their wealth and the canons, none on the Bible and the Holy Land:

> *For this* [*the florin*]
> *The Gospel and great teachers laid aside,*
> *The decretals, as their stuff'd margins show*
> *Are the sole study. Pope and Cardinals,*

Intent on these, ne'er journey but in thought
To Nazareth, where Gabriel oped his wings.
                                      (Paradise, 9)

The end of the world was coming now for Clement, and a subtle change set in. Perhaps he was going back to the faith of a child who had declared for God at the age of ten, or the abrupt death of thousands all around him from the plague may have sobered him down. To posterity, laying self away, he wrote:

"If, since we were elevated to the Papacy, we have advanced in our writings or in our words propositions contrary to religion or to morals, we revoke them and submit them to the correction of our successor." The infallibility of the Popes is here denied. Perhaps he remembered how the first great Fisherman erred.

In the same vein, he defended the Mendicant Friars, stood before his Cardinals, many of them chosen by himself and whose character was closest to his own, and preached in favor of their enemies, those upholders of the triple vows:

". . . And if the Friars were not to preach to the people, what would you preach? Humility? you, the proudest, the most disdainful, the most magnificent among the estates of men, who ride abroad in processions on your stately palfreys! Poverty? you who are so greedy, so obstinate in the pursuit of gain, that all the prebends and benefices of the world will not satiate your avidity? Chastity? of this I say nothing! . . . your bodies are pampered with pleasures. If you hate the Begging Friars and close your doors against them, it is that they may not see your lives . . . Be not surprised that the Friars receive bequests made in the time of the fatal mortality, they who took the charge of parishes deserted by their pastors, out of which they drew converts to their houses of prayer —

houses of prayer and of honor to the Church, not seats of voluptuousness and luxury."

Surely Clement knew that he must include his own name in the indictment.

Toward the end of 1351, Clement was taken ill. He was up and then down again. "Our Pope returns from death and goes back to it," wrote Petrarch. On March 13 of the following year, he addressed this to Clement, who had a fever: "What makes me tremble . . . is to find your bed surrounded by doctors who never agree, because it would be a shameful thing if the one who speaks second thought the same as the one who speaks first, and only repeated what the first one has already said . . . Doctors learn their business at our expense. It is through constant killing that they perfect themselves in the art of healing; they are the only people who are allowed to murder with impunity." He then tells the Pope to make a choice among them; to choose, not the best talker, but the one most attached to himself. Again, he reminded Clement of an Emperor who had commanded as his epitaph: *Turba medicorum perii* — Felled by my physicians. On Clement's doctors, Petrarch commented later: "They delivered him from the perplexities of the Papacy, by uncalled-for remedies and too frequent bleedings."

After a long illness, and toward the end a continuing fever, Clement died. His death came suddenly, on December 6, 1352. Mollat, from a distance of six hundred years, says it was due to an internal tumor and consequent hemorrhage, denying the charges of Villani, Mathias de Neuenburg and the *Chronicle of Melsa* that Clement died of a venereal disease brought on by his immoral life.

Clement's burial was splendid, like his feasts. It unfolded in three solemn acts, one played in the great chapel of the Palace, one for nine days in Our Lady of the Lords, and one the long ceremonial journey to the grave in La Chaise-Dieu. Gifts were distributed as part of the mourning: florins, pounds of Avignon and bread. Fifty priests celebrated special Masses for nine days and the courtiers received thin black mourning robes of sendal silk. The catafalque was draped in sendal too, and standing guard about it were funeral urns and black-swathed candelabra; on his bier the black drapery was embroidered in gold, with his coat of arms against a field of red silk, and they had placed escutcheons at the catafalque's four corners. Nevertheless all this was dwarfed by the blaze of lights flickering, fanning and beating over him where he lay in state.

Afterward they sewed Clement's body in a deerskin and carried it to La Chaise-Dieu. He had himself supervised the stone carving for his mausoleum there, as the work went forward at Villeneuve. His wheel of faith had turned full circle; it was fitting that the man should be buried where the boy had taken his vows.

In 1562, the Huguenots broke open his tomb and kicked his skull around for a football, and we hear that later on it was made into a drinking cup; so that, from that bowl of eloquence, passion and wit, the wine flowed out.

※ ※ ※

· THE CLOSED VALLEY

AFTER Laura died, Petrarch came back
again to Vaucluse. It was spring. "The
west wind comes, bringing back fair
weather; bringing the grass and flow-
ers, its gentle family; the song of Procne and the tears of
Philomela, the white and the vermilion spring. The meadows
laugh, the sky is calm again . . . Air, water, earth are filled
with love; each living being turns to love again. Alas, for
me there are only sighs, the heavy sighs that she drags out of
my heart, who has carried its keys away to Heaven. And the
songs of little birds, and the flowers of the riverbanks, and the
sweet gait of chaste and fair ladies, all these are nothing but a
desert to me, nothing but as the sight of beasts, savage and
cruel."

"Since she left me, there is no other place," he wrote of

the valley, "where I can see so clearly her whom I seek; where the sky is full of so many cries of love. No, I never knew another valley to include so many private places where one could sigh; I do not believe that in Cyprus or anywhere else Love could ever have found such tender nests. The waters here tell of love, and so do the branches and the airs, the birds, the fish, and grasses and the blossoms — they all cry together, Love, love forever."

He kept on as he always had, from the first day, looking for Laura.

"And then I see her, a nymph or a goddess, coming up out of the clearest depths of the Sorgue, coming slowly, and sitting herself down on the bank, or gently walking over the fresh grasses, her feet among the flowers, like a living creature; and her look tells me of her pity."

There she still was, the one for whom he had "scattered so much ink, so many tears," his laurel tree, "more fragrant, more luminous than the bright and perfumed East, than fruits and greenery, than grasses and flowers." How could it be, he asks, that her eyes should be changed now to a little darkened dust. And then he tells her to look down "at the great rock where the river pours out, and you will see him there in the grass by the water, who lives on his anguish, and your memory."

Laura, his youth, his work, are all a part of this strange fountain. "Valley forever filled with my moaning, torrent that, many a time, my tears increase, animals of the forest, light birds, fish who live in these waters with the green banks, air that my long sighs turn calm or burning, sweet path so full of bitter memories, hills that I once loved, that I hate now, and where Love, from custom, still carries me . . . It was from here I used to see her, and in this same retreat I see once more the place from which, leaving here below her lovely dust, she climbed to Heaven."

"All the works that have come out of my pen," he has written, "were either entirely composed, begun, or conceived at Vaucluse." Like the headwaters of the Sorgue River, his writings welled out from under the sheer cliffs, into the tourmaline pool.

※ ※ ※

Petrarch had not always been unhappy here. He had the capacity for enjoyment that is a part of genius, and there had been good years in this place.

"As for me," he wrote, "when I am outside Italy, I breathe only at Vaucluse."

The only thing he did not like about Vaucluse, he informed his new friend Boccaccio — whom he met, probably for the first time, at Florence in 1350 when going to the Jubilee in Rome — was that it was too far from Italy, and too near "Babylon." Elsewhere he gave still another reason for his choice of this valley: "Too well-known, too sought-after in my own country, praised, flattered to the point of nausea, I seek a place where I can live alone, unknown, without glory . . ."

During some of this time, the Papal Court was at its most brilliant, largely because of the influential Cécile, Countess of Turenne. When she arranged a marriage for her younger sister Eleanore to the Pope's nephew, the Count of Beaufort, Petrarch chafed at having to attend the magnificent wedding; he could not wait to get back to Vaucluse.

"These men," he wrote of Clement and his Court, "that look down at everyone from the heights of their grandeur, that address Princes, even, in a superior tone, have deigned to lower themselves to the point of showing me an unclouded face, and telling me obliging things. It is to my reputation that I owe this singular reception — I know it well, but I would never have believed that my fame could have produced such a great effect." He refused the post of Apostolic Secretary, telling them Horace had similarly refused to be the secretary of Augustus.

He was always pursued, if not by the powerful, then by hordes of would-be writers. "Every day, verses and epistles rain upon me from every corner of my country; but that is not enough, I have to get them from France, Germany, England, Greece and so on. I don't even know my own self, yet people take me for the judge of everybody else." Everyone, he complained, was going in for "Apollo and the Muses." ". . . if the delirium should spread, soon the shepherds, fishermen, laborers and even the oxen will do nothing but rumble and ruminate poetry."

In 1352 he was called back to Avignon by him "who opens Heaven with his fingers and governs the stars by the movement of his cap." It was, once again, the post of Apostolic Secretary that was offered. Only they told him that his (Latin) style was too highflown, and that something more down to earth would be required. This saved him, he says: he turned in a sample letter so high toned that they could not understand it at all, and went back to Vaucluse.

※ ※ ※

An old servant and confidant, Raymond of Clermont, called Monet, was the custodian of Petrarch's precious library, assembled here and there in the course of many journeys. Monet could not read. "When I would entrust a book to him, he would show a great joy, and would hug it to his breast, and sigh; and sometimes he would speak the author's name in a low voice."

Probably only a few of these books were in French. Petrarch knew that language hardly at all; when Milan sent him as Ambassador to Good King John, to return the ring John had lost at the battle of Poitiers, he apologized to John in Latin for his inability to speak French. Provençal, however, was something else again. The troubadours — finders of their own material — had made it popular on both sides of the Alps. Saint Francis of Assisi even called his disciples, from the troubadours' name *jugleor*, the "jugglers of God." In the *Purgatory*, Canto 26, the dead troubadour Arnault Daniel addresses Dante in this tongue, telling him: "Jeu sui Arnautz, che plor e vai cantan." I am Arnault, who passing weep and sing.

France's South in the olden time had been ahead of the North, light streaming from it on a day when Paris was "a fishermen's straggling village . . . hidden under its island reeds." This was because of the fresh Muslim brilliance so close at hand. Chivalry reached in through Muslim Andalusia, the Virgin rose higher, the Prophet's daughter Fatima was known as Our Lady of Light, such as Nazhun and Zainab, Hamda and Safia and Mariam and many another, were accomplished Muhammadan gentlewomen of Spain. Unconnected with classical antiquity, a new system of manners and concepts marked by the changing status of women had been spread by the troubadours. The Vatican has a manuscript with the poems and lives of these masters of the "Gai Saber," which belonged to Petrarch once, and is full of jottings in his hand.

Besides, when very young he had passed at the foot of the Pyrenees "an all but Heavenly summer," as the guest of Bishop Giacomo Colonna, and may well have attended the Floral Games of Toulouse, a poetry contest founded in 1323 to preserve the language-of-*oc*. (This language, a dialect of which was Provençal, comprised the tongues spoken south of the river Loire, while the northern tongue was the language-of-*oïl*, and Italian the language-of-*si* — each being named for its manner of saying yes.) The games were put on by a group of poets calling themselves the "Consistori del Gai Saber"; they featured works by the troubadours, and the prize they awarded was a violet of gold.

Certainly Petrarch's *Triumph of Love* shows that he was familiar with all the most famous of the "finders"; Arnault Daniel, whom, like Dante, he placed first; then the two Peters (Pierre Roger and Pierre Vidal), and the lesser-known Arnault (de Marueil), and the two Rambauts (d'Orange and de Vaqueiras), and old Pierre d'Auvergne, and Giraud, and Folquet (of Genoa) "who bestowed his fame on Marseilles, and then exchanged his clothing and condition to gain a better land" — who, that is, having lost his mistress, entered into holy orders and became a Bishop. Among others listed in the *Triumph of Love* are "Geoffroy Rudel, who spread out a sail and rode to his death, and that William who, singing, cut down the flower of his days."

Petrarch imitated them all, their ideas, their rhythms, their style, even up to their word play. He would pun, for instance, on the names "Laura" and "Colonna" much as Pierre Milon had divided "Amor" into two parts: "A!" to denote lamentations, "Mor" to mean death — and had concluded: "He then who truly loves, dies weeping."

Petrarch's library may have included works on the Kabbala, as spread by Jewish and Muslim philosophers, but no demoniacal magic such as the impounded book of Bernard Délicieux. Petrarch commented on alchemy: "What do you expect from alchemy, except smoke, ashes, sweat, sighs, words, trickery and ignominy?" He was also harsh to astrologers. While speaking one day at the Visconti Court, he was interrupted by the official astrologer, whereupon he refused to continue.

Dark notions of this sort were then invariably ascribed to

the Muslims. Not all was astrology and magic in the Muslim
world, but a double wall of Arabic and prejudice (which still
stands) was reared between the rest of Europe and the Islamic heyday in Spain. In the Christian Middle Ages, the Devil
and the Muslim were thought of as joined together; it followed that people taught by the Muslims were taught by
the Devil. Gerbert, afterward Pope Sylvester II, who studied
in Cordova was one of these. The medieval story (in the
twelfth century *Gesta Regum*) had it that this scholar made a
pact with the Devil, reaching his earthly ambition by barter-
ing away his immortal soul.

Meanwhile, as one example among hundreds, Seville's La
Giralda remains in eloquent rebuttal: built as an observatory
under the superintendence of the mathematician Jábir ibn
Afíah in 1190, it was, when the Moors were expelled, turned
by the Spaniards into a belfry; for they had no idea what else
to do with it. To Islam, ignorance was not "the mother of
devotion," for Muhammad had taught: "Seek knowledge,
even unto China."

How vividly near and real the Devil was in those far-off
times can be judged by the fact that to millions he still is.
Every day, Baptism and Extreme Unction rites still exorcise.
The priest still drives out evil spirits in cases of "demoniacal
possession." On June 11, 1958, a Church of England commission, after a five-year study, decided that human illness
caused by demons may be possible: ". . . they would not like
to assert a priori that no case will ever be found of such an
unusual character as suggests the need for exorcism." Small
wonder that witchcraft was terribly feared in those times,
that the Devil lurked in medieval libraries, that one of the
Avignon Popes thought Petrarch a sorcerer. (Shipley, most
entertaining of etymologists, derives "sorcerer" from the
Late Latin *sortiarius*, from *sors*, lot: "One who attempted to

arrange someone's lot.") The timorous great of the four-teenth century did not want their lots rearranged by the wrong people.

Historians were no doubt well represented in Petrarch's collection. To them he was partial, "though I could not but be revolted by their discrepancies." He planned a complete history of Rome, and also collected coins and studied geography, even writing the Englishman, Richard of Bury, to ask the whereabouts of the Romans' Island of Thule.

Books on the law, the study of which he had abandoned, were probably not in evidence; these he disliked "because their application is vitiated by the chicanery of man. This made me reluctant to learn what I scarcely could practice without dishonesty . . ." Medicine, however, must have been there; he seems to have known a good deal about it, which is perhaps the reason why he ridiculed the doctors of his time, and scandalized them by drinking water, eating fruit, and often fasting. To Boccaccio, he proposed as a controlled experiment: two battalions of one hundred men each should be selected, one to be served by doctors and the other not; and he affirmed that the group without benefit of medical aid would have better health and fewer deaths.

Another of his ideas was that literature should be used therapeutically; Cicero's *Tusculanarum* should be taken as follows: the first book to overcome the fear of death; the second to control physical pain; the third to calm the ailments of the soul; and the fourth to uproot the passions. To one of his friends he prescribed the second book for gout.

He had little use for the empty disputes and barren dialectics of the Schoolmen, popular in his day. "In my own judg-ment," he said, "the merit of one's lips, compared with that of one's life, is of very inferior account." He mocked the doctoral dissertations: "A young fool enters the sanctuary.

His tutors eulogize him, relatives and friends applaud him. He receives a command to go up on the rostrum. He already looks at everything from above, anyhow. He murmurs some confused statement or other; his elders outdo one another, praising him to the skies; he has spoken like a god. During this time bells ring, trumpets blow, he is kissed, they put a round black bonnet on his head. When all this is accomplished, he who was a fool when he went up, comes down wise. Admirable metamorphosis, unknown to Ovid!"

His library was studded with the Classics. Plato was then little heard of, but Petrarch collected him. In the late treatise *On His Own Ignorance and That of Many Others* he condemned his Venetian critics for hating Plato and believing he had written only one or two little books, and added that he, Petrarch, had "sixteen or more of Plato's books at home." Pushed to the wall for a pronouncement on Aristotle, whom any intimate of Robert the Wise must have read through Averroës, Petrarch finally dared to comment that Aristotle was only human and could not have known everything, and proceeded to criticize his lack of style. Petrarch, however, knew virtually no Greek, although he tried to learn it twice; and the translations were imperfect, a fact which he should have recognized, since he quotes Saint Jerome to the effect that Homer is lost in translation. But Homer, Petrarch said at one time, was dumb to him, and he deaf to Homer. Nevertheless he wrote a letter to Homer, informing him that he, the blind poet, did not have more than ten friends in all Italy: five in Florence, two in Verona, one in Bologna, one in Mantua, one in Sulmone, none in Rome. Nicolas Siger sent Petrarch the first Homer to come from the Orient to the Occident since the division of the Church.

Petrarch has been allotted, with his friend Boccaccio, credit for giving the initial modern impulse toward the study of

Greek. This, as much else written about him, is perhaps overly generous. Greek philosophy reached into Europe in eleventh century Toledo, when Latin translations were made from Arabic translations of Greek. Palma's remarkable Raymond Lully, the "Enlightened Doctor" (died 1315), who knew Arabic, founded a Franciscan school of Arabic and Chaldean studies at Miramar, and went on missionary journeys to North Africa, Armenia and Palestine, had long since asked Philip the Fair in Paris to establish a college for instruction in Arabic, Greek and Tartar.

Boccaccio was indeed studying Greek in Naples, and Petrarch took lessons in Avignon from the monk Barlaam, Ambassador of the Emperor Andronicus. He also wrote to his correspondent in Constantinople for Hesiod and Euripides, and attempted further study with the Calabrian Leonce Pilate. (It was Boccaccio who brought Leonce from Venice in 1360, established him in his Florence home, put up with his dirt and misanthropy and his disdain for the Latin Church, had founded for him "the first Chair of Greek in the Occident," and heard from his lips the first explanations of Homer that modern Italy knew.)

Cicero first — who was not widely read in Europe before Petrarch — and then Virgil, headed Petrarch's hierarchy: the two authors that his father, who wanted him to study law, had once torn out of his hands and thrown on the fire. Horace, Terence, Statius, Pliny, Seneca, Quintilian, Aulus Gellius, Macrobius, Lactantius, were also among his possessions. If this last was the Christian Father of that name, Petrarch could read here about the heretical doctrine of the world's being round: "Is it possible," said Lactantius, "that men can be so absurd as to believe that the crops and the trees on the other side of the earth hang downward, and that men have their feet higher than their heads? . . .

They reply that . . . heavy bodies tend toward the center like the spokes of a wheel, while light bodies, as clouds, smoke, fire, tend from the center to the heavens on all sides. Now I am really at a loss what to say of those who . . . defend one absurd opinion by another." It is interesting that Dante, when on his mystical journey he reaches the center of the earth, follows his guide Virgil who "with pain and struggling hard, Turn'd round his head where his feet stood before," and the travelers could now lift their eyes to the Hell they had just left and see Lucifer upside down. Virgil explains to Dante: ". . . when I turn'd, thou didst o'erpass That point, to which from every part is dragg'd All heavy substance."

Petrarch wrote letters to these long-dead ancients on his shelves. To Livy (known then only in mutilated form) he said, "I read you whenever I seek to forget these places, these times, these manners . . . You cause me to disregard present ills, you usher me into happier ages." (This Livy was, in the next century, the treasured friend of Machiavelli. Confined to a villa near San Casciano, he would come home muddy and dirty from a day spent hunting thrushes, cutting wood or talking with peasants in a tavern, change into Court dress, and thus appropriately clothed spend four hours in his study, reading the men of classical times: "Received by them with love," Machiavelli reports, "I nourish myself with the food that is the only reality for me, the only thing for which I was born.")

We do not see much, in Petrarch's library, of Christian theology, but Petrarch was sure that Cicero would have embraced Christianity if its truth could have reached him. Such an eventuality was highly improbable, however, as Cicero's equivalents did not recognize the Carpenter's Son in the early days; scholars are usually as blind to truth from the unlettered, as the rich are blind to truth from the poor. It took

three hundred years for that highly conservative class to begin responding to the Galilean summons.

※ ※ ※

King Robert of Naples and many Princes and Cardinals
were Petrarch's guests in the Closed Valley. Two Queens,
Sancie of Aragon and Clémence of Hungary, made the journey to see him.

"I have clothes to cover me," he wrote, "provisions to feed
me, horses to carry me, a piece of land to lie down on, stroll
on, and lay my remains in after my death. What more did a
Roman Emperor have?" He had health, books, friends, and
no enemies "except those that envy has made for me." Among
his riches, he said, was the good will of many excellent people
throughout the world, many of whom he had never seen and
probably never would see.

His letter of invitation to Cardinal Colonna said: "If to the
uproar of the city you prefer the quiet of the fields, come
and enjoy it here. May the coarse fare I eat and the hardness
of my beds not put you off! . . . But if you disagree, then
what would prevent you from bringing along more delicate
foods, wines from Vesuvius and your silver plate . . . I
promise you a bed under the shade trees; a concert by nightingales; figs and grapes, water freshly drawn out of the river
— in a word, everything that can be had from Nature's hands,
the only fountain of true pleasures."

He also gardened. He would ask friends to send him peach
and pear trees from Naples to plant at Vaucluse. He
grafted trees along the Sorgue, and planted laurels brought
from abroad. Writing of his garden as enameled with flowers,
he tells of fledglings trying their wings there; of the river on
one side, the rocks on the other; of moss and leaves, and an
enclosing wall.

In all, he and his faithful Monet were together about fifteen years at Vaucluse — three lusters, Petrarch says. Perhaps the old man's death broke the last link that held him to France.

※ ※ ※

A letter in Latin verses, also to Cardinal Colonna, describes Petrarch's "War with the Nymphs of Vaucluse." He had, he wrote, wrested a garden from the Naiads of the river, and while he was away in Italy they conspired to get it back. The water kept reclaiming his bit of contrived, green meadow. Years went by. Fish swam in his garden. Then he mobilized the shepherd, the laborer and the fisherman. With iron tools they moved great boulders, rolling them around to shore up the land, and the nymphs retreated.

"Near the headwaters of the Sorgue, gigantic rocks lift into the sky on either side, where they receive the winds and clouds. Fountains pour out at the base of these rocks, and that is where the nymphs hold sway. The Sorgue comes out of a cavern, and with a mighty noise rolls its sweet and icy waters over a bed carpeted with small pebbles that look like emeralds. In the midst of these waters I possess a little, stony field, where I have undertaken to establish the Muses, that people everywhere are driving away. This is the reason for my great war with the nymphs. They take it ill that I should wish to put strangers in their place; that I should prefer nine old maids to a thousand young virgins."

· ROOT OF ALL EVIL

CARDINAL'S world in terms of fourteenth century Avignon must have been hard to renounce. Dying, they would leave pious wills, and it is from these documents that their possessions can be assessed. For example Cardinal Lagrange had to part with, among other things, beautiful gardens outside the Gate of St.-Michel, a great vineyard near the Gate of Miracles, many town houses, and a château at Sorgues. The brother of Clement VI, Cardinal Hugues de Roziers de Maumont, left an iron-bound coffer containing vessels of gold and silver, rich jewels and ornaments, and 144,173 gold florins. The Bishop of Cahors was relatively poor: all he had was a retinue of clerks, two porters, one steward, one cook, three runners, two grooms for his palfreys, one fisherman, three wine stewards. Prelates richer than he kept in addition troupes of buffoons to make them laugh; singers, male and female; musicians to play concerts for them. And we hear repeatedly of Oriental carpets; of silk and gold cloth from England; of such attendants as officers of the hunt and falconry; of captive monkeys and even lions; of swarms of *damoiseaux* — apprentice knights — who, curled, short-skirted and simpering, walked out in their master's wake.

John Visconti, who became Archbishop of Milan, was eclipsed by only three or four Cardinals at Avignon. He lived in vast palaces surrounded by fairytale gardens, and he had 637 servitors of all grades: chaplains, secretaries, equerries, pages, cupbearers, musicians, singers, knights. He also had immense quantities of falcons, goshawks, sparrow hawks, rare hunting dogs, and Arab horses.

Certainly this prelate could have stood up well to such a nonclerical man of wealth as the Duc de Berry, brother of Charles V, remembered because he refused to die until he should own the most beautiful Book of Hours ever created. Besides possessing at death ten and a half pages of this book, pages painted with ground-up lapis lazuli and pure gold, the Duke owned northwestern France, a dromedary, an ostrich, and a bear that followed him on his journeys in a small chariot. His staff included embroiderers, clockmakers and glassmakers, and it is reported that what should have been his daughters' marriage portion was spent on pampering his nightingales.

It was Petrarch's opinion that the Cardinals were blinded by the piece of red cloth on their heads. If not, they might have been dazzled by their dress: a sky-blue gown, perhaps, and a vast, violet cope; or, as the decades passed, short, tight coats, spurred boots, bonnets with plumes, long hair artistically arranged, a mantle with big green checks. It was hard to tell a prelate and a noble apart; not all were so neatly dichotomized as Bishop Hatfield of Durham, whose seal, dating from about 1350, shows him dressed in episcopal garb on one side, and on the other riding to war in full armor.

A decree of Pope John XXII, *Etsi deceat*, came down hard on the rich and voluptuous holders of Church livings who dressed in worldly clothing and hid themselves like birds of the night from the eye of the Great Shepherd. John himself, be it said, is usually described as frugal and abstemious; but few of the fat and easy-living are seen aboveground by his age. It is not so much that one gives up the world as that the world gives one up. "What," asks in another connection a classic Persian author who was a contemporary of John's, "can an old prostitute do but renounce whoredom, or a deposed official but cease from oppressing the citizens?" Even John had, besides his enormous wealth in money, those seven million florins' worth of dishes, crosses, miters, and jewels. And he had built himself a splendid, high-walled and towered summer palace at Sorgues, with elaborate frescoes and gilded woodwork, and curtains of his favorite green. He paved his chapel with costly glazed tiles, ornamented and colored, showing cocks and peacocks and griffons, imported from Lyons. He had precious Eastern and Spanish rugs for his rooms, and to use as trappings for his horses, and Mongolian hangings on his walls.

※ ※ ※

In the town where they ruled supreme, the Cardinals were rich in houses, one possessing twenty-one, another half a hundred. A typical mansion would boast a large reception room, a banquet hall, a study, bedrooms, chapel, and galleries one above the other around a court. Often there would be an adjoining, humbler house and courtyard for retinue and servants. These princely establishments were fortlike, each with its tower as a symbol of strength, though some Avignon houses were tiny, one being a little over twelve feet across and twelve deep. After the Papacy came, makeshift dwellings had grown up under boomtown conditions even in the streets and graveyards, and hugged the city's walls. On the site of the Dominicans' sprawling monastery, a whole quarter later developed. There were few open spaces, none, for example, before the Papal Palace. Cemeteries were therefore in demand for gatherings both sacred and profane, including the conduct of legal business, fairs and cattle auctions; they did not, apparently, serve their primary purpose too well, since as late as 1359, scavenging pigs could root out the new and shallow-buried dead.

There were continual difficulties between owners and tenants, and many as high-placed as Bishops would leave town without paying their exorbitant rent, thus bringing on themselves the threat of excommunication. Under John the fast-diminishing space was allocated by a commission, which made lists, taxed rents, and distributed housing. Each resident was obliged to limit himself to the number of rooms absolutely necessary to his station and the size of his household, and one assumes that every man's home was the commissioners' castle. Houses "delivered up" to Pope or Cardinals were called "liveries," says Girard, and previous owners were compensated.

Lusty, gusty Avignon was a-bulge with humanity. By road and water, the world came to its doors. For boats, the main landing place was under the Bridge, and near this main port inns and taverns abounded. The narrow streets were jammed. Circuslike sideshows featured at one time an armless woman who could sew and spin, toss a ball and play at dice with her toes. There were visiting Kings and Queens to see, Tartar Ambassadors, victorious generals with spoils, defeated enemies, prisoners in chains, pilgrims and saints. Favorite spectacles were the Pope's *cavalcatas:* these included the Pope's white palfreys, led by grooms; equerries carrying the *pallium*, or white wool band worn by the Pontiff on his shoulders as a symbol of might — and three red hats set on poles. Then would come the two papal barbers, each holding a red case, one containing the Pope's garments, the other his tiara in its box. After a subdeacon holding up the Cross, followed a horse or mule bearing the Corpus Christi, and then came the Pope himself on a white horse, half a dozen nobles around him holding a canopy over his head, behind him an equerry carrying a *montatorium* to help him mount or dismount. A great crowd of courtiers, prelates and members of the Pope's household were next, the most useful being, perhaps, the Pope's almsgiver, whose function was to break up traffic jams by scattering little coins, the Roman emperors' *missilia*, to the people. This and many other such details are vividly present in the illustrations of the fifteenth century Richental *Konzilschronik* to be seen at Constance.

New walls were thrown up from 1355 on, as the Companies and other marauders threatened the treasure-filled city; the security they offered made Avignon second only to Paris, and its tidal pull tended to depopulate the countryside and swell the deaths from epidemics. Not only the ecclesiastics but the lay rich came and built their palaces here too, personages such as the Prince of Orange, and Queen Joanna of Naples whose mansion was out in the lists, the strip of land bordering the walls near the Boquier Gate.

By day a spectacle, at night the streets were a perilous adventure. There was a curfew, and those braving the winding alleys on their lawful occasions thereafter were supposed to carry a lantern or torches. If cries were heard, or blows and thumping feet, here and there a window would light up. Mu-

nicipal officers such as the marshal and constables kept a
makeshift order. High up on the Lookout Tower of the
Pope's Palace — the Tour de la Gâche — a watchman blew
on his trumpet when he began his nightly vigil, and again
blew up the dawn.

The great wealth of the fourteenth century clergy attracted proportionately violent, immediate and daily hate.
Under Pope Benedict XII, the White Cardinal, there was a
parable by Jean de la Roche Taillade, to illustrate the luxury
of the prelates: "A Cardinal is an arrogant, naked bird, which
the other birds deck out with their most beautiful plumage."
It was noted by some that the Popes were practising not the
imitation of Christ but of Caesar. Complaints, jokes, anec-
dotes, proverbs, always on the same theme of clerical greed,
have come down to us. "Priests, monks, nuns, and poultry,
never have enough," said the Italians. "The monk that begs
for God's sake begs for two," said the French and Spanish.
And the Germans: " 'Oh, what we must suffer for the
Church of God!' cried the Abbot, when the roast fowl

burned his fingers." Even the Persians had: "Beware of a thin doctor and a fat priest."

The tenderly cultivated acceptance, in the mass of mankind, of these excessive inequalities as the Will of God — the Duc de Berry's splendid Book of Hours routinely shows a number of his peasants in tatters — did not prevent observers like Petrarch from noting them. And of the rich in general, England's John Ball was preaching from 1360 to 1381: "By what right are they whom we call lords greater folk than we? On what grounds have they deserved it? . . . If we all came of the same father and mother . . . how can they say or prove that they are better than we, if it be not that they make us gain for them by our toil what they spend in their pride? They are clothed in velvet and warm in their furs . . . while we are covered with rags. They have wine and spices and fair bread; and we oat-cake and straw, and water to drink. They have leisure and fine houses; we have pain and labour, the rain and the wind in the fields."

By way of elaboration, here is a banquet, lay or ecclesiastic, of the fourteenth century: "To open the appetite," limes, cherries and salads; then almond paste with cream; crayfish or poultry pasties; various broths, or chopped meats cooked in beef or lamb bouillon; soups variously made of hemp seed, oats, millet, herbs, fennel, mustard, tripe, pears, quinces; roasts with sauces, cooked with cinnamon, parsley, garlic, young shoots, cherries, plums, broom, roses. After that, dry roasts or venison; gosling pie; all kinds of pastry — the Crusaders had brought back sugar from the Muslims — cooked with pumpkin, rose leaves, flowers; then all kinds of fruits. In the salon, sweets, wine from Corsica sweetened with honey, hippocras with cloves. The dining room floor was strewn with sweet-smelling flowers, and hanging decoratively from the ceiling were branches with the ripe fruit on them. Greek wine was served with a slight admixture of fragrant resin, of mastic or turpentine and was much prized by gourmets, as was a Greek stuffed lamb cooked with glacé onions, garlic or leeks, in a liquor called *garum*, which is a sauce of fermented fish.

☧ ☧ ☧

Not money but the love of money is the root of all evil, warned the Bible. This pursuit of money for its own sake was a declaration of secularity. It meant that the Church had opted for this world instead of the next. The Abbé André writes: ". . . in the French pontifical period we note the end of the sacerdotal age, and the principle of the predominance of secular power. The idea of a Kingdom of God to be established on earth, under the universal suzerainty of the Roman Pontiff, was abandoned forever beneath the Palace arches at the Rock of the Lords."

Certainly in what followed, money was deeply implicated. Possessions are the propagandist's likeliest target, there are so many more voters among the have-nots. As ecclesiastical wealth accumulated, the reformers, even blindfolded, could hardly miss their aim: the soft underbelly of the Church.

☧ ☧ ☧

Even Alphonse Daudet must have sensed that something had been wrong, and decided that whited sepulchers are better than soiled ones, centuries afterward when, in his story called "La Mule du Pape," he gave the world its favorite picture of the Avignon Popes. For his own whole-cloth Pontiff of those fabulous, golden times, when there was, he says, neither war nor want, and the prisons were used only for cellars to cool the wine, was the gentle old Boniface who, with a sprig of marjoram in his biretta, smiled at you no matter who you were and blessed you politely as he trotted past on his mule. This Boniface's only love was his little vineyard, planted with his own hands, and Sundays after Vespers he and the Cardinals would ride out there and he would sit and his Cardinals would stretch out around him in the good southern sun. Boniface would uncork a bottle of ruby wine, and sipping, gaze tenderly about at his vineyard. On their way home in the twilight, crossing Avignon's Bridge, his mule would skip to the music of the farandole, and with his biretta, to the scandal of his Cardinals, the Pontiff would beat time to the dance.

No doubt to find this Boniface again one would have to conduct one's researches as Daudet himself did, flat on his back for a week in the lavender-smelling Grasshoppers' Reading Room, which was located just outside the door of his famous mill in Provence.

※ ※ ※

· REVOLUTION WITH AN IF

HAT Clement who knew how to be King had vanished, and the Cardinals were locked in again. All the windows were bricked up, to twenty-six feet above the ground. It looked like a long sentence. Beds were curtained off to secure a measure of privacy, and each Cardinal was allowed two members of his household staff to serve him. The new rules of the late Pope had made things a bit more comfortable for the Conclave, but they were still irksome enough. The fare was plain, judged by the standards of Avignon: nothing but clear or thick soup, some hors d'oeuvre, meat, eggs, fish, bread, cheese, and wine.

It was not, however, their haste to get home to better menus that set the members feverishly to work. Nor was it the word which had seeped into the Conclave, through locked doors and bricked windows, that John II, King of France, was on his way to Avignon; John, with his own ideas about who should be Pope. Perhaps they so hurriedly got down to business because their purpose was not the business at hand.

Here in this prison, they made a revolution. They proceeded happily to bind up the Pope and unloose the College. Not without conflict, but ultimately in agreement, they fashioned chains for the future Pontiff, and each one promised under oath, should he be elected, to fetter himself. The shadow of this brief and busy Conclave, whose aim was control of the Pope, would stretch forward in time to the Councils of Pisa and Constance.

During the debate there were some who questioned the right of the Sacred College to impose restraints on the supreme Head of the Church, presumed to receive his power from God, not the Cardinals, and who remembered the Constitutions of Gregory X and Clement V, limiting the Cardinals' actions during interregna to the choice of a new Pope. These more conservative Princes inserted an escape clause before they signed, the clause reading, "If it conforms to the law." Most, however, had no misgivings, and glowed at the thought of a necessary task well done.

According to their Manifesto the Pope would henceforth be prevented from creating Cardinals at will, thus packing the College; no new Cardinals could be named unless the number fell to sixteen. The total could then be brought up only to twenty, no more, and the selection of any new Cardinals must be approved by those already in office. No Cardinal could be arrested or deposed without the unanimous consent of the others. The Pope could not seize a Cardinal's property under any pretext, either during his lifetime or after his death.

Concern for their own property led the Fathers on to consider whether the Pontiff had too much freedom in disposing of what belonged to the Church. They decided that the approval of two-thirds of the Cardinals should be required for the transfer or the donation of any feudal or Church estate, quit-rent, or long lease. Next they reinstated the decree of Pope Nicholas IV which allocated to the Sacred College, with no exceptions, half the revenues: taxes, fines, all the Church's emoluments. Also, and on the same authority, no one might be established in or removed from office in any domain of the Papacy without the consent of a majority of the Cardinals. To reduce nepotism, no relative of the Pope, either by blood or marriage, could be Marshal of the Court, or Governor or Rector of a papal domain. Except with the approval of two-thirds of the Cardinals, the Pope might make no grant of tithes or other subsidies, nor set up any Reserve for the profit of the Papacy. Finally, decided the Cardinals, should questions of interpretation arise regarding these rulings, the Pope should set forth such explanations as were agreed upon by two-thirds of the Cardinals. They stopped at this point, feeling they had done enough. The truth is, they had done too much.

Here in this swift Conclave the Cardinals fashioned one of the wedges which at a later time was to split the Church apart. Whether their rulings were well advised, whether the Cardinals had the right to formulate them, whether they could be enforced — all this is unimportant beside the overriding fact that a majority of the Cardinals assumed they had jurisdiction over the actions of a duly invested Pope. This was an old struggle for power. The great misfortune of the Church is that it was revived in a situation already fissured by the move to Avignon.

Even those doubtful ones who qualified their signatures with "If it conforms to the law" hardly apprehended the vast implications of this act, or they would not have signed at all.

One of these was Etienne Aubert, a man with a Roman nose and curly beard, who was Bishop of Ostia and Velletri, as well as Grand Penitentiary and Administrator of the diocese of Avignon. He said little, but in his private mind he was already thinking of himself as Innocent VI. He became a possible choice for Pope when Cardinal Talleyrand-Périgord swung votes away from Jean Birel, General of the Carthusian Order, severe and disciplined both with himself and others.

"Let us see," said Cardinal Talleyrand to the Conclave, "if you want to return to the simplicity of the early Church. Depend upon it, a few days after his election, the new Pope will hitch your beautiful horses to the plough . . . He is a lion when it comes to God and the honor of the Church."

Thus damned, Birel was dropped. And the Cardinals, still warm from their revolution and fearing that the oncoming King of France would enforce his own choice, hurriedly agreed to a compromise candidate, the bearded Etienne Aubert. Since the time when they were first locked in, three days had passed.

※ ※ ※

· THE HAT

LONG before the Reformation, and before the Great Schism of the West, there obviously was a rising tide of protest against the worldly Church, and the thousands who withdrew from the world to attempt some other way of life were in effect on strike.

The comment is often heard that "in any case the Church would have reformed itself." From one standpoint this is against nature and contrary to what happened. From another, of course, the Church did reform itself, since those who began the dynamics of change were Catholics. Petrarch, Dante, Boccaccio, Catholics all, were among the most virulent critics of the Church, not of its teachings but its morals. They were in this sense early Protestants. As for early critics of dogma, Wycliffe was a Catholic priest, and Huss affirmed till they burned him that he had not renounced Catholic doctrine. Luther was still a long way in the future. His birth would follow Wycliffe's death by some hundred years.

In protesting Dante's Hell are "Popes and Cardinals, O'er whom Avarice dominion absolute maintains." (Canto 7.) There we find such Popes as Nicholas III, Boniface VIII, and Avignon's Clement V.

One of Boccaccio's stories in the *Decameron* — stories which, a Scheherazade in reverse, he is believed to have written to entertain Queen Joanna — further expresses the position of enlightened contemporary opinion toward the fourteenth century Church. Boccaccio neither wept nor beat his breast. His was the far deadlier light touch. And in his First Day, Second Tale, he was obviously revealing nothing new:

Giannotto, a merchant of Paris, had tried to win over the intellectual Abraham to Christ. It was quite clear that Christianity was true, he said, for it was prospering, while Judaism was so diminished it would soon vanish away. Abraham was moved. He would go to Rome, he said, and see for himself. Appalled, Giannotto begged him to stay in Paris, where there were plenty of learned Christians to teach him. But Abraham left.

Once in Rome (and probably for Rome we should read Avignon) Abraham quietly set about observing Pope and Cardinals, the other prelates and the Court. When he got back Giannotto went to see him anyway. Nervously he asked what Abraham thought of the Holy Father and the Cardinals. Abraham answered that he had found among them neither holiness nor devotion nor good works; that the Shepherd, and consequently the rest, seemed to be exerting all their talents to "reduce the Christian religion to nothing and thrust it out of the world." And still, said Abraham, this religion grows brighter and greater day by day; therefore, it must be the Holy Spirit which sustains it, and this being so, nothing would stop him from becoming a Christian.

Interestingly enough, by this Italian, Paris is here given the beau role. But then even Petrarch is sometimes, as the French have noted, "caught red-handed" praising France.

※ ※ ※

Petrarch hoped, but could not have believed, that being at Avignon was all that ailed the Church. Once, talking to his friend Cardinal John Colonna, Petrarch "announced as coming in the near future, the fatal day when the pride of this order, having wearied out the patience of God and man, would be cast down and destroyed . . . he [the Cardinal] answered with a sardonic laugh that he hoped I had the blindness of Tiresias and not his prophetic gift. He cited as against my statement these words of the Gospel: 'Simon, I have prayed for thee, that thy faith fail not.' " (Luke 22:32.) Petrarch replied that his meaning was, not that faith would fail, but that it would tend to be increased "by the ruin of the destroyers of faith."

"From childhood," he wrote, "when I was brought . . . by my fate to these regions, I have up to now passed the greater part of my life groaning here in indignation . . .

"I know from experience that here is no piety, no charity, no faith, no respect, no fear of God, nothing holy, nothing just, nothing fair, nothing sacred, in short nothing human. Friendship, modesty, decency, candor, are banished from here. I say nothing of truth; for what would truth be doing in a place where all is full of lies, the air, the earth, the houses, the towers, the streets, the halls, the squares, the porticoes, the vestibules, the courtyards, the bedrooms, the panelling of the ceilings, the cracks in the walls, the shops, the sanctuaries of the temples, the chairs of the judges, the throne of the

Pontiffs, in sum the faces of men, the movements of their heads, and their gestures, and their very voices — those images of the soul?"

Cardinal comes from *cardo*, the hinge of a door. Petrarch writes: "Two Roman senators, on whom the globe of the world and the door of the House of God turn as on a hinge," were coming down with an army of servants from the Palace of the Pope. An immense crowd of petitioners, "of whom this wretched city, odious in God's sight, is particularly full," waited at the entry. Seeing their chiefs approach, they clamored to know "what their lot was, and how their business was going with the Pope." One of the Fathers "began at once to report a whole flock of impostures . . . He invented something to satisfy each one's hopes, and made up the Pope's answer to this or that one's request, discussing it all without the slightest hesitation, impregnably brazen." The other, who could, says Petrarch, "have been a decent man if he had not belonged to this order," said jokingly, "Aren't you ashamed to mock these simple people and fabricate the Pope's replies to suit yourself, when we weren't even able to see him . . . ?" The first one answered, laughing, "Aren't you, rather, the one to be ashamed for having such a slow mind that in all this time you haven't been able to learn the tricks of the Curia?" Petrarch reports that he listened to this with stupefaction, while the others present burst out in laughter and praise.

He wrote of Avignon as a place "whence no one has returned better for the example he found here, and whence thousands have come away worse."

Once (under Innocent, next after Clement VI), the poet even called on Emperor Charles IV of Germany for help with the to him vital transfer to Rome: "O most invincible of the Kings of our time . . . You who . . . can drive out of their unwholesome dens . . . these somnolent foxes, and

draw the bride of Christ from her mud and chains . . .
This shepherd grown dull with age, sleep and wine, will
never of his own will come out of his lair and his well-loved
lupanars. You alone shall take him by the hand, shall rebuke
him, and flog him with the whip, and set him back in his ancient domicile."

This from the same man who would get up in the night
and pray barefoot.

It seems obvious that Petrarch's very belief was at the root
of his long anguish. A nonbeliever would not have mourned
over the state into which Christianity had fallen.

But there was something else as well, that never let him
rest: had not Petrarch's own nameless sister been seduced by
one of the Popes? Mézières sidesteps it all by claiming that
Petrarch never had a sister, "in spite," he says, "of the formal
testimony of Léonard Arétin and Gamurrini, in spite of the
marriage contract of a daughter of Petracco [Petrarch's
father], that Baldelli discovered and published . . ." He says
Petrarch would have spoken of her, had she existed. This
argument is weak, for shame is an effective silencer.

The plaque set up in Petrarch's memory by the people of
Vaucluse is incorrect: it was not to flee "the pleasures of the
age" but the anguish of it, that Petrarch retired to his Closed
Valley.

᠅ ᠅ ᠅

Here is Petrarch's account of the Stuttering Cardinal, written in 1358 under Innocent VI.

Virgil's statement, he says, that an old man is of ice for the
Goddess of Love could not be falser, "so ardent are all these
old men, and so inclined toward Venus; to such an extent have
they forgotten their age . . . so much do they throw themselves into all the vices, as if all their glory were not in the
Cross of Christ but in the pleasures of the table, and the orgies

and indecencies which result in their bedrooms; so much do they hold back with their hands escaping youth . . . On the one hand a heady wine, on the other the properties of Oriental berries procure for them this ardor and these nerves. O vines of Liguria and the Campania, O sweet sugar cane and black shrubs from the Indies, created for the advantage and the honest delights of human beings, to what uses have you now been put for the ruination of souls? Satan, laughing, sits in judgment between these old men and their young girls." Husbands are first sent into exile, then forced to take back now pregnant wives, then after the birth forced to give them up again.

There was in Avignon a stuttering Cardinal, one of whose "purveyors of young girls," a person known to Petrarch, operated in this fashion: "His traps and snares laid siege to every street, to every house and chiefly to those of the poor. Here he would distribute money, there ribbons, here rings, there caresses, here the remains from the table, there all kinds of dainties, and whatever he judged likely to seduce a woman's mind. Himself, when he was at the end of his expedients, would sing: for, as a matter of fact, he was a choir leader, but he had transferred his voice from the altar to the dances and brothels."

His master was long past seventy, bald and with only seven teeth. He could not sleep alone, comments Petrarch, "perhaps because he was afraid of rats or haunts." On one occasion the procurer brought him a very young girl. At the sight of him she set up a loud wail. She had been promised a Cardinal, a great and illustrious being, not an old, bald, dilapidated priest. Unmoved by arguments, she stubbornly fought him off, whereupon the old prelate ran into his cabinet and returned in his hat.

· BLUE LAWS OF INNOCENT VI

THINKING of Innocent VI, who purportedly represents the Church's effort to reform itself, we find starkly varying opinions to reconcile. Was he indeed a "Judas"? Was he "the best of the Avignon Popes"? He seems rather to have made gestures in various directions, perhaps like an aging dancer who can only sketch out his intent, but seldom follows through.

Upon his election, this old man of uncertain health and guarded views was welcomed by Saint Bridget of Sweden who commented that he was made of better metal than Clement VI and that the material of which he was cast was capable of receiving the most beautiful colors. She had, however, changed her mind by the time he died, and buried him in terms which incline one to think she disapproved of him:

"Pope Innocent has been more abominable than the usurious Jews, more treacherous than Judas, crueller than Pilate. He has swallowed down the ewes and cut the throats of true shepherds. In the end, for his crimes [Christ] has heaved him into the abyss, like a heavy stone, and has condemned his Cardinals to be eaten up by the same fire that devoured Sodom."

Nor did Petrarch think well of him, for to Innocent, Petrarch himself was a sorcerer. When he was Cardinal of Ostia, the Pope had often heard Cardinal de Talleyrand joking with Petrarch as to the latter's reputation for magic — Petrarch probably being guilty by mental association, since he was a reader of Virgil, called in medieval legend a magician. Petrarch steadfastly avoided Innocent, his excuse being: "I was afraid that I might hurt him with my witchcraft, or that he might hurt me with his gullibility." When powerful friends urged him to come and congratulate the new Pope, who would certainly change toward him since he loved persons of merit, Petrarch answered: "I hope that is true. If the Pope loves only persons of merit, he loves very few people: I do not flatter myself that I am one of them — but I would rather be one of them, than be Pope."

Ignorance of the Classics only proved that Innocent was a man of his day and shared in the common superstitions. He was certainly not against learning, although the bounds he set to it were narrow. He had been a professor of law, and as Pope founded the college of Saint Martial at Toulouse and a chair of theology at the University of Bologna.

On being elected, he had not waited long to dispose of the limitations laid upon him as future Pontiff at the Conclave. To him the oath of a Cardinal did not bind the same Cardinal once he turned Pope. He now saw the work of the Conclave as contrary to the rights of the Papacy and he proceeded to show up his former colleagues with all deliberate speed by adding a new Cardinal; this new member was, of all people, his nephew Aldoin Aubert. This was not the last time a Pope would discard his previous oath as of no moment, once he reached the papal heights. In fact, it became standard practice during the Great Schism of the West.

He began to inveigh against the rich absentee clerics who thronged Avignon, neglecting their flocks. As his comment on the Oriental luxury of Clement VI, he cut down the personnel of the Palace, sold off the best horses, stopped the feasts. "Austere and righteous," Pastor would call him, adding, "he emptied the Papal Palace of a crowd of useless courtiers, whose only occupation was intrigue and money-making . . . he banished all splendour from his Court . . ."

Many an ecclesiastic found himself bustled away from the delights of Avignon to a congregation whose faces he had almost forgotten. It was that or risk excommunication. Things were spoiled for a time in the papal city. The Cardinals had to cut expenses, set a moderate table, appear in public with diminished pomp. No more were streetwalkers overlooked on condition they were prompt with their payments, and murderers who had managed to buy off their victims' relatives could no longer buy absolution as well. Even gambling was forbidden and heavily penalized.

Nevertheless, like most cleanups, this too was temporary. Things improved. Houses called "of tolerance" by the French (who define tolerance as "indulgence toward what one cannot or does not wish to prevent") steadily multiplied, paying protection money to various officers of the Curia, whom the Pontiff ousted, with no visible result.

Innocent was fond of saying: "Ecclesiastical dignities should follow merit, not birth," and he tried conscientiously to obey his rule, except of course with his own relatives.

Those who brought up their kinsfolk for preferment could expect such treatment as was meted out to a favorite chaplain, who presented his young nephew to the Pontiff in the hope of getting him a living. Innocent's hand reached musingly for his bearded chin. "One of the seven benefices which you hold will do very well," he said. The chaplain seemed depressed. He was then asked which three of his remaining six livings he considered the best. He named them off. "Good," said Innocent, "with your other three I shall be able to reward three of the poor and deserving clergy."

Toward the middle of his reign he had a chance, tenuous but certainly exploitable, to repair the breach between the Latin Church and the Greek. Innocent's handling of this was typical of the man.

John Paleologus, Emperor of the East — urged on by his Empress mother, Anne of Savoy — renewed to Innocent the old idea of uniting East and West. Things were not going well with John and he needed help. He had even sat down to a royal banquet that amounted to penury; it was served on earthenware and pewter; glass and gilt leather had done duty for gold and jewels and although there were indeed some true pearls to be seen they were "very thinly sprinkled."

John's envoys sailed all the way to Avignon about this matter of unification in 1356. What John offered, sworn to on the Gospels and written in purple ink, was complete obedience to the Pope, both his own and his peoples'. He would give a palace and church to the Papal Nuncio in Constantinople, with power to confer benefices on all clergy returning to the Latin rite. He would spread the Latin tongue. He would send his eldest son and successor Andronicus to Innocent as a hostage, and the Pope should raise him as an adopted child. In exchange all that John wanted was five hundred men-at-arms and a thousand archers, some funds for his soldiery, and enough galleys to carry them, one of which would be returned, bearing back the Crown Prince.

Even this little, however, Innocent could not provide. What he did was to send off letters recommending John to the Venetians, the Genoese, the King of Cyprus and the Grand Master of Rhodes, letters which might as well not have been written at all.

Then there was the problem of the Archpriest. He was a gentleman soldier of fortune from Périgord whose real name was Arnaud de Servole. He had fought against the Black Prince at Poitiers, was wounded and taken prisoner, but had survived to turn brigand and ravage the countryside. Under him was a corps of élite officers, all relatives of the late Clement VI and bearing such noble names as Amiel des Baux and Bertrand de Bidosse, and under them were brigands in their thousands. The knightly courtesy of old had by now disappeared, and marauders such as these spared neither women nor aged men nor children any more, in a France that had with the Hundred Years' War become "one vast expanse of fire and carnage."

The Archpriest eventually fastened on Avignon and would not be shaken loose.

Innocent invited him to dinner. Not once but several times he ate with the Pope and Cardinals and was treated by the Pontiff, according to Froissart, "as reverently as if he had been the son of the King of France." Finally, his sins forgiven but not discontinued, he left with a present of 40,000 crowns.

Meanwhile, France's Good King John was a prisoner of the English in a Bordeaux jail and the Dauphin was struggling to save his ravished country and at the same time prevail on Innocent to get his father free. The Pope sent a couple of Cardinals to Emperor Charles IV, then sojourning in Metz. Proceedings, not too energetic, anent the King's ransom were set in motion, but came to nothing because of the Black Prince's understandable desire to exhibit in England his illustrious spoil of war.

Good King John was not returned to France until 1360, when he signed the treaty of Brétigny and left a son as prisoner in his stead. This youth contrived to escape, whereupon John was preserved in history forever with a proud act and comment: He made himself prisoner of the English again and he said: "Were good faith to be banished off the face of the earth, still should it live in the heart and on the lips of Kings."

A brighter event of Innocent's reign was the return to Avignon of the victorious Gilles d'Albornoz, back from conquered Italy with trophies. At a point long commemorated by a cross, *la Croix de Noves*, he was met beyond the city by Pope and Cardinals, and had his welcome over flower-carpeted ways.

Thanks to his warrior Cardinal Innocent possessed the Papal States again, though sadly overrun. The efforts of Albornoz had proved costly not only in blood — there was always plenty of that — but treasure as well. Clement VI had so depleted the splendid sums piled up by his predecessors that Innocent had been obliged to melt down silver and gold ornaments and cunningly designed pieces of jewelry to finance the Italian campaign. Beauty, religious or historical importance, all had to be sacrificed.

Now Innocent, needing funds, bethought himself of Germany again. He would tax the German clergy still further and get money for his Papal States. With this in mind he sent off Philippe de Cabassole. But the German clergy refused the Pontiff with one voice; Emperor Charles gathered all the Princes of the Realm together at Mainz, with lawyers to advise them, and everyone agreed to resist the tax.

Philippe de Cabassole had to listen to an impassioned spokesman who told him: "Let us stop this new and overwhelming evil at its onset. Let us push off at least in part this sore, humiliating yoke now thrust upon us. Too long, too long has Rome considered Germany a gold mine. It is enough. What, pray you, does Rome offer us in barter for our gold? Blessings that are ineffectual; anathemas; wars; a shameful bondage. The Court of Rome is an abyss, a bottomless abyss where all our riches leak away. From Germany rivers of gold flow in . . ."

Enumerating some of the uses to which this endless gold was put, the German spokesman said it was for solicitation or purchase of a benefice; the confirmation of prelates; lawsuits; the infinite number of appellations, dispensations, absolutions, indulgences, privileges — "in a word for innumerable forms of slavery adorned with the fair name of acts of grace."

On the following day, even Emperor Charles assailed the unfortunate de Cabassole. "Lord Bishop," he said, "how does it happen that the Pope demands such sums of money of our clergy, yet dreams not of reforming them? You see for yourself how our prelates live, you see their outward show, their unblushing luxury and pomp!" As he spoke the Emperor turned his furious gaze on Conrad, Canon of Mainz. Approaching him, Charles snatched from the ecclesiastic's head his magnificent hat encrusted with jewels and gold. Pushing his own cloth hat on Conrad's denuded head, the Emperor put on his prize and cried: "What do you think? Is not such a hat more becoming to a knight than a clerk?"

This gesture was a symbol of the Emperor's threat: that he would sequestrate the revenues of the Church and have them administered by lay princes instead.

Innocent got no funds from Germany. His only riposte was a somewhat weak letter, written by way of routine admonition to the clergy of Mainz, Trier, Cologne, Bremen and Salzburg.

"For some time word has been reaching us that in your provinces . . . even certain Bishops have forgotten the holy preeminence of their estate and taken on the ways of laymen; that they participate in jousts and tournaments and other military exercises; that they show in their behavior, in their clothes, and even in their shoes, a magnificence which is forbidden them. Thus do they dissipate the patrimony of the Church and of the poor to the great scandal of everyone. That is why we entreat you and we order you at one and the same time to repress these abuses in all the ecclesiastics of whatever rank and dignity they be, and oblige them to live according to the gravity and the modesty of their calling . . ."

Whether he begged or commanded, the result was the same.

The Free Companies now increased Innocent's money troubles. Bands of them, temporarily out of war work, were as usual robbing, murdering, and laying the country waste. Perhaps remembering the Archpriest's welcome, they bore down on Avignon where neither the Pope's anathemas nor his hasty attempts to build up the ruined walls produced salutary results, and recourse was finally had to a bribe of a thousand florins. Some two years later, in 1361, they were back again, and their price had gone up to 14,500 florins (or, according to one souce, to 60,000, with a plenary indulgence thrown in). The mercenaries, called *Tard-venus* (latecomers, or perhaps Johnnie-come-latelies), had captured Pont St.-Esprit, thus cutting the road to Avignon and providing an excellent location for robbing Church dignitaries on their way to the Pope. Innocent laid siege to them, then decided if he could not defeat them he should hire them; they gladly went off to fight in Italy, and Innocent was well out of an explosive situation.

Avignon was overwhelmed at this period by a series of disasters. In 1359, the Rhône and Durance washed over their banks, ruining crops and crumbling part of the new walls. Worse, a gang of terrorists known as the *Alparuches* took over the winding streets. Dressed as animals or demons, they worked in the dark, committing their nightly atrocities, and when the streets yielded too few opportunities for robbery and rape, women were heard to scream out in their own invaded houses. Curiously, the band of hooligans was made up of students and young nobles and supposedly solid burghers, as well as the rabble. These last eventually had their heads cut off, while the more distinguished were sewn in sacks, and thrown by night into the hurrying black Rhône.

The same definitive treatment was later accorded a group of *Tard-venus* who ungraciously returned from Italy, slipped into Avignon, and attempted to open one of the gates. The Pope's spies caught them in time, and a prompt exhibition was put on for the benefit of their fellows waiting outside the walls: ten were drowned, eleven hanged. The hint proved broad enough. The *Tard-venus* traveled on.

This constant harassment of the countryside by unemployed mercenaries impelled thousands to crowd into Avignon for protection, and the resultant withdrawal of large numbers from agriculture, besides the driving off of livestock and pillaging of crops, led toward the end of Innocent's reign to a serious famine. Boats bringing provisions from the North were intercepted by the vicious Companies; at such a time Innocent excommunicated the merchants of Marseilles and laid their city under an interdict, because they had put an embargo on Italian shipping, thus preventing the transport of wheat to his suffering metropolis.

Overcrowding as well as undernourishment contributed more thousands of victims to the new plague which devastated Avignon. Between March 28 and July 25, 1361, 17,-000 persons succumbed. It is reported that this plague was most virulent in places that had best weathered the visitation of 1348, that casualties were proportionately greater in locations with high ground and good air. Nine Cardinals died.

※ ※ ※

Old and gouty or frugal, weak or an able administrator, often well-intentioned or of shifting moods, pitiless to underlings and heretics — Innocent's cruelty to the Fraticelli was one reason for Bridget's revising her judgment about him — or a stern reformer, whatever Innocent was, his story was coming to a close. Certainly "weak" is the word that recurs for him. He lacked the panache of the man who preceded him, and the virtue of the one who came after.

Somewhat irrelevantly, the still youngish Luigi of Taranto, Queen Joanna's second husband, died before he did, whereupon Innocent sent down as his Legate to Naples the Abbot of Saint Victor, Guillaume de Grimoard. He could hardly know that in a little while the throne he sat on would be warmed by this very Guillaume.

Innocent died September 12, 1362, having reigned nine

years, eight months, and twenty-three days. That winter was the worst in memory. The Rhône stopped in its course so that people and horses could cross over it on the ice, and trees froze to death. At last spring came, and they buried him with pomp, out at the Charterhouse of Villeneuve-lès-Avignon, which he had founded and where he expressed the wish to lie.

Centuries rolled by, the Revolution came, a peasant turned the Pope's empty sepulcher into a rabbit hutch. Where the Carthusians had been, cattle passed. These were matters the King of France had not foreseen, on the day he led Innocent's funeral procession out to the tomb.

· URBAN THE GOOD

BEFORE Urban V was chosen Pontiff, another man was elected by mistake. Without feeling out the strength of the various factions and doing some preliminary trading, the Cardinals had taken a vote, and it chanced that fifteen out of the twenty agreed on a candidate who was unacceptable. Each must have thrown away a vote on Hugues Roger, brother of the late Clement VI, believing him safely out of the running.

Cries of outrage were heard from a majority of the voters when it turned out they had elected Hugues. "Another Limousin! Hugues! Never!" Roger's party insisted he had been legally elected, but he himself, either out of largeness of spirit or merely political wisdom, decided not to accept. In the subsequent voting, an English faction developed around the

Gascons, subjects of the King of England, and a French faction arose to withstand it; chances of solving the deadlock diminished daily, tempers flared, at last it was found necessary to look beyond the Sacred College for someone agreeable to all. Fifteen days after Innocent's death, they elected Guillaume de Grimoard, Abbot of Saint Victor at Marseilles.

The Cardinals' ultimate vote was carefully concealed from the world, and to keep it a secret they stayed on, blocked up in the Conclave. For the man they had chosen was out of the country, bearing the dead Innocent's condolences to widowed Queen Joanna; and should the Italians discover that the new Pontiff was at that moment on their soil, they would kidnap him and keep him prisoner in Italy where they were sure God wanted him to be. Couriers were rushed off to Naples. Guillaume, now changed into Urban V, took to the sea as the shortest and safest way back, arriving at Marseilles October 27, 1362, one day less than a month after he had been chosen Pope.

His first act at Avignon was to refuse to lead the usual mounted procession through the streets. Plans had been completed, the horses shone, silks and satins and jeweled trappings were laid out, three Kings (of Navarre, Cyprus and Denmark) stood by. But Urban remained indoors. He had work to do.

※ ※ ※

Urban was young for a Pope, only fifty-two. He had a strong face, with the bony structure, especially the cheekbones and square jaw, notably prominent. It is easy to imagine that chin jutting, but historians report that his disposition was compliant. A man of contemplation, of prayer and study, he was a theologian rather than a lawyer, and had a mind not coruscating but careful. He had taught "science" and law at the Universities of Montpellier, Toulouse and Paris, and was known as a good speaker.

Although his life was packed with work, he still made room each afternoon for his books. His schedule followed this pattern: mornings, before saying Mass, he made a full confession of his faults, and remained kneeling for a long period of prayer during which he begged for mercy and aid. The Mass over, he held audiences and occupied himself with Church affairs until his simple lunch. Then he slept for half an hour, on waking signed approved petitions and sent off his mail. After this he put aside work for study, and concluded this period with prayer. The day's business claimed him again until a short while before dinner; in that interval he enjoyed walking in the gardens with various Cardinals and high Church officials. During the evenings he read, discussed the lives of saints with close friends, and talked over the state of the world (it was not good then, either).

His bed was no less rigid than his day, for he slept on bare boards in his clothes — his Benedictine robe was on him at all times. To close a door each night on the worldliness of the Papal Court, he had chosen as his bedchamber a monk's cell built out of wood. When he entered there and lay down on the hard bed, he became, so far as it was possible for the Head of the Church to become, simply another monk.

Surely, however, the day's problems slipped through into his cell. There was the continuing struggle for power between France and England, the marauding Free Companies, the need to hurry the building of Avignon's walls, the unsteady reign of Queen Joanna, the unwillingness of Europe's rulers to carry the Cross to the Holy Land again, the papal war with Bernabo Visconti whom Urban had personal reasons for hating, the frenzied proliferation of heresy, the question of returning to Rome. If the Pope tossed and turned, it was not only because of his bed.

Gibbon says he was "mild and virtuous." Contemporaries called him learned and saintly, or spoke of his justice, his punctuality, his kindness to the poor. He was the one Pope whom Petrarch eulogized. The poet told him he had been chosen by God: "Don't think that any of the voters ever thought of investing you with the Pontifical purple . . . God alone elected you. In spite of themselves, He made them pronounce your name."

Full of hope at Urban's advent that he would transfer the Holy See to Rome, Petrarch considered him worth urging onward: "When you shall appear before the tribunal of the Lord Christ, when you shall have come to that place where you are no longer the master and we are the servants no more, but where only He is Master, and all of us but equal in servitude, do you not think He will say: 'You were poor and I raised you up, I brought you out of your lowliness, not only did I seat you beside Princes but above Princes, and desired that they should bow themselves at your knees and your feet. And where now have you left this Church that I gave into your hands? You whom I adorned with many a special gift, what have you brought Me in exchange, that was more than others brought? You have sat yourself down on the Rock of the Lords, and forgotten Tarpeia's!' "

※ ※ ※

The new Pontiff was opposed to "concubinage in all orders, especially the clergy." He was no more responsible for the immorality of the day than Hercules for the stalls of Augeas. Many factors were involved here, among them being the relative youth of civilization, and not the least of them, the Church's attitude toward marriage and celibacy.

Early Christianity had not enforced celibacy on the clergy, and (Draper says) "the life of the hermit or monk was unknown in the Church for more than two hundred years after its formation . . . " Monachism came from Egypt, contributing to the view that marriage was sinful; people who have abstained from something tend to begrudge it to others. Other factors promoted celibacy as an ideal: the position of woman was very low — not till Islam did religious law begin to improve her status. Gnostics, Manicheans and such were antimatter, really anti-life. The mother of Jesus was virgin (and the Catholic Church refuses to accept Matthew 1:25 and 12:47, and Mark 3:32, regarding her giving birth to other children as the wife of Joseph). Jesus Himself did not marry. Saint Peter was, embarrassingly enough, married, but the antimarriage idea got around this — he and the other married Apostles, it was affirmed, gave up their wives upon being converted. The influential Paul was against women and against marriage. Zealots, when it was objected that without marriage the human race would die out, replied that "there would always be sinners enough in the world to avoid that disaster." And Saint Jerome added that though marriage replenishes the earth, virginity replenishes Heaven.

Celibacy, however, was not imposed on the clergy until 1073, more than a thousand years after Christ. A tenth century Italian prelate had already commented that if he were to enforce the canons against unchaste persons administering Church rites, no one would be left to perform such offices but the boys; and if he were to enforce the canons against bastards, these would have to be excluded too. The Council of Palencia anathematized laymen who forced their pastors to take concubines; Lecky refers to this insistence of the flock as arising from "the significant prudence of many lay Catholics . . ."

By the fourteenth century monks roistered, and might keep a tavern in the monastery, while nuns went out at night; for instance, a complaint was made about the nuns from the Abbeys of Hoemburg and Erstein, who regularly visited the courts of neighboring Barons and Counts, for no good. In 1350 the beautiful nuns of Neuss invited Leo von Rozmital to a party, and proved they were skilled in all the latest dances.

Marriage was officially regarded with dubiety. As for a second marriage, that was unspeakable. Saint Jerome, who apparently was not thinking very far ahead, had pointed out that of the unclean animals, only one pair each was received into the Ark, so that a second marriage would prove impossible for them. The fourteenth century was hilarious about second marriages. The fourth statute of the Church of Avignon, 1337, imposed a fine of ten pounds of Tours on all clerics who engaged in charivaris, the saturnalias put on at second weddings. Participants would smash church equipment, benches, the lights for the service, would howl like animals, take the bride and groom prisoner and lead them through the streets wearing bonnets of suggestive shape, make them buy themselves free and then use the extorted money for a sumptuous feast.

Emphasizing the meritoriousness of priests renouncing their wives, Saint Gregory the First (d. 604) was wont to describe the piety of a priest who had virtuously abandoned his wife forty years before and now lay dying. His former helpmeet, hurrying to the deathbed, leaned over the old cleric to see if he was still breathing, at which he gasped out: "Woman, be gone — take away the straw — there is fire yet!"

᛭ ᛭ ᛭

Divided for convenience into Seven Deadly Sins (pride, covetousness, lust, wrath, gluttony, envy, sloth), licentiousness of all kinds, although not the whole picture, understandably took up much of Urban's canvas.

As usual with a new Pontiff, it is reported that Urban swept the Bishops out of his capital and back to their dioceses (apparently they never stayed away from Avignon very long) and he allowed them to keep only such benefices as they could deal with themselves. Preying on spendthrifts, gamblers and the like, usurers had swarmed to the Papal Court. Urban forced them to make restitutions which in a few days piled up into a total of 200,000 gold florins. He attacked pomp and luxury, simony, lawyers who manipulated the law's delay.

It was no time for a relative. Surprisingly, Urban favored neither other people's nor his own (except that he named his brother to the diocese of Avignon). The matter of his father's pension from the King of France is typical: Urban said that a favor to one of his family might be construed as placing the Pope under an obligation, and the pension was renounced.

He finally decided to improve his times by reviving the old Provincial Councils, and himself attended the one he summoned to Apt in 1365, representing all of Provence. The clerics assembled in such gatherings inveighed against clerical drunkenness and debauchery, against the clergy having their illegitimate sons assist them at the altar, against their employing buffoons and tumblers or themselves functioning as such. Ecclesiastics, said the Council of Apt, must limit the number of their servants; their pages must wear a robe reaching to the heel, with sleeves buttoned at the wrist; pointed shoes were banned, especially in the new long-toed style that curled up in front and jutted out, spurred, in the back; and particolored stockings were forbidden as well. The average man appeared then in a long garment with a monklike hood, but elegance was snipping away at this robe until at last it barely covered the hips.

This Council also emphasized that the clergy should not keep hunting dogs or falcons or maintain other pets while the poor went hungry. To surround oneself with animals was a favorite pleasure and proof of status, and we read of pilgrimages undertaken to pray at a shrine for the recovery of a sick hawk, and of English nuns being reprimanded for bringing rabbits, birds and hounds to church. This keeping of pets had once led to a classical disaster in the city of Cologne.

On a certain day, two Canons of the Cathedral there invited a rich bourgeois named Evérard Gryn to dinner. After he had enjoyed a succulent repast, they took him into a room where there was a ravenous Sahara lion in a cage, opened the cage door and threw him in. The animal attacked. Evérard seized his dagger with his right hand, and wrapping his left hand in his mantle thrust it down the lion's throat, stabbing him all the while in the shoulder. The lion fell, and Evérard came out of the cage.

For some reason he did not turn the other cheek. A mob

took his side, but the Archbishop took the Church's. Burghers and Churchmen fought. Everything was finally settled, the French account says, "*à l'aimable*": the Senate put Evérard to death, and the Archbishop hanged the two Canons at the city gate.

※ ※ ※

Urban also instituted and spread throughout Christendom a secret moral and religious inspection along with which went whip and thumbscrew, the rack and Spanish Donkey and devouring flames, and he established three enormous prisons. After all, he was harassed by unkillable Fraticelli, by revived Beghards and Beguines, and by converted Jews who were going back in great numbers to Moses. Someone had to silence all these preachments. In addition, he destroyed whenever possible the pagan art forms of antiquity; he was a builder — he re-established the Vatican, repaired the ruined palace at Montefiascone and completed the Avignon one — and into his foundations went broken pieces of Greek and Roman handiwork, including the shattered marble of a statue of Hercules.

But the new Pope, besides his repressive measures, furthered education as well. He founded and endowed a college at Montpellier, and during his reign universities were also opened at Cracow, Orange and Vienne. He supported 1400 students and when he was reproached for this expense he said he wanted the Church to "abound in learned men." Urban knew that not all the students would go into the Church; some would become monks, others lay priests, others would drop out of the religious life altogether and become heads of families. No matter. Whatever they should take up, even manual labor, "it will always be useful to them to have studied."

Christendom was still in its Dark Age. It had hardly begun to unravel fact from fancy — a task still not completed. Relics included two heads of John the Baptist and a flame from the Burning Bush. Magicians were malevolently busy over wax images; most men were tied to the soil or forced away to the wars; such democratic ideas as Rienzi's were pagan wickedness. Against this, Urban looks advanced. It is true that like the currency, like every other factor, almost, we cannot easily equate his colleges with their modern counterparts. As is memory or a dream alongside reality, much was the same, yet subtly different; for the past, though recognizable, is a foreign country. Nevertheless, we should clearly give him credit for saying: "It will always be useful to them to have studied."

He was busy with matchmaking along with everything else. Among the Princes of Europe who honored him, Good King John arrived in person, asking for the widowed Queen Joanna, the Pope's vassal, as a bride for his fourth son. Urban, who had been carefully staving off aspirants to that fair, jeweled hand, concealed his disapproval and pretended to comply. But the Queen, fearing French influence perhaps, and bypassing Urban, proposed marriage to Jaime of Aragon, titular King of Majorca, who owned nothing but his cape and his sword. The Pope's later matchmaking was more successful: striking at England, he refused the Princess Margaret and a large chunk of France to a son of Edward III, and married her off instead to King John's son, Philip the Bold.

He also found time for the monks of Cluny. At a time when Avignon was ringed about with bandits, no provisions could be brought in, but the monks had thoughtfully smuggled in some Burgundy wine for the beleaguered Pope and Cardinals. Once the countryside was cleared again, they expected, reasonably enough, that their gift would no longer be needed. Officers of the Pope's Court, however, who knew a good thing when they had it, enforced on Cluny the heavy burden of keeping up the supply. Urban now granted the monks a dispensation releasing them from this. He also gave them a *hôtel* where they could stay when they came to Avignon — the palace built by Hugues des Baux as seneschal for Queen Joanna. Before, the monks on their frequent visits had lodged in the crowded taverns with jugglers, buffoons and girls of the streets.

Less easily solved was Urban's basic problem, one which plagued him throughout his reign: how, he wondered, could he contrive to turn everyone — quarreling Princes, English invaders, Free Companies, brigands — into one great package Crusade against the Muslims. On a day in March, 1363, with Kings in the audience, Urban preached his Crusade so effectively that John, his eyes brimming, cried out that he for one would arise to avenge Lord Jesus. In true evangelistic style the King was thereupon ushered, iron-hot, down to the altar where he was made to swear on the consecrated Host that he would go into Asia at the head of 150,000 men.

An Italian tyrant, however, Bernabo Visconti, the Pope's enemy and a man who wanted all Italy for his province, stood in Urban's way. This Bernabo was the grand uncle and prototype of that Duke of Milan who went around with a pack of killer mastiffs, which — laughing to bursting — "he would loose against anyone whose face he disliked." Bernabo, too, was fond of dogs. And if he held life cheap, it was no wonder, for he was called — and with awe — the father of everybody north of the Po.

Pope Urban would never forget the occasion when, still only an Abbot, he had been sent with a message to Bernabo from Innocent VI. After the Abbot had formally read out the Pope's letter, Bernabo said to him: "Swallow it this moment, or fall down dead." The Abbot swallowed it.

Urban now accused his adversary of a long list of crimes. One of these was that he had forced a priest of Parma to climb a high tower and from there to excommunicate, with many anathemas, the entire Papal Court, while down below, the Duke and his courtiers roared with laughter. When the Archbishop of Milan had opposed the Visconti excesses, Bernabo summoned him and cried in a fury: "On your knees, scoundrel!" The Archbishop kneeled. Then: "Don't you know, you foolish pedant, that in my dominions *I* am Pope, and Emperor, and Lord of all? Don't you know that neither the Emperor nor God Himself can do anything in my states except what I have willed, and that I have no intention of letting *them* encroach?"

Excommunicated, Bernabo implored pardon, and with the aid of various sovereigns, a truce was made between him and the Pope; the interdict on his cities was raised, and he was absolved. But not for long. He broke his word and went to war again, whereupon Urban preached a crusade against him instead of the Muslims.

Various intermediaries again arose and made attempts to reconcile Bernabo with the Pope. It was high time, because by now he was threatening Bologna. Bernabo was not precisely the negotiating type, and as might have been foreseen, the would-be arbitrators soon withdrew, highly incensed. But Archbishop Peter Thomas of Cyprus and a colleague did not give up. Two days after the others had gone, Bernabo summoned these envoys to an isolated chamber, away from his usual haunts. He sat them down, one to either side, and told them: "Speak to me of peace."

This meant he deigned to be bought off. He would collect from the Pope, over a period of eight years, the sum of five hundred thousand gold florins, and of course, receive absolution. In exchange he would quiet down, and disgorge many a fortified castle and stronghold.

With Italy thus cleared, old King John now felt that he could lead the Pope's Crusade to the Holy Land, but his ministers would have none of it. They pointed out that Europe's populations were decimated by plague and famine; that there would be no funds; that the King's predecessors had laid France bare with the Muslim wars and, asked the ministers, what did they all have to show for it? Not one inch of Asian ground.

☙ ☙ ☙

The Free Companies were Bernabo many times over. These "errant military states" were international armies of mercenaries who roamed the countryside, hiring out to any contender that paid the most. A body of them even helped Avignon in time of need and were known as "Brigands of the Pope."

There was, for example, the already mentioned "Archpriest," whose many bands preyed on the Provence area, and later, 40,000 strong, devastated Alsace and Lorraine, and finally butchered their chief when he got too old to fight.

Or, to look closer at a typical leader, there was Sir John Hawkwood, to whom, after his death, Florence erected a black marble statue for having restored military discipline. Employed by other Italians, including Bernabo Visconti, he founded, appropriately enough, an English hospital in Rome.

Hawkwood was once in his castle at Montecchio when two friars approached him with the usual greeting, "God give you peace." "God take away your alms," was his immediate reply. "Why spake you as you did?" they asked, surprised. "We thought that we said well." "What!" exclaimed Hawkwood, "when you wished that God might make me die of hunger? Know you not that I live on war as you live on alms? I have but returned your greeting in like sort as you gave it."

When two of his English corporals fought over a nun, between them on her knees in prayer, Hawkwood, drawing his sword, slashed her down the middle, saying, "Half for each."

A Company was well-organized. The plunder was held in common. Under a Captain General were four Lieutenants, who executed plans in turn, and the Company had its secretaries, clerics and money-lenders. Most of the personnel was of the outlaw variety. Important matters, such as a truce, or war, or peace, were decided in a general council by plurality vote.

We read in one of Urban's decrees a list of the Companies' crimes. They exacted huge levies from the cities; burned harvests; destroyed vines and trees; stole flocks and farm animals; slaughtered masses of the peasants; tortured the rich to force out ransoms; butchered infants in the cradle; raped virgins consecrated to the Deity; violated women and young girls; turned noblewomen into serving maids in the camps, forcing them to carry weapons when on the march, and to perform the most revolting services. Urban anathematized them, stripped them of all a citizen's rights and ordered that they be boycotted.

Not all the women who accompanied them were unwilling. Their camp was a market, Gregorovius reports, where crowds of merchants sold their spoils. Great Italian banks did business with their captains, who deposited plunder at interest. They negotiated with Princes and states as equal to equal. Treaties with the seals of perhaps twenty of their condottieri appended in a row are preserved at Florence and Siena; and the object of it all was the extortion of money.

Like many a weapon, they were dangerous to the user, and their employers found it necessary to appoint overseers, on the order of Commissars, to see that they fulfilled their agreements, and did not "throw" a battle to opposing mercenaries of their own kind, or arrange a simulated victory.

Now the King of France, wishing at the same time to destroy Peter the Cruel, King of Castile, in order to avenge the death of Queen Blanche, appointed the doughty Frenchman Bertrand Du Guesclin as a sort of Pied Piper to lead the Companies out of France. It is said the bands totaled 30,000 men. Du Guesclin took on (perhaps without too much difficulty) their language, behavior and attitudes; and their joint Chiefs, Arnold d'Andrehen, Hugues de Courrelay, Jean d'Evreux, Olivier de Mauny and another called only the Green Knight, after many a flowing bowl of Burgundy, elected him as generalissimo, and they marched on the South.

Avignon shook in its poulaines. Urban hastily ordered the small, surrounding states to raise an army, but with pitiful results. Meanwhile, like the Cardinals, the Companies were enjoying France and its good wines, and it was proving as tricky a job for Du Guesclin to pull them out as for the reformers to pull out the Holy See. He then used his big argument. He "showed them the necessity, for the salvation of their souls, of attacking the Moors of Spain and winning those indulgences which were granted to men who fought the evildoers." Thoroughly understanding his fourteenth century mercenaries, he told them: "It is better for us to do thusly, and save our souls, than to damn ourselves and hand ourselves over to the Devil. For as each knows in his own case, we have all sinned far too much, and committed far too many

crimes, and it is right that we should put an end to it all."
With this he contributed to their general fund the monies the
King of France had sent to get them out of the country.

They reached Villeneuve, and camped across the river
from Avignon. A Cardinal was sent out to them, to ask that
they respect the Holy See. He assured them that he brought
a plenary indulgence for all. "But have you brought any
money?" an English officer asked. The Cardinal repeated
that he had brought a plenary indulgence, and desired to confer with their Chiefs. Marshal d'Andrehen replied that they
were off to fight the Saracens at Granada, and wished the
Holy Father, God's Lieutenant, to give them 200,000 florins
for their journey, as well as absolution for their sins. The
Cardinal answered they could be certain of the absolution.
Du Guesclin told him: "Sir, it is needful to deliver what the
Marshal asks, since here are many who will do without the
absolution, and would much rather have the money. For we
are making them virtuous in spite of themselves, and are leading them into exile, that they may not harry Christian folk."

There was consternation below the Rock of the Lords.
Urban fingered his bony jaw. He finally said, "It is the custom in Avignon to bring *us* rich gifts of gold and silver to absolve a man; and must we now, as these ask, both absolve
them and pay them as well? Certes, this is beyond all reason."

But the 30,000 were there, across the river. Like modern
businessmen passing an extra expense along to the customer,
Urban imposed a capitation tax on the citizens of Avignon to
raise, forthwith, the 200,000 florins. His own funds, he said,
were gone: there had been the Italian wars, the building of
Avignon's ramparts, the additions made to the Papal Palace,
the sum that had been gouged out by the "Archpriest." Europe was in disorder, his revenues had not been coming in:
the annates, the reserves, Peter's penny. King Edward of

England had failed to send him the annual thousand pounds sterling for Ireland, now due these thirty years.

Having collected the money somehow, Urban signed the bull of absolution, sealed it with the Great Seal, and sent it out by a chamberlain to Villeneuve.

Du Guesclin said to the envoy: "Tell me now, Brother, and keep nothing back: where does this treasure come from? Did the Pope get it out of his treasury?"

"No," was the reply, "the people of Avignon have paid out the money, each his allotted share." Du Guesclin was pained. He said that the sum he wanted must come "out of the Pope's money, and that of his rich clergy . . . We desire that this collected money be returned to those who paid it, without anyone losing aught of his own; and tell the Pope that he see to this; for if I should hear to the contrary, it would make me sorry indeed, and even if by then I had crossed over the sea, I would come back again this way."

Thus Urban had to do something that had surely never been done before: he had to return the vast sum to the people. The members of his Court were made to reach deep into their own pockets, and the amount was raised. Royally paid, cleansed of all sins, the guests at last moved on toward Spain.

※ ※ ※

·THE LIFE AND DEATH OF BOOKS

ETRARCH'S love was not the whole story, there was still another insubstantial woman in his life. We hear of her because, less adamant than Laura, she bore him two children — John and a younger sister, Francesca. The Pope legitimized them both. Petrarch confided to posterity that at forty he renounced women and counted his celibacy "among my principal blessings." But he wrote from Avignon in 1351 of a "friend" who was trying to re-establish her previous rights over him, who did not believe in his vow of continence and thought he had deserted her for someone else. She stormed his door by day, sometimes by night.

John was born in 1337 and his document of legitimization was signed by Clement VI on September 5, 1348. Later on,

Petrarch got the boy a benefice from the ever generous Clement: Canon of Verona at fourteen, John was.

Although satisfied with Francesca, Petrarch and his son never hit if off. He wrote of John: "So far as I can judge, he has a good enough mind; but this is only a suspicion, because I hardly know him. When he is with me, he maintains a stubborn silence, either because my presence awes and troubles him, or else because the shame of his ignorance closes up his mouth. One thing I see only too clearly, his antipathy for Letters . . . He fears, he hates nothing so much as a book . . ." Again, he wrote: "A book has the same effect on him as a snake. Neither prayers, nor caresses, nor threats, nor blows with the ferrule, are any use . . .

"Sometimes I make rather sharp jokes about him . . . When I take this tone with him, he looks down at the ground and blushes."

Petrarch hoped that if the Canon of Verona could not be clever, he could at least be good. "Not everyone can be Cicero or Plato, but everyone can be good. I prefer the man without education to education without the man."

John, however, could not be good either. He was forced out of Verona in 1354, apparently because of the local Prince's hostility to Petrarch, and showed up at home in Milan. Here, the Abbé de Sade thinks, John went so far as to rob his father's house, banding together with the servants for this purpose. There was Petrarch, working up to sixteen hours a day, while John roused himself from his torpor, scepticism and indifference only to mock at whatever his father loved. Petrarch finally put him out of the house. "Love is defeated," he had written his son, "hope is used up, patience has run out. My threshold can no longer support you, the walls of my house can no longer contain you, my roof can cover you no more, nor my ears hear you, nor my eyes behold you." He had reached the point where he hated John's walk, his voice, his way of moving his hands, of frowning, of shaking his head. Even this letter ended, however, in the hope that John would repent and come home.

John did repent. The repentance did not last, because it was cut short by the boy's dying of the plague, at twenty-four, on the very day they had given him back his benefice at Verona. And the father thanked God for his death, "which freed me, but not without sorrow, from a long affliction."

❉ ❉ ❉

Books — hated by his son, condemned on religious grounds by his brother — were Petrarch's way of life. He was always on the lookout for manuscripts, hunting them down in faraway cities. He enlisted friends, relatives, foreign visitors, the learned who were sent as ambassadors to the Pope, and widened his search till it included all Europe, and even the Orient. He traveled to distant monasteries as did Poggio in the next century. Urging a Florentine monk related to him, to help in the searching of monasteries, he wrote that he was curing all his passions except one: the overwhelming desire for books. ". . . books charm us to the marrow of our bones, speak to us, counsel us, make themselves part of us . . ." He was always inviting someone to come and share his studies: ". . . no house is little for two men who share one soul. You will find neither riches nor poverty here, but innumerable books."

Many a time if he wanted a copy of some work, he had to make it himself. He tells in a letter how he once stopped off at Liège, hearing that the city contained many books, and there obliged his companions to wait until he had accumulated two orations of Cicero, one in a friend's hand, one in his own.

Reminiscing about this, Petrarch adds, "I can tell you that it was a considerable task to find some ink in so fine a barbarian city, and that when it was found, it was very much the color of saffron."

Once, wearied out with copying Cicero, his fingers refused to push along and he was about to stop when he chanced on a passage in which Cicero describes how he himself had copied Cassius. At this Petrarch went on with his task, saying to himself, "What! Cicero copied out the lectures of another, and *you* cannot copy those of Cicero!"

Cicero was not always kind. Petrarch had a manuscript copied by himself, of the *Letters;* to keep it handy, he propped it against his library door, but several times as he brushed by, it toppled over and hit him, always on the same spot on the left leg. At first he paid no attention to the bruise, but finally as it worsened had to go to bed with it and nearly lost the leg.

※ ※ ※

Libraries, like other things composed, must die. Their elements separate and drift away. Petrarch watched over his like a mother, carried it about with him and tried to will it security beyond his death. When, in 1362, the plague drove him out of Padua and with his daughter and son-in-law, Brossano, he looked for a refuge in Venice, he willed his collection to the Republic: "Francis Petrarch," he wrote, "would wish to have the blessed Mark, the Evangelist, as heir to the books he has, and will have, on condition that these are neither sold, nor scattered, and will all be deposited in a secure place, where they will be protected from fire, and the rain, and carefully kept safe in perpetuity, to his honor and for the use and pleasure of the nobles and lettered of the city." He asked for a house where he and his could remain with the library. The Senators responded by a decree which

begins: "In consideration of the offer made us by Sir Petrarch, whose reputation is so great that one does not remember having seen in Christendom a moral philosopher, or a poet,
who could be compared to him —" and assigned him the
Palace of the Two Towers. Tomassini reports that the books
were later stored over the Church of Saint Mark "where
they were almost completely reduced to dust, and some of
them were even as it were petrified."

❧ ❧ ❧

What actually happened to Petrarch's books is not clear.
For five years or more he lived in the "vast palace — flanked
by two square towers." This is identified as the Palazzo Mo-
lin, on the Riva degli Schiavoni, near the Ponte del Sepolcro.
The poet was, however, not entirely pleased with Venice.
Perhaps it was another case of this place no good.

· JOANNA AND THE PAPAL ROSE

ᴏʀ Italians, and especially Petrarch, that conscience of the Avignon Popes — Urban's great reform was that he went back to Rome. Too much significance has perhaps been placed on this remove. Most writers claim that he went because he was afraid of the Free Companies. This is doubtful. The walls of Avignon were pretty well built up by now; the unfinished part, from the Gate of the Rhône to the structure housing the military stores, had in any case a natural protection of river and Rock. The large bribe paid Du Guesclin rescued not Avignon so much as the outlying crops, cattle and the Court's rich country estates from his pillaging troops.

It is certain that when Urban left, the great treasures of the Church stayed behind in a walled-up room. This argues that he was not making an irrevocable move; more likely he was only dabbling a pontifical toe in Roman waters.

After all, the Papacy had vast interests in Italy and if it would consolidate the gains already made there by Cardinal Albornoz, the warrior Cardinal who had won back so much territory for the Pope, why not change over for a while? The great danger, and one that Urban at first overlooked, was that his death, should it occur on Italian soil, might force the French Cardinals to choose an Italian Pope, rather than elect a Frenchman and risk violent death at the hands of the Roman mob.

Whatever his reasons, and whether his plan was for a temporary stay or not, the battle lines formed over Urban's decision. Controversy along the Rhône drowned out the wind.

By now Avignon, with Villeneuve across the river, had grown larger than Rome. The lovely "liveries" of the Cardinals studded the bright hills. The silver-green of olives, the soft flowers of Provence, the shining sky, the swan-white snow on Mount Ventoux, the rapid slide of Alpine water under the great Bridge — all these were easy on their eyes. And Rome lay ruined.

Among all the arguments against going to Rome, the most potent, apparently, was the Cardinals' cry: "But Burgundy will not be there!" They could not part with the wines of France, and they knew that good wine does not always travel well. Petrarch, in all seriousness, tried to console them with a flow of words about the excellence of Italian wines, but rhetoric was not enough. When they got to Rome they disagreed with Petrarch, and the wine with them; Urban had to send back to France for a proper vintage. We have no record of how it stood the trip.

The slogan "Where the Pope is, there is Rome" was heard

everywhere in Avignon until the day when Urban had his mail forwarded from the Rhône to the Tiber.

The King of France sent one of his finest orators down to Avignon to dissuade the Pope. Ever since the Druids, Nicolas Oresme declaimed, the Gallic people had shown a constant and natural inclination toward religion. His witness was no less than Julius Caesar. Moreover, he continued, the very Christian Kings of France had long granted asylum to the Pontiffs. After many a reference, as erudite as farfetched, to the Scriptures, he finally ended with this: Jesus had never left *His* homeland, therefore the Pope should not leave his.

Notwithstanding, on April 30, 1367, Urban left behind the naturally religious French, the wine of Beaune, the fairy landscapes of Avignon, its lovely ladies, the Palace of the Popes, his zoo, his fragrant gardens where he loved to walk, his library, the wooden cell, the papal treasures.

At Marseilles, the Cardinals made a last-ditch appeal to him not to quit French soil, soon changing to threats.

He replied by creating a new Cardinal, a man of twenty-eight — thus letting them know that if need were, he could draw still others out of his cowl.

On May 19, the fleet of twenty-three galleys (Urban's being supplied by Queen Joanna) and some smaller boats sailed out of Marseilles. Petrarch reported that the sobbing Cardinals behaved as if they were being dragged away in chains by Saracens. As the anchors were irrevocably raised, hideous cries rang out: "Evil Pope . . . impious Father, where are you taking your children?"

They made stops at Toulon, Villefranche, St.-Etienne, Albenga and other ports, arriving at Corneto June 3. Here nobles, Church officials and a clamoring mass of people greeted the flotilla. The sky was bright with promise of the new day but the sun still below the horizon when Urban stepped ashore and rested briefly under a silk tent embroidered with silver and gold. An altar had been set up in the flower-spangled fields by the sea, and as the sun rose in splendor that June morning the Pope said his first Mass on Italian soil. People murmured to each other about how auspiciously Urban's advent had begun.

The murmurs were different, however, a few days later, after the party had marched inland to Viterbo. The townspeople here were loyal to Cardinal Albornoz, whose energetic campaigns and shrewd politics stood out all the brighter against the gloomy foreign-office record of Innocent VI, and except for whose successes, Urban would not now be in Italy. Albornoz was ill, from disenchantment. He was soon to die. He had made the mistake of failing to protect himself at the Papal Court, and expecting the gratefulness of two Popes to be his safeguard. While he fought, day and night, to win back the Pope's possessions in faction-torn Italy, jealous Cardinals, at peace in Avignon, attacked him from behind. And the Pope listened. He now demanded an accounting from the gallant prelate. He wanted to see the books.

Not long thereafter, Urban heard the clatter of horses, the ring of iron wheels on the cobblestones below his window. He stepped to the balcony and there, standing beneath him in a wagon heaped with heavy locks and keys, was Cardinal Albornoz. In his two hands, the Cardinal lifted up the jangling ironware.

"Most Holy Father!" he cried out. "Here are my ledgers! Here is how I have used the monies of the Church! These are keys to the fortresses that I conquered for the Pope. My one regret is this: that I served you far too well. I leave you now — forevermore!"

Rioting broke out in uneasy Viterbo. Whether it was touched off by a brabble between a Cardinal's mistress and one of the townspeople, or whether it started when some of the Cardinal's servants washed in the public fountain, is not known. Whatever its cause, the treatment of Albornoz must have been a factor. The Cardinals ran for their lives to the citadel that sheltered Urban. A mob besieged the Pope for three days, yelling up at the barricaded castle, "Death to the Church!" He was delivered, and seven hangings helped to quiet things, but his auspicious welcome was clearly over. Urban knew for certain that he was back in Italy.

The Pope's arrival in Rome that October was greeted with manifestations of delight. After all, the Papacy had been gone sixty-three years and the Romans love a good show.

He came in preceded by two thousand precautionary men-at-arms, and he saw the flowery-walled Lateran fanning with bats and owls. Petrarch was displeased with this martial entry, and wrote: "His dignity, his holiness, would defend him better than swords and breastplates. The weapons of priests are virtue and fasts and good morals, prayers and tears." But then, Urban was there, Petrarch was not.

※ ※ ※

The ever controversial Queen Joanna, old acquaintance not forgot, now came on a visit, and Urban honored her with the Golden Rose, an award given on *Laetare* Sunday to the most distinguished personage then present at the Papal Court. He placed it on the Queen's head — a spray of roses made out of gold, one of them formed into a tiny vial for balsam and powdered musk. Over it the Pope had prayed that the Church might bring forth the perfume of the Savior and the fruit of good works.

The immediate fruit of the Pope's action on this occasion was a rousing complaint from Urban's Cardinals, who claimed that no Queen had ever received such a flattering distinction before. They, to a man, were particularly critical because a Queen had been chosen for the honor when a King was available. (The King of Cyprus was indeed present — because he had been banished from his throne.) The Cardinals also reviewed, but among themselves, Joanna's somewhat checkered past. The Pope stopped them with: "If no one has ever seen a Queen thus honored before, it is because no one has ever before seen an Abbot of Saint Victor in Peter's Chair."

And so Joanna rode out for her triumph, surrounded by Lords and Cardinals for all Rome to honor, and the bells rang.

※ ※ ※

For three anxious years, Urban stayed on in Italy, far away from his safe Palace on the Rhône. He rebuilt the Lateran and other ruined places, and he summered in the cool of Montefiascone, facing the Apennines. But he longed for Avignon. Meanwhile, at the Italian advent, Petrarch had seen the dream of his life come true. He would say, later on, of Urban: "In the midst of the corruption of this century . . . he was a good man." He wrote the Pope to tell him:

"In a single day, you have redeemed the wrongs done by five of your predecessors in the course of sixty years." And he hailed him with these lines from the Psalms: "When Israel went out of Egypt . . . then was our mouth filled with a gladness and our tongue with joy."

The aging poet set out for Rome, but was stricken on the way, and fell into a thirty-hour coma at Ferrara. They laid him in an open boat, for he could not sit a horse, and got him back to Padua, his welcome to Urban unspoken.

The French Cardinals ached for France and each one daily depicted a gloriously idealized Provence, with ever sunny skies, ripening wine grapes, and no wind, only the cool sweet air off the river. True, the people of Avignon were somewhat short of religion, but their homely complaisance made them all the easier to get along with. They had the gift of laughter; and really, life was altogether too pleasant to get stirred up about things when you could eat *coq au vin* for dinner and there were plenty of dusty bottles down cellar. How many riots could Urban remember in Avignon? And in Italy? And those three days shut up in the citadel at Viterbo when he had hardly yet gotten rid of the motion of the sea — they had been only a sample of troubles to come.

The Italians had no moderation. The people rebelled against every restraint, even that of the Church. The Cardinals pointed out how ungrateful the Italians were. Had not Urban re-established some order? Church property had lain in ruins and he had restored it; no longer could a cow graze all the way up to the altar of Saint Peter's. The Romans should be taught, all over again, that "the Pope has no need of Rome, but Rome has need of the Pope."

The constant repetition of such reasons for leaving had their effect, but the truth is, no people are bound tighter to their own country than the French, and Urban was homesick. Even stronger, however, was the uncertainty as to what would happen next, should he die in Rome. This had not been a consideration when he left Avignon. He did not feel old then. And he intended to return. This last point is emphasized by French writers who list the items he left behind: all the furnishings and palace paraphernalia, the celebrated library, and most important of all, the papal treasure.

The possibility of neighboring death had brought on a new problem. We cannot say Urban feared a schism — that clairvoyance was given to Gregory ten years later; but he unquestionably expected that serious trouble would follow his dying in Italy. There would then be great pressure on the Cardinals to elect an Italian Pope. As early as 1368, he named only one Italian out of eight new Cardinals, thus lessening the chance that threats of violence would seat an Italian on the throne. The danger of mob action was always there.

In the spring of 1370, something happened which served to point up his insecurity. The Pope loved to go to Montefiascone; it was the next best thing to being back in the South of France. At the very time most Italians were pleading with Urban to stay, the Romans, who had the most to gain if he did, were with fine illogic driving him back to Avignon. Now the Perugians rebelled against the Church and joined up with the Romans; Hawkwood and his mercenaries were hired; the Pope had to flee from Montefiascone to Viterbo where he had been besieged before. Nothing more was needed to reinforce his yearning to get out of Italy.

Then, in the guise of the redoubtable Saint Bridget of Sweden, even Heaven stepped in. This was the same Bridget who denounced Pope Innocent; the one who compared the clergy of the fourteenth century to "pitch, which stains and blackens all it touches." Some of her lines on the clerics and cloisters of Rome, the historian is afraid to remove from their Latin wrapping: *"Nunc autem clerici manifeste laetantur ex eo quod meretrices eorum, intumescente ventre, cernunt inter alias ambulare . . ." "Et ideo talia loca similiora sunt lupanaribus quam sanctis claustris."* The saintly woman was greatly reverenced; her pronouncements, believed to come directly from on High, had almost the strength of Scripture. She addressed Urban with a precision not always available in prophecies: "The Will of God is that the Pope should not leave Italy, but that he remain here until his death. And if not, he will soon be struck off from the number of the living and go where he will be called to account by the terrible Judge of Heaven."

※ ※ ※

Considering himself God's Vicar on earth, Urban felt that if need be he could overrule even Bridget; but her fateful prediction weighed on him, and perhaps shortened his life. Would the way back spell death? Some say he made a vow to return to Rome if Providence restored his health. Finally, in spite of all opposition, whether spiritual or temporal, he got together thirty-four galleys loaned by Queen Joanna, the Kings of France and Aragon, the Lords of Provence and the jubilant citizens of Avignon. He sailed from Corneto September 5, 1370, and making excellent time, landed at Marseilles eleven days later.

Back in the Papal Palace by September 24, Urban worked at a feverish pace. He set up special councils for each branch of Church administration and attended their sessions; he tightened law enforcement, which had grown lax during his absence; took measures to protect the poor against the exactions of Church officials; insisted that all cases be tried with speed and justice. To his great disappointment he was unable to make peace between France and England; for he had said that his main reason for leaving Rome was to mediate between the two powers and in this he failed.

Nevertheless he toiled on. October passed, and then November, and Urban was still in the world. Half of December went by, with Bridget's prophecy unfulfilled; the Pope was out of Italy, and lived. But then, on the 19th of December, Bridget won.

As Urban lay in his brother's house, where he had asked them to move him when he noticed death coming, he requested that the doors be thrown open to any who wished to enter. They could watch him lying there on his hard bed, dressed in the robe of Saint Benedict, the Crucifix in his veined hands.

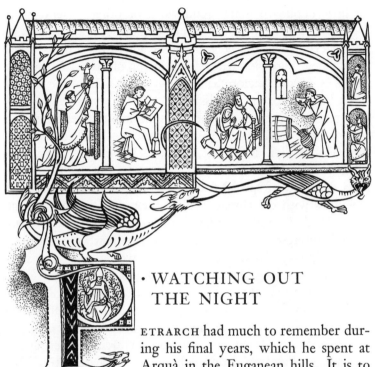

· WATCHING OUT
THE NIGHT

ETRARCH had much to remember during his final years, which he spent at Arquà in the Euganean hills. It is to be expected that his spirit would be strong there, in that place where Shelley later heard the rooks calling over the sunlit woods, saw them flying through the broken mists, their purple feathers starry with gold rain. He tells how he stood there looking down over the plain of Lombardy, and watched Venice's towers and spires as if in a furnace of light — and Padua's domes, and all the rest; Petrarch's love is still burning there, the Englishman wrote, a lamp that will never go out, for the heart to see by.

As ever, people gathered around him, appealing, Nolhac says, "to his memory and his books . . . there were many visitors, many written requests, and he always had by him 'in his little cupboard' some good work or other to lend . . ."

His one regret, Petrarch wrote Gherardo, was the lack of a Charterhouse in the neighborhood where his brother could live. They were closer now than in the old time, when they stood, as it were, back to back: Gherardo a man of the Middle Ages, Petrarch of the Renaissance.

Often in leisure hours he thought about friendship and friends. He had lived in so many places — Arezzo, Carpentras, Montpellier, Bologna, Avignon, Vaucluse, Parma, Verona, Milan, Venice, Padua — that naturally he had often been deprived of special friends. Then he would people his loneliness with the absent, evoke "their qualities of face and soul." True friends, they had been to him. Anyone friendly for self-interest was only "a clever salesman of cosmetics." Friendship was its own spur and great reward.

As his days lengthened out, he had to mourn his friends, one following another. There were the Florentine Mainard Accurso and the Roman Luca Cristiano, and that scene in his study at Parma, he waiting impatiently for them to come. At last, in a heavy downpour, the servant arrived. Seeing the man's face, Petrarch dropped his pen. "What is it? What news?" The servant, weeping, tried to say it: both men attacked by brigands in the Apennines; Mainard surrounded, butchered. Luca, one against ten, pulling out his sword, cut down, left for dead among the rocks.

Or there was Boccaccio, still precariously thriving. Boccaccio who called him Sylvanus for the Latin god of fields and forests, a cheerful old deity in love with Pomona, who is goddess of fruits that grow on trees. Petrarch could recall with enjoyment the episode of his and Boccaccio's message from Jesus. Oddly enough, Petrarch reflected, Jesus had sounded very much like the anti-intellectual clerics of the day. What happened was that a holy Carthusian of Siena, being on the point of death, dispatched one of the monks of his monastery to Boccaccio with a warning: Christ Jesus had appeared to the holy man, and directed the author of the *Decameron* to repent as to the scandal his writings had caused, and to undergo penances in order to repair the wrongs he had done, since he had not long to live. A similar warning was to be sent Petrarch. Boccaccio hurried off a panicky letter to Petrarch, saying he was going to sell his books, give up Letters, and retire to a monastery. Petrarch, who had often advised the plump and pleasure-loving Boccaccio to mend his ways, now cautioned him against overdoing it. Boccaccio insisted that Jesus had said he must give up poetry. Petrarch replied that such an injunction could hardly have come from a Divine source: It is a great matter, wrote Petrarch, if Jesus has spoken, but has He? Many think or say they have seen Him, but what does that prove? Petrarch would have liked to question the monk who brought the message. Meanwhile, what was so extraordinary about it? It said Boccacio would die. Had Boccaccio not known this already? Did you, Boccaccio, need the monk to tell you that every day you must prepare for death? As for the study of Letters, why should we let ignorant counsel or the approach of our end keep us from it? In what way are our studies contrary to Faith? "I know that many men have arrived, unlettered, at an admirable state of holiness, but I know of no one who has been excluded from holiness by education. I believe . . . that ignorance offers a smooth, but cowardly path to virtue. All good men have a single goal, but there are many ways to reach it . . . ignorance, however pious it may be, does not compare with *educated* piety. And in this flock of unlettered men you cannot show me a single saint that I cannot match with one more saintly in the other group." After all this, Petrarch smiled to himself, his winning argument was doubtless the offer to take over Boccaccio's books.

"You are always with me," he wrote still another friend,

Barbate di Sulmone, whom he had not seen for many a long year; "I make use of the privilege of those who love: absent myself, I behold and hear you . . . Set between us the Alps and Caucasus, and Atlas and Olympus higher than the clouds, and the great sea itself, yet these can never hinder us from meeting, from speaking together, from walking together, from eating supper and watching out the night."

"Not only the ones who are far away," he wrote, "but even those who are gone forever and already changed into sifted dust, I see them before me: they live again."

⚘ ⚘ ⚘

Francesca, his daughter, with her Milanese husband Brossano, was a consolation to him in these years. She was so good a daughter as to have left no history, unless one counts a letter from Boccaccio, full of her praise.

She had a child in Venice in 1366, Franceschino, delight of Petrarch's life, and handsome as the poet himself, long gone. Then, when the boy was two, he died. As always, Petrarch tried to write it out: "Those who go thus, in their unblemished bloom — we miss them more, we weep for them more, than if they had lived on to turn against us, to afflict us." He asked himself if he had ever loved anyone as much, if anyone had ever filled his hours so full, as that small being. He built the dead a little marble mausoleum in Pavia, and composed twelve Latin verses to be carved on it in golden letters: ". . . I was a fair child, my parents' joy and now their sorrow. It is that alone which saddens me . . . so easily did I reach eternal life. Twice did the sun, four times the moon, go round the universe, and then death, or rather life, drew on. Venice gave me to the world, and Pavia took me away . . ."

There was no one left to represent Petrarch directly in the world, and it was time he made his will. By April, 1370, he was planning to leave on his abortive trip to visit Pope Urban, taking advantage, as he informed the Pontiff, of his "first ray of health." Although he was almost sixty-six, an age when many hearts are cold from long disuse, he thought at length and tenderly, as he wrote out his testament, about the people he loved.

There was Gherardo, first of all, the brother forever worried about Petrarch's salvation. The poet had not failed to report to Gherardo as to his prayers, confessions and vigils, and his fears of any association with women "which I once thought I could not live without." With age, Petrarch had gone a long way back from the chivalry of his youth; Madonna Laura was in the sky, and he now regarded woman as the Fathers had: as the destroyers of God's image — man. Gherardo had continued to make progress in the monastery, he remembered with satisfaction, and had sent him a present, a boxwood box carefully polished on the lathe.

Petrarch, bearing in mind the severe rule of Gherardo's Order, said in his Will: "Immediately after my death my heir [Francesco da Brossano] is to give written notice of this event to my brother . . . and let him choose whether he wishes one hundred florins [at once] or five or ten florins annually, as he may please." (A part of this bequest, twenty florins, was used in 1377 in the monastery of Montrieux to endow a Mass for Petrarch's soul.)

Thanks to his Church benefices, Petrarch was not a poor man, although the Will ritualistically apologized for his poverty, saying: "Let my . . . friends accuse not me but Fortune — if there be such a thing as Fortune." (Petrarch believed that "Fortune by herself does not exist.") He was able to support relatives and guests, servants, five or six copyists, at least two horses in the stable, and he had plenty of possessions to refer to. One of his treasures was a panel of Mary

by Giotto, "the prince of painters of our era," which he
willed to Francesco da Carrara with this appraisal: "The
ignorant do not understand the beauty of this panel but the
masters of art are stunned by it."

In his own hand he set out bequests like these: he left to his
literary executor, Lombardo della Seta, "my little round cup
of silver and gilded," saying he could drink water from it and
adding approvingly that Lombardo preferred water to wine.
An attendant, Pancaldo, got twenty ducats, and the words
"may he not use them for gambling." And Boccaccio, perhaps closest of all, was to buy, with his fifty gold florins, "a
winter garment to be worn by him while he is studying and
working during the night hours."

He added that "no one is to weep for me . . . but to address prayers for me to Christ," and give alms to Christ's poor
to do as much. For tears, he wrote, are harmful to the living,
and useless to the dead.

※ ※ ※

Few writers in history, before or since, could match his
long momentous life. Four Popes, Clement VI, Innocent VI,
Urban V and Gregory XI, had wished him for their service.
Two Kings of France, Good King John and Charles V, had
begged him to live at their Courts. King Robert of Naples
had lamented that he could not crown him with his own hands
at Rome. Great Italian princes, the Viscontis, Carraras, Gon-
zagas, kept him by them; at a public ceremony, Venice had
put him in the place of honor, at the Doge's right. To tell
him she had borne a daughter, a German Empress wrote him
in her own hand. A blind schoolmaster walked half the length
of Italy to find him in Naples, missed him there, and went
back to Parma across the Apennines, only to hear his celebrated voice. A goldsmith of Bergamo placed his portraits

through the house, gilded the room in which he would be received, and swore that none should ever sleep again in the purple-spread bed in which Petrarch passed one night.

Besides, he had given his time a new slant. He had helped to bring back the past, and transmitted the new energies from Spain and beyond the Inland Sea. He had looked forward to an Italy that would not come about for five hundred years. He had, in Chaucer's words, "Enlumined all Itaille of poetrye." He had loved, and told his love to the human race.

Now that he was feeble, and old, and sick ("Oh, I am used to hearing the names of my ailments, and to enduring the surgeon's hand!"), his one desire was to get on with his work.

On July 18, 1374, they found him in his study, his head bowed over a book. At first, they did not know he was gone.

※ ※ ※

And so the crowning at Rome was not the only time when Petrarch, with his simple tastes, went sumptuously dressed and companioned. They clothed him in a flame-colored cassock, garb of the Canons of Padua, and sixteen learned scholars carried him on a bier that was covered with ermine-lined cloth of gold, to the parochial church of the village, and laid him down. Later they raised a marble monument there, carving on it the epitaph written by the poet for himself:

"This stone covers over the chilled bones of Francis Petrarch. O Virgin Mother, receive his spirit. O Virgin's Son, be Thou indulgent. And may his soul, now so long wearied of this earth, find rest in the retreats of Heaven."

· GREGORY THE GRAVE

T ABOUT this time in Avignon's life — that is, in the life of Christianity's capital — yet another woman would take charge of events, perhaps most doomfully. None could evade this; it had all been prophesied, long before.

Urban's successor was chosen by unanimous vote, one day after the Conclave opened, December 30, 1370. If the previous Pope had been, by Church standards, a young man, this one was almost a boy. He was thirty-nine. Gregory had become accustomed to high office rather early in life — at eleven, to be exact; for he was the nephew of Pope Clement VI (of Avignon's first seven Popes, two were Pope's nephews) and had been made Canon of Rodez and Paris at that tender age, Cardinal at eighteen. He had, however, never been ordained, and was now, shortly before his crowning, made a priest.

On the Feast of Epiphany, as that Cardinal who was Prince of Auvergne placed the tiara on the eleventh Gregory's head, he pronounced these traditional words: "Receive the tiara adorned with the three crowns, and know that thou art Father of Princes and Kings, Ruler of the world, and Vicar on earth of our Savior, Jesus Christ, to Whom be honor and glory, world without end."

The new Pope was a man short of stature, pale, with grave gestures and sorrowful eyes. A paragon in many ways: intelligent, approachable, pious, clean-living, desiring peace. He had many of his uncle's qualities, but lacked that kingly attitude toward the Papacy, and that sensuality as well. His only weakness where women were concerned was perhaps that he let himself be influenced by good ones.

Along with some affability, he had ability too, a way about him that got things done. He had been a brilliant student of canon law and his juridical equipment was extraordinary. Nevertheless, he was modest too; feeling, perhaps, not physically up to it, he did not seek the Papacy but tried to have someone else named in his place.

The negative list seems almost bare: nepotism was a hereditary fault, he was timid when boldness was needed, suffered from habitual melancholy. When one looks closer at his other side, however, one stumbles into unexpected horror; was his untiring zeal against the heretics only a desire for the Church's welfare, or did he sluice off against them black emotions, leaving the remainder of his personality quiet and gentle? Besides, this zeal was the cause of his historic mistake: paradoxically, a worldling like his uncle might at that moment have been better for the Church.

During his reign, he had to watch the Muslims flourishing

in Andalusia, moving on Dalmatia, threatening Sicily. They seemed to be everywhere, but Christian rulers would never stop fighting each other and turn on the followers of the Prophet. Meanwhile, busy Venetians and Genoese sold the Muhammadans food supplies and arms.

Unable to protect Christianity from without, Gregory tried to crush the heresies that weakened it within. Torture and flame had not put down the Spirituals, who continued to insist on the poverty of Christ, and, by extension, of those who said they ruled in His Name. In spite of massacre after massacre, the Albigensian heresy was rising again from its ashes. Various other sects of the Cathari, and descendants of Peter Waldo's Poor Men of Lyons, all needed to be punished. Even converted Jews wandered into new fields of unorthodoxy and had to be dragged screaming back onto the straight path with red-hot irons.

Aware of how past Popes had failed, Gregory still followed the same blood-drenched road, ignoring as they had the sickening fumes of burning human flesh. If he can be excused, it must be because he was trained in the dictator's credo, so widely upheld throughout the ages, that man's spirit really can be enslaved by law if only this law is rigidly enough applied. It was impossible that he should succeed in France; the individual is too strong there. And those who had to carry out the law had begun to doubt its wisdom, and perhaps its truth. The "secular arm" was tiring. There was a mounting dislike of doing the dirty work of the religious, especially when the lay power began to see churchly hands reaching into areas of jurisdiction that had formerly been reserved to states. Executioners knew their duty but grew lax. Partly, also, the work slowed because it had proved fruitless. Martyrs' blood continued to generate ideas. The bones of dissidents who had died at the stake were being collected and cherished: chapels were raised to honor them; belief in them went on.

For over a century in France, from the days of Gregory IX, it had been common to witness brave men and women going up in flames, while out of the nauseating smoke and fire they continued to voice their beliefs. Whether they were right or wrong — whether they had embraced an error, succumbed to a person, or to collective insanity, or been blinded by a self-engendered vision, or whether they had actually seen what ordinary men cannot often see — the fire had burned away their flesh but not their faith.

The secular arm was tiring; it was hardly withered up. (Long afterward, when the mentally disturbed Damiens sought immortality by knifing Louis XV, the Legate of Avignon eagerly offered Paris his own city's dreaded *Veille*, an indescribable horror machine housed in the Palace, together with the local hangman to run it. Unfortunately, the would-be assassin succumbed to other refinements of applied agony before the *Veille* reached Paris.)

Nevertheless, whipped on by the unwearying Gregory, increasingly reluctant civil authorities were for the moment persuaded, and the Pope piled up victims.

Early in Gregory's reign, bands of men and women suddenly came dancing and singing into Flanders from the Rhineland. Immense multitudes were affected. They kept up a continual, rapid dance, laughing uproariously and giving out hoarse cries. A performer would leap into the air, spring and dance till he fell in convulsions. Someone would then revive him by jumping on him; or if he wore a cloth tied around his middle, it helped to twist this cloth with a stick. When, at Herestal, a large company of the dancers got together and consulted about killing all the clergy of Liège, the Dancing Mania was revealed as dangerous. Gregory sent his inquisitors to look into it; these reported that the malady was due to demoniacal possession, caused by baptism at the hands of country priests too ignorant to pronounce the formula correctly; once they proceeded to rebaptize the victims properly the disease, said the inquisitors, tended to abate. The masses did not quite agree; they said the dancing was due to defective baptism brought on by the fact that the priests kept concubines.

Meanwhile, the eternal question remained: Would the Pope, would he not, go back to Rome?

A third plague now struck Avignon and it was followed by famine. Gregory left the city, but he did not make this an occasion to take the Papacy away. Perhaps there was no time. Did he really want to go back? He himself said that from the beginning of his reign he had intended to make the change; yet after he had reigned six years, he was still in Avignon. Indubitably, he entertained the idea of going, but like any other Frenchman was in no hurry to leave France. Certain conventions were regularly observed during the long stay of the Popes in Avignon. It was always wise to assure the Italians, with a wink at the French, that the new wearer of the tiara wished to return the Papacy to Rome. The valuable States of the Church in Italy, the loyalty of Italian ecclesiastics, the income — all could be more firmly held, regained or enlarged if it seemed likely the Pope would soon come back.

In 1374, the year of the third plague, Gregory published in a bull his intention of leaving for Rome during the autumn or early the next year. But his departure was put off until July, 1375, and again until spring, when it was postponed once more.

Meanwhile, events in Italy could be blamed for the latest delays. Florence was in rebellion and carrying her neighbors with her under the flag of "Libertas." This revolt of the

Pope's long-standing ally resulted from an attack on that city engineered by the very Papal Legate, Guillaume Noellet, who was entrusted with her protection: Guillaume had ordered Hawkwood and his mercenaries to take Florence at a time when he knew she was unarmed.

Gregory tried hard to repair the damage his Legate had done. He wrote to Siena, declaring he had never aimed at Florentine territory. "We are told that some among you wish the people to believe that the Holy See would lay hold of Tuscany. Than this calumny, nothing is farther from the truth. How wrong, to think that shadows could emanate from the Center of light, that evil could come from the hands of a Father who dispenses only good . . . Content with what we already possess, we have ever refused those territories belonging to the Empire that Charles IV has wished to give us. Nothing do we long for with such ardor as to see all the cities of Italy living together in peace."

We may believe Gregory, but the acts of his Legate could not be canceled out. The Republics of Siena, Pisa and Lucca joined with Florence, and named a directing committee which they called the Eight of the War. Under the word "Libertas," in gold, their troops invaded the Papal States, assuring all that they wanted nothing for themselves. There would be no conquests. They had only the one desire: "Libertas." So strong was the wish to be freed from papal control that within ten days eighty cities and towns rallied to the golden word, and the dual cry rang out: "Down with the priests! Libertas!"

Before Bologna, "Pearl of the Romagna," should be lost, Gregory, though he had an army, offered peace. The Eight of the War refused, and sent Count Bruscoli into the city to arm and stir up the people. The papal troops were ousted, the Legate imprisoned, and, timid though he was, the Pope finally decided to fight.

At this point, however, that mysterious virgin, Saint Cath-

erine of Siena, intervened. Catherine clamored for peace.
Florence accordingly sent her confessor, Brother Raymond,
on a mission to quiet down the Pope. Gregory duly agreed
to suspend hostilities, and gave the Florentines a month to
answer for their misdeeds or be excommunicated. They replied to this with an embassy, who stood before Gregory
and instead of asking indulgence began to accuse his Legates.

"Their speaker, Donato Barbadori, recalled with bold eloquence all the real or pretended causes of the revolt . . . 'If
we started the war, it was to save our country, our wives,
our children, our life . . . We do not deny the revolt that
has spread to the Church lands, but the cause of it was the
governors' avarice and pride!' "

Eloquence is not always well placed, a fact which should
comfort the inarticulate, and it probably works better on
mobs than on minds. The Pope's reply was to excommunicate Florence. Barbadori then turned to the Crucifix, in-
voking the Lord: "O our God! We deputies of the Florentine people, we appeal to Thee and to Thy justice against the
unjust sentence of Thy Vicar. O Thou . . . Who lovest
the freedom of peoples, not their slavery, guard Thou the
Florentines as they defend their freedom; turn Thou away the
cruel anathemas now hurled against us."

The terrible effects of the excommunication and interdict
soon darkened the lives of all in Florence. Upon the more
spiritually sensitive, and those who felt themselves in danger of dying without absolution for their sins, or who feared
that their newborn might perish unbaptized and so be
damned forever, the wholesale excommunication was an intolerable weight. The majority, given to regarding remote
consequences, however eternal, with less concern than present
danger, felt the restraints on trade like cords around their
throats. A nation excommunicated was so to speak outlawed.

The Pope's weapons of embargo and economic strangulation went into action. The essentials of life must not be supplied by other Christians to the excommunicated: no wheat for bread, no meat, no cloth, no firewood. All financial transactions with Florence and the Florentines were forbidden. Thus, money owed them need not be repaid, and their property could be confiscated, wherever it might be. To a commercial people with merchants and brokers all over Europe, these were mortal blows; many went bankrupt in a day.

But worse even than the loss of goods and money, to say nothing of Heaven, Gregory commanded that they be seized and turned into slaves. The Pope had terrifying powers and he was bringing down the full weight of them on the Republic which had dared to revolt, and raise against him his own Church States.

· AND IF YOU DIE
IN ROME

HRISTIAN opinion was massing against Pope Gregory, forcing him actually to leave for Rome, to make the journey in a galley, not just in ink across the page. It began to look as if the seventy-year-old promise would have to be implemented at last. Disillusionment over his failure to leave Avignon had certainly contributed to the rebellion in the Church States; then the rebellion itself became the cause of further delay, but meanwhile the pressure for action was steadily building.

It showed in small things as well as large. For instance, Gregory issued a bull in 1375, ordering all Bishops to remain at their Sees. One day he noticed a prelate in Avignon who should have been at work far away. Gregory chided him with the question, "Lord Bishop, why do you not go to your

See?" The Bishop, pausing only a moment, replied, "And you, Holy Father, why do you not go to yours?"

Of one such episcopal broadside, Gregory quietly remarked: "Our dear Bishop has passed the night in some tavern, surrounded by daughters of joy, and has abandoned his reason in the depths of a wine jug."

He might, by judicious postponements, have managed to tide things over, and stay on in his homeland. But Catherine ruled otherwise: Catherine of Siena, whose magic was stronger than the Pope's.

⚜ ⚜ ⚜

Two centuries before, Saint Malachy — the same who in 1148 died in the arms of Saint Bernard of Clairvaux — had made a prophecy about all the Popes to come. Each man was signalized by a Latin device, and Gregory's device was *Novus de Virgine Forti*. The strong virgin now proved to be a young woman, sickly, unlettered, unknown; her father was a dyer of Siena, but she was not subdued to what he worked in. She entered the Third Order of Saint Dominic, attracted a circle of men and women "Caterinati" about her, and served the poor. From this she was drawn into politics and began to issue commands to Kings and Popes, Queens and Cardinals — in short, to the heads of the Western world.

Mysticism, a phenomenon which occurs in every religion, was strong in the Christian fourteenth century, providing an opposite pole to the materialism of the Papal Court. Instead of worldly power, the emphasis with the mystic was on love. Overt or disguised, sex might be here as well, in every degree.

A canticle of German Flanders portrays the Cross as a May tree that flowers for the salvation of the world. A nightin-

gale perches upon it, singing out his love for a young girl.
He weeps and laments over her, and dies. The nightingale
is Christ, the young girl is the Church. In another canticle,
Christ is a bridegroom, running at night after the souls that
long for Him. Someone cries out: "O Mary! Look out for
your Son! See how He is capturing the young maidens!"

A nun of Utrecht says: Love goes, love comes, love stays,
love sings. Love rests in love; love sleeps, love wakes; love
takes away all else but love."

So personal was this love at times that Saint Laurent Gius-
tiniani composed a treatise on "the chaste marriage of the
Word and the Soul," in which one chapter treats of "the visible signs by which the espoused may know in her own
entrails the lawful love of the Word."

When Catherine of Siena was married to Jesus He slipped
on her finger a wonderful ring set with three precious stones,
that only she could see. He tore out His heart and placed it
where hers had been, taking her own away.

Midnights, when the heavenly Groom would visit Catherine, she tells us: "He enters then into my cell, my sweetest
Spouse. He sings holy hymns to me, and then He lays himself
down upon my couch and makes me drunk with the delights
of Heaven. He came to me once in the dress of a mendicant
friar, that I might not know Him; and thus disguised, he
begged for alms in a voice so filled with anguish that, having nothing else, I passed Him my cowl, my robe, my sash, to
comfort that sore-afflicted One whose urgencies and prayers
had grown ever more piteous. Then at last when I had taken
away the final veil that wrapped me, He assumed His godly
shape, and caught me away with Him to the Seventh Heaven."

Catherine left over four hundred letters, which have been
called one of the glories of Italy. She often dictated without
hesitation to two secretaries at once, different letters on com-

plicated themes, and some she composed while in a state of ecstasy. Her confessor, Raymond of Capua, said that at first he had doubts of her marvels, until one day as he gazed at her he saw her change into Jesus Christ.

One of these letters, addressed to Raymond, tells how she had prepared a man to face his execution. She took him to Mass the day before, and he received the Eucharist, which he had previously avoided. The rest of the day was passed in spiritual transports. He leaned his head on her bosom. "Stay with me," he told her. "I shall be content." The next morning she came first to the scaffold, and laid her own head on the block. What she longed for was withheld. At length he came. He received the blade like a lamb, speaking Christ's name. She lifted his head in her two hands, and at that moment saw Jesus. He shone out like the sun, and He accepted the man into His Kingdom. Catherine could not bring herself to wash off the rich red blood from her clothing.

Now she addressed the Pope, and directed him to return to Rome. "Be the true successor of Saint Gregory," she exhorted. "Love God. Be bound neither to father nor mother, nor friends, nor the requirements of the world. Go forward. Complete what you have well begun. Make haste and tarry not, for delay has caused a spate of ills, and the Demon spends his wits to thwart you. Raise high the flag of the true Cross, through this alone shall you win peace . . . Resist no more the will of God, for the famished flocks are waiting, longing to see you back in Peter's chair. Come without fear, for God is with you. Wait not for time, because time waits for none. Answer the Holy Ghost. Come as the Lamb Who with His unarmed hand brought down His foes, when weaponed but with love . . . Be brave. Redeem the Church from evil and from rifts; the very wolves will draw to you like sheep, and wail for mercy, and hide against your breast."

He must, she wrote again, like Christ forgive his enemies, his Italian foes: "You know well that one does not drive the Devil away with the Devil, but only with good." She addressed the Ruler of the world as her "Babbo."

Written exhortations, however, were not enough for the Saint's vehemence. Catherine would come in the flesh to Avignon. Florence's harried people had made her their Ambassadress to the Pontiff and her approaching advent was the talk of the town. The sophisticated prelates were vastly annoyed; why, they asked almost audibly, should the Florentines send them a weak young woman, perhaps not quite right in the head? They let it be known that they were not going to be influenced by trances.

On June 18, 1376, Catherine entered the city. She came accompanied by twenty-two disciples, with Raymond as her interpreter, and Gregory put a splendid house at her disposal, with a rich chapel. Two days after arriving, she stood before the Pope in her nun's poverty.

It was one of several audiences they had together. They talked about the sad state of Italy. The burden of what she said was always the same: Go back he must, or the Church was finished. At other times, she pressured Gregory in writing: "Play a saintly trick; make as if to delay your going, then all of a sudden — go!" She exposed a letter, purporting to come from some pious individual, actually a forgery, which, to frighten the Pope away, prophesied that he would be poisoned in Rome. Again she addressed him: "Suppose there is danger of death, must we not sacrifice life?" But she had prayed for him, and after the prayer, "I saw neither death, nor peril, nor any of those dangers of which your counselors tell you." (Strange that she did not see him, a year after his return to Rome, lying cold in the Vatican.)

※ ※ ※

Avignon looked at Catherine. The Pope's sister, Countess of Valentinois, became her patroness, but various prelates, fearing her influence on Gregory, said her wonders were mere symptoms of ill health. An Archbishop questioned her, and with some disappointment could find no heresy. The Pope's young niece, Elys de Beaufort, applied a more scientific method to solving the enigma: once when Catherine was caught up in an ecstasy, Elys jabbed her in the foot with a needle. Catherine did not stir. Elys, making a face, had to acknowledge the validity of the trance condition.

And Catherine looked at the Papal Court. She became, during her stay, less a young woman thinking of Gregory's benevolent fatherliness, more a saint speaking down to him in plain terms. She ticked off his failings, especially the way he favored his relatives and promoted them regardless of worth. She told the Cardinals that where she had expected a Paradise of virtue she could now detect the stench of Hell.

Avignon was used to being denounced: such tirades did no real harm. What the town could not abide was all this talk of moving back to Rome when everyone was so comfortably installed here. Yet the Pope seemed to be listening. He sounded as if he had been won over by this woman. Maybe he really meant to leave. Avignon was not a mob-raising town, life here was too pleasant for that, but her constant drumming on the one theme brought them close to mobbing Catherine. What saved her was that Gregory treated her with marked respect.

"I have had several interviews with the Holy Father," she wrote the Florentines, exhorting them to send official ambassadors promptly. "He has listened to me with the most moving kindness and has shown the keenest desire for peace. He is a loving father who thinks not of his son's offense, only of his repentance, that he may grant him forgiveness and mercy." Gregory never doubted Catherine's pure intentions, but he mistrusted the Florentines, and mockingly referred to them as "those merchants." Perhaps they trusted him as little, for they sent him no ambassadors empowered to conclude a peace.

It would not be long before they turned on Catherine as well. When she got back to Florence she found that the Eight of the War were branding as traitors whoever talked of unity with the Church. A bare-armed Florentine, waving his sword, shouted to the people to avenge themselves on "the Madwoman," and she had to run for her life.

But in Avignon, the Saint got what she came for. If for no other reason than to restore peace in Italy, Gregory at last felt he must leave. His later bitterness is itself the measure of her influence. He had been deeply moved by some quality she had which moved everybody.

Departing, she said to the Pope with quiet authority: "Into your hands I give the interests of the Church; husband its glory." Strange words, coming from the daughter of a dyer to the head of Western Christianity. One could either laugh at her complacent assurance or believe that she had a Heavenly right to it. Gregory did not laugh.

Prudently, she later enlisted the aid of Saint Bridget of Sweden and Peter of Aragon, both of whom had tried to keep Urban in Rome. They laid down a heavy fire of letters which contributed to Gregory's decision. This was hastened, too, by envoys who came in August, warning that an anti-Pope would be elected if Gregory stayed away much longer; news which was confirmed by the Papal Legate in Rome, and further supported by the actions of many of the Italian clergy, who had joined the rebellion of the Papal States and were urging their charges to throw out the Pope's officials. We know, what Gregory did not, that the Abbot of Montecassini was ready to assume the office of Roman Pope.

The King of France, meanwhile, had sent down his own brother, Louis, Duke of Anjou, to dissuade Gregory. As he left the Pontiff, having failed like all the others, Louis addressed him sadly: "Where are you going, Holy Father? You leave a Kingdom where religion is honored more than in any land on earth. You go into a country where you are anything but loved." He then added the prophetic words: "If you should die there, which is likely, the Romans will make themselves masters of the Cardinals' persons, and to prevent the Papal Court from returning to Avignon, they will force them, with daggers at their throats, to elect a Pope perhaps fatal to the Church."

· THE GREAT SCHISM
OF THE WEST

S THE century opened, the Popes had
deserted Rome. Earlier Popes had
many times sought refuge on French
soil, but only as a temporary asylum;
this time they moved the Holy See. And except for the short
and quickly repented stay of Urban, Gregory's predecessor,
one after the other seven Popes had remained away. They
had stayed for seventy years, enjoying Provence, freed from
the fear of Roman mobs. Now, because of a woman, the
seventh of these Popes was to venture back. Actually, he
too might have again abandoned Rome for the Rock of the
Lords had the choice been his.

Gregory's act would still influence mankind when six
long centuries had passed, for it was the immediate cause of
the Great Schism of the West, and this in turn set off the Prot-

estant Revolution. What the Great Rift did was not so much
to create new abuses as to extend those already there — and
most of all, it advertised them to the world.

This struggle for the papal throne would not remain a far-
off quarrel, a matter for hair-splitting between theologians.
There would be, in fact, no difference over dogma. Rather,
a choice of loyalties would be forced on the individual.
Which would he have, the Pope of Avignon or of Rome;
and later which of the three, him of Pisa, Rome or Avignon?
Each would be defended by eminent doctors who would
prove that he was the true Christian's only true Pope. Meanwhile the Schism lasted forty years and more. Men began to
say there could well be ten or a dozen Popes, perhaps a
Pope for each country, and from there logic carried them
to the consideration of whether there need be any Pope at
all.

Look ahead into the future, past Gregory's death, to a day
in April, 1378; see the next Conclave in Rome. Hear the
Lords Banneret, rulers of the city, shouting to the captured
Cardinals: "Take heed, take heed, give us a Roman Pope, or
we will turn your heads redder than your hats!" They speak
from strength, they have thousands of furious peasants, each
with his murderous farm tools, massing close at hand.

Another voice lifts up: "Ever since Pope Boniface, France
has gorged herself on Roman gold. Now it is *our* turn. We
will feast on French gold for a change!"

Before the windows, twenty thousand jam Saint Peter's
square. "A Roman or at least an Italian, or we cut you to
ribbons!" they chant.

Look closely at Cardinals Robert of Geneva and the calm
Pedro de Luna. These two in succession will be Avignon's
next Popes, but perhaps not the world's. Except for these
two — de Luna because he never knows fear and Robert

because he has chain armor under his robes — the prisoner Cardinals sweat and shake.

Among them there are four Italian votes, and there are twelve for France, but split. The voters turn against each other and their mutual screams drown out the mob. Suddenly below stairs hooligans splinter the doors, roar down the halls, break into cellars and drink the wine of Beaune. They pile up bundles of sticks, dry branches, straw, and set the Vatican on fire. One of the Cardinals cries: "Better to elect the Devil himself than die!"

Among the voters is old Tibaldeschi, who, unable to walk, had been carried into the Conclave. Very old, Tibaldeschi, but a man of Rome. Somehow the Cardinals balance the miter on his shaking head, bundle the red cope across his shoulders; anything, anything to snatch time; they hold him up before the people, force him to act as if he were Pope. The jubilant Romans seize his swollen, gouty hands, and the old man shrieks with pain.

In panic, the Cardinals then elect Bartolomeo Prignano, Archbishop of Bari, and one after another, by secret exits, flee away. They do not want Prignano for Pope, but as one Cardinal says, speaking for them all, "I would rather be of those who suffer for the Faith than of those who die for it."

The new Pope takes the name of Urban VI. He reigns as Pope. Intolerably he reigns, with a glint like madness in his angry, bloodshot eyes. At last the same Cardinals who, pressured by Roman mobs, had chosen old Tibaldeschi and then this almost mad Archbishop, flee to Fondi. Here they elect again. They declare Robert of Geneva their third Pope for that year. As Clement VII this Pope will come back to Avignon and reign, while the furious Urban keeps on as Pope in Rome, and men coin the new words "Urbanist" and "Clementine." Pedro de Luna, as last Avignon Pope, will not abandon his Palace there until March, 1403, will never abandon his tiara.

Finally at Constance, more than a century after the first Pontiff came to Avignon, the West will assemble, cut the papal knot which there is no way to loose, and somehow splice the line. But this is sealed in many dark tomorrows.

※ ※ ※

Meanwhile, Pope Gregory was leaving Avignon. The last day came, September 13, 1376. Another woman tried, once more, to influence him now. As the Pope quitted his apartments his mother, her hair unkempt, her clothing in disorder, threw herself down before him, blocking the door. Weeping, tearing at her dress, she bared her breasts to her son. But Gregory forced her aside and walked on; and her love, more truly prophetic than Catherine, cried after him, "I shall never see you again!"

At the Palace steps, when he went to mount his horse, it shied and curvetted till they could hardly get Gregory on, and once he was in the saddle the animal froze. Grooms pulled at the bridle in vain. The Pope had to climb down. Alas, he let the omen by, and they brought up another mount.

Did Gregory remember these things, as he lay in the Vatican during the second spring after his return to Rome? Did he go back in his mind to the country where the Mistral blows, to the flowing hills, the tender skies of France? It is certain that he left this world lamenting his safe Palace on the Rhône, the massive fortress out of which he had led his Church. As he grappled with his final hours, those at the bedside heard him muttering at his own folly, for having "listened to the prophecies of pious women," for having turned back again to Rome.

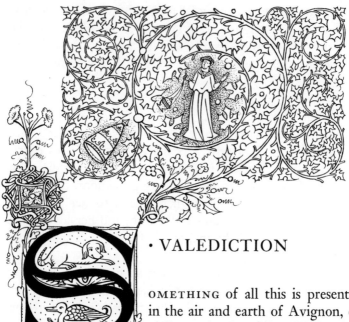

· VALEDICTION

SOMETHING of all this is present yet, in the air and earth of Avignon, especially as the day falls. Walk where a street of plane trees reaches to the Gate of Saint-Roch, near where the plague victims were buried, in the Champ-Fleury. Come to the empty, swirling Rhône. At intervals along the lonely bank are posts, for mooring boats. Up in the sky beyond the fourteenth century wall stands Our Lady of the Lords, queening it over the Palace; and further along is the broken-off Bridge, spanning only time. Voices reach out of the shadows: "Advanced something," they whisper, "relating to the happiness of the Saints in the other world"; or, "My predecessors did not know how to be Popes"; or again, "Suppose there is death, must we not sacrifice life?"

At sunset the wind is gentler here, and there may be a mo-

ment when it brings down the memory of another voice saying:

"That hair, now bound with pearls and precious stones,
now loose in tresses blonder than fine gold, she spread it
out with such grace, she gathered it back with motions so
charming that my heart still leaps at the thought of it." When
the low sun gilds the water and the Rhône ripples off in light,
and it is Laura's hair that the Mistral is blowing away.

CHRONOLOGY

Avignon Popes during Petrarch's lifetime:

CLEMENT V	(1305–1314)
JOHN XXII	(1316–1334)
BENEDICT XII	(1334–1342)
CLEMENT VI	(1342–1352)
INNOCENT VI	(1352–1362)
URBAN V	(1362–1370)
GREGORY XI	(1370–1378)

1302 Pope Boniface VIII issues the bull *Unam Sanctam*.

1303 French force under de Nogaret captures Boniface VIII, with help of Colonnas. Boniface dies. Benedict XI succeeds him.

1304 Petrarch born July 20 at Arezzo. Benedict XI dies after a reign of eight months. Poisoning suspected.

1305 Bertrand de Goth becomes Pope Clement V. The Papacy is moved to France.

1307 All Knights Templars in France arrested. Edward II becomes King of England.

1308 Henry VII of Luxembourg is Holy Roman Emperor.

1309 Clement V transfers the Holy See to Avignon. Robert the Wise becomes King of Naples.

1310 Henry VII conquers Bohemia and places his son John on its throne.

302 CHRONOLOGY

1311 Clement V erases from papal records the bulls against Philip the Fair. Petrarch at Pisa. General Council of the Church meets at Vienne.

1312 Order of Knights Templars abolished. Petrarch's family settles at Carpentras, near Avignon.

1313 Henry VII breaks with the Papacy. He dies. Boccaccio born.

1314 Clement V dies. Philip the Fair dies. Louis IV of Bavaria and Frederick of Austria both take the title of Holy Roman Emperor. Louis X the Quarrelsome becomes King of France.

1315 The papal throne is vacant.

1316 Louis X dies. Philip V the Long succeeds him. John XXII elected Pope, ending two-year papal vacancy. Petrarch studies law at Montpellier.

1317 Assembly at Paris rules that no woman may sit on the French throne.

1320 Petrarch studies law at Bologna.

1321 Death of Dante.

1322 Charles IV the Fair becomes King of France.

1323 John XXII issues the bull *Cum inter nonnullos*.

1324 John XXII tries to remove Louis IV as Holy Roman Emperor.

1326 Petrarch settles in Avignon.

1327 April 6, Holy Week, Petrarch first sees Laura. Edward II of England deposed. Edward III begins his reign. France and England agree on the Peace of Paris. Louis IV of Bavaria marches into Italy.

1328 Philip VI the Bold becomes King of France. He defeats the Flemish at Cassel. Treaty of Northampton recognizes the independence of Scotland. Anti-Pope Nicholas V created by Louis IV of Bavaria.

1329 David II rules as King of Scotland.

1330 Petrarch summers in Lombez, Gascony, with Bishop Giacomo Colonna. Edward III becomes King in fact as well as name. Mortimer and Isabella the Queen Mother overthrown.

1333 Petrarch travels in France, Germany and Flanders.

1334 Benedict XII becomes Pope.

1335 Petrarch appointed Canon of Lombez.

1336 Petrarch climbs Mount Ventoux. John, his son, born.

1337 The Hundred Years' War begins, between France and England. Petrarch withdraws to Vaucluse. Froissart born. Giotto dies.

1338 German Diet declares the election of the Holy Roman Emperor to be independent of the Pope. Petrarch begins *Africa*.

1340 Muslims defeated at the battle of Tarifa. Edward III claims the title King of France. French fleet defeated at Sluys. Chaucer born.

1341 Petrarch crowned at Rome.

1342 Clement VI becomes Pope. Petrarch begins *Secretum*. Cola di Rienzi first in Avignon? Petrarch Papal Ambassador at Court of Naples, after the death of Robert the Wise. Petrarch's daughter Francesca born.

1343 Joanna I becomes Queen of Naples.

1344 Petrarch at Parma.

1345 Petrarch returns to Vaucluse. Joanna suspected of murdering her husband Prince Andrew.

1346 French defeated by English at Crécy. Charles IV of Bohemia chosen Holy Roman Emperor.

1347 Rienzi assumes power in Rome as Tribune. Petrarch starts out on a visit to him but stops at Genoa. Naples invaded by Louis of Hungary.

1348 Year of the Plague. Death of Laura. Massacre of the Jews in Germany.

1349 Petrarch prepares the Sonnets. Peter the Cruel becomes King of Castile.

1350 John II the Good ascends the French throne. Petrarch in Verona, Mantua, Rome, Arezzo. Rienzi in Prague. Jubilee held in Rome.

1351 Zürich joins the Swiss Confederation. Petrarch in Padua. Florence-Milan war.

1352 Innocent VI elected Pope.

1353 Petrarch at Court of Visconti in Milan, remains eight years. Boccaccio completes the *Decameron*. Berne joins the Swiss Confederation. Genoa-Venice war.

1354 Fall of Rienzi.

1355 Petrarch Ambassador to Prague. Coronation of Charles IV as Holy Roman Emperor, in Rome.

1356 French defeated by English at Poitiers. John the Good captured by the Black Prince.

1358 Peasants revolt against French nobles.

1360 Treaties of Brétigny and Calais.

1361 Petrarch in Paris on mission. Returns to Milan.

1362 Urban V becomes Pope. Petrarch moves from Padua to Venice, where Senate assigns him a palace. Langley works on first version of Piers Plowman. English Parliament opened by a speech in English.

1363 Philip the Bold becomes Duke of Burgundy.

1364 Charles V the Wise ascends the French throne. Petrarch begins to arrange his Letters.

1365 Statute of *Praemunire* in England.

1367 Urban V returns to Rome.

1368 Petrarch settles at Arquá with daughter and son-in-law.

1369 The Hundred Years' War is renewed.

1370 Urban V comes back to Avignon. Dies. Gregory XI becomes Pope. Petrarch makes his will and testament, at Padua.

1372 Chaucer takes his first trip to Italy. War renewed between Venice and Genoa. British fleet defeated off La Rochelle by Castilians.

1374 Petrarch dies.

1375 Boccaccio dies.

1376 Gregory XI leaves Avignon for Rome. The Good Parliament in England. Wenceslas the Worthless made Holy Roman Emperor. The Eight of the War raise the Papal States against the Pope.

1377 Edward III dies. Gregory XI condemns the teachings of Wycliffe. Richard II becomes King of England.

1378 Urban VI elected Pope in Rome by a Conclave under duress. September 20, the Great Schism of the West begins at Fondi.

On the throne of:

	THE PAPACY	FRANCE	THE HOLY ROMAN EMPIRE	ENGLAND
1305	Clement V	Philip IV, The Fair	Albert I	Edward I
1307	. . .	. . .	. . .	Edward II
1308	. . .	. . .	Henry VII	. . .
1314	. . .	Louis X, The Quarrelsome	Louis IV	. . .
	No Pope			
1316	John XXII	Philip V, The Long	. . .	. . .
1322	. . .	Charles IV, The Fair	. . .	. . .
1327	. . .	. . .	. . .	Edward III
1328	. . .	Philip VI, The Bold	. . .	. . .
1334	Benedict XII	. . .	. . .	. . .
1342	Clement VI	. . .	. . .	. . .
1347	. . .	. . .	Charles IV	. . .
1350	. . .	John II, The Good	. . .	. . .
1352	Innocent VI	. . .	. . .	. . .
1362	Urban V	. . .	. . .	. . .
1364	. . .	Charles V, The Wise	. . .	. . .
1370	Gregory XI	. . .	. . .	. . .
1377	. . .	. . .	. . .	Richard II
1378	The death of Gregory XI	The Great Schism of the West		

BIBLIOGRAPHY

Ameer Alí, *The Spirit of Islam*. London, 1949.

André, J. F., *Histoire de la Papauté à Avignon*. Avignon, 1887.

———, *Notes sur l'Histoire dans le Département de Vaucluse*. Avignon, 1876.

Aquinas, Saint Thomas, *Summa Theologica*. Translated by the Fathers of the English Dominican Province. Vols. 1–8. London, 1911–22.

Arnavon, F. de, *Pétrarque à Vaucluse*. Paris, 1803.

Arnold, T. W., *The Preaching of Islam*. London, 1935.

Baddeley, St. Clair, *Joanna I of Naples*. London, 1893.

Bahá'u'lláh, *Kitáb-i-Íqán* (*The Book of Certitude*). Translated by Shoghi Effendi. Wilmette, Ill., 1931.

Bémont, C., and R. Doucet, *Histoire de l'Europe au Moyen Age*. Paris, 1931.

Boccaccio, G., *The Decameron*. Translated by Richard Aldington. Garden City, N.Y., 1930.

Brewer, E. C., *A Dictionary of Miracles*. Philadelphia, 1884.

Bridget (Saint Bridget of Sweden), *Revelations of St. Bridget*. London, 1873.

Brisset, Fernand, *Laure de Pétrarque*. Paris, 1931.

———, *Les Sonnets de Pétrarque à Laure*. Paris, 1933.

Browne, E. G., *A Literary History of Persia*. 2 vols. London, 1902.

Browne, Lewis, *Since Calvary*. New York, 1931.

Catherine (Saint Catherine of Siena), *Lettres de Sainte Catherine de Sienne*. Translated from the Italian by E. Cartier. 3 vols. Paris, 1858.

Christophe, J. B., *Histoire de la Papauté pendant le XIVe Siècle*. Paris, 1853.

Cochin, Henri, *Le Frère de Pétrarque*. Paris, 1903.

Cosenza, Mario Emilio, *Francesco Petrarca and the Revolution of Cola di Rienzo*. Chicago, 1913.

Coulange, L., *The Life of the Devil*. Translated by S. H. Guest. New York, 1930.

Creighton, Mandell, *Epochs of the Papacy*. 16 vols. London, 1886–98.

Cummings, C. P., *The Revelations of Saint Birgitta*. London, 1929.

Dante, Alighieri, *The Vision; or, Hell, Purgatory and Paradise*. Translated by H. F. Cary. New York, 1880.

Draper, J. W., *The Intellectual Development of Europe*. 2 vols. New York, 1876.

Gaillard, G. H., *Histoire de François Premier*. 4 vols. Paris, 1819.

Gallotti, Jean, *Le Palais des Papes*. Paris, 1949.

Gauthier, J. S., *Vieilles Maisons*. Paris, 1937.

Gay, Jules, *Le Pape Clément VI et les Affaires d'Orient*. Paris, 1904.

Gibbon, Edward, *The History of the Decline and Fall of the Roman Empire*. 3 vols. Modern Library edition. New York, 1932 (?).

Girard, Joseph, *Evocation du Vieil Avignon*. Paris, 1958.

Gregorovius, Ferdinand, *History of the City of Rome in the Middle Ages*. Translated by A. Hamilton. 10 vols. London, 1894–98.

Grunebaum, G. E. von, *Medieval Islam*. London, 1953.

Hallmann, Eduard, *Die Geschichte des Ursprungs der Belgischen Beghinen*. 1843.

Hollway-Calthrop, H., *Petrarch, His Life and Times*. New York, 1907.

Hansen, H. H., *Die Kostümgeschichte Aller Zeiten* (Knaurs Kostümbuch). Zurich, 1957.

Hassall, W. O., *How They Lived*. Oxford, 1962.

James, Croake (pseud. for Paterson, James), *Curiosities of Christian History Prior to the Reformation*. London, 1892.

Jameson, A. B., *Legends of the Monastic Orders*. London, 1852.

———, *Memoirs of Celebrated Female Sovereigns*. London, 1831.

Joudou, J. B., *Essai sur l'Histoire de la Ville d'Avignon*. Avignon, 1853.

———, *Histoire des Souverains Pontifes qui ont Siégé à Avignon*. 2 vols. Avignon, 1855.

Jundt, Auguste, *Histoire du Panthéisme Populaire au Moyen Age*. Paris, 1875.

Kelly, W. K., *Proverbs of All Nations*. Andover, 1869.

Kirstein, Lincoln, *Dance*. New York, 1935.

Labande, L. H., *Avignon au XIIIe Siècle*. Avignon, 1908.

———, *Le Palais des Papes*. 2 vols. Avignon, 1925.

Langdon-Davies, J., *A Short History of Women*. New York, 1927.

Langlois, C. V., *La Vie en France au Moyen Age*. 4 vols. Paris, 1924–28.

Lea, H. C., *History of the Inquisition of the Middle Ages*. 3 vols. London, 1888.

Lecky, W. E., *History of European Morals*. 2 vols. New York, 1898.

Luce, Siméon, *Histoire de Bertrand du Guesclin*. Paris, 1876.

———, *La France pendant la Guerre de Cent Ans*. Paris, 1890.

Mézières, A., *Pétrarque*. Paris, 1895.

Mérimée, Prosper, *Notes d'un Voyage dans le Midi*. Paris, 1835.

Milman, Henry H., *History of Latin Christianity*. 9 vols. London, 1864.

Mollat, G., E. Baluze, Nouvelle Édition d'après les Manuscrits. 4 vols. Paris, 1914–27.

——, Étude Critique sur les Vitae Paparum Avenionensium d'Étienne Baluze. Paris, 1917.

——, Les Papes d'Avignon. Paris, 1920.

Mosheim, J. L. von, Institutes of Ecclesiastical History. Translated by J. Murdoch and H. Soames. 3 vols. London, 1863.

Nolhac, Pierre, Pétrarque et l'Humanisme. 2 vols. Paris, 1898.

Pastor, Ludwig, The History of the Popes, Vol. I. London, 1891.

Pennington, A. R., Epochs of the Papacy. London, 1881.

Petrarca, Francesco, Epistolae. 1914.

——, Letters to Classical Authors. Translated by M. E. Cosenza. Chicago, 1910.

——, The Rhymes of Francesco Petrarca. Compiled by T. G. Bergin. London, 1954.

——, Sonetti et Canzoni. In Vinegia. Appresso Gabriel Giolito de Ferrari. 1547.

——, Poésies Complètes. Paris, 1900.

——, Mon Secret. Translated by V. Develay. Paris, 1879.

——, Petrarch's Secret. Translated by W. H. Draper. London, 1911.

——, Testament. Translated and edited by T. E. Mommsen. New York, 1957.

——, The Triumphs of Petrarch. Translated by H. Boyd. London, 1807.

——, Des Visions. Six Sonnets. Translated by C. Marot. Lyon, 1544.

——, Lettres sans Titre. Translated by V. Develay. 2 vols. Paris, 1885.

——, Les Oeuvres Amoureuses de Pétrarque. Translated by P. L. Ginguené. Paris, 1875.

——, Lettres . . . à Jean Boccace. Translated by V. Develay. Paris, 1891.

——, Lettres à Rienzi. Translated by V. Develay. Paris, 1885.

Phelps, R. S., The Earlier and Later Forms of Petrarch's Canzonieri. Chicago, 1925.

Pichon, J., Le Ménagier de Paris. 2 vols. Paris, 1846.

Reinaud, J. T., Description des Monuments. 2 vols. Paris, 1828.

Robinson, J. H. and H. W. Rolfe, Petrarch. New York, 1914.

Rocal, G., Châteaux et Manoirs. Paris, 1938.

Rudwin, M., The Devil in Legend and Literature. Chicago, 1931.

Sade, de, Abbé, Mémoires de la Vie de Pétrarque. Amsterdam, 1764–67.

Sa'dí, The Gulistán (The Rose Garden). Translated by F. Gladwin. London, 1808.

Salzman, L. F., *English Life in the Middle Ages.* London, 1945.

Schiedlausky, G., *Essen und Trinken. Tafelsitten bis zum Ausgang des Mittelalters.* Munich, 1956.

Schmidt, Charles, *Histoire et Doctrine de la Secte des Cathares.* 2 vols. Paris, 1849.

Shipley, J. T., *Dictionary of Word Origins.* New York, 1945.

Simonde de Sismondi, J., *Histoire des Républiques Italiennes du Moyen Age.* Vol. III. Paris, 1826.

Spinka, M., *Advocates of Reform.* Library of Christian Classics, Vol. XIV. London, 1953.

Suetonius, *The Lives of the Twelve Caesars.* New York, 1931.

Tabarí, 'Alí, *The Book of Religion and Empire.* London, 1922.

Tatham, E. H. R., *Francesco Petrarca.* 2 vols. London, 1925.

Tilley, Arthur, *Medieval France.* Cambridge, 1922.

Touron, A., *La Vie de S. Thomas d'Aquin.* Paris, 1737.

Villani, Giovanni, *Villani's Chronicle.* Translated by R. E. Selfe; selected and edited by P. H. Wicksteed. London, 1906.

Weiss, Charles, *Laure et Pétrarque.* Paris, 1935.

Whitfield, J. H., *Petrarch and the Renascense.* Oxford, 1943.

Wilkins, E. H., *The Making of the "Canzoniere."* Rome, 1951.

——, *Studies in the Life and Works of Petrarch.* Rome, 1955.

INDEX

Catherine of Siena *cont'd:*
290; trance condition of, tested, 291; censures Gregory XI and Cardinals, 291; Gregory XI listens to, 291; Florence turns against, 292; farewell of, to Gregory XI, 292; enlists aid of Saints Bridget and Peter of Aragon, 292
Catherine, Princess of Taranto, 138
Cauvin, Maistre Symon, 184
Cavalcata, 51; description of, 214
Celestine V, Pope, abdicated, 29; given to levitation, 29
Celestines, Church of, burial place of Saint Bénézet, 69
Celibacy, 244
Cemeteries, business conducted in, 213
Champagne, Countess of, 146
Charles of Durazzo, 138; 153
Charles IV, Holy Roman Emperor, 166; hands Rienzi over to Clement VI, 167; 226; resists papal tax, 234–235; censures luxury of German clergy, 235; 283
Charles V, King of France, Adamites burned by, 38; 264; 270; 276
Charles the Hammer (Charles Martel), 21; 22
Charles the Lame, King of Naples, 119
Charonton, Enguerrand de, 180
Chaucer, 146; 277
Chivalry, 145; 201
Chopinel, Jean, 147
Chronicle of Melsa, 195
Cicero, 44; 206; 207; 259; 260
Cigisbéisme, 142
Cistercians, Order of, 101; 106
Clémence, Queen of Hungary, 208
Clement V, Pope (Bertrand de Goth), meets the King of France, 7–10; 13; coronation of, 14; triumphal progress of, 14; at Poitiers, 15; reviews charges against Templars, 16; moves Holy See to Avignon, 16, 18, 19; 23; 26; 27; 29; 30; committed to Templars' guilt, 31; presses Edward II to torture Templars, 32; bull of, on Templars' guilt, 33; Templars' property transferred by bull of, 33; cursed by de Molay, 35, 41; delays trial of Boniface, 36; declares Boniface

innocent, 37; 39; ill, dies, 39; body of, despoiled, 40; charges of Italian Cardinals against, 40, 41; 47; 49; 54; 119; 220; in Dante's Hell, 224
Clement VI, Pope (Pierre Roger), adds to Papal Palace, 3, 126; statue of, 3; private apartment of, 3–5; receipts from Papal States, 79; background of, 125; lavishness of, 126; and women, 126–27; compared with Caesar, 127–28; Court of, 128; library of, 128; banquet for, 129–130; and Queen Joanna, 131; 132; 138; 139; 152; acquits Queen Joanna, 152–53; obtains Avignon from Joanna, 153; and Rienzi, 155, 157, 160, 161, 165, 167, 169; 171; 187; and the plague, 188; protects the Jews, 188; Devil's letter to, 192; views of, on Papacy, 193; retraction of possible errors by, 194; condemns Cardinals, 194; death and burial of, 195–96; 199; 233; 234; Petrarch's son legitimized and appointed by, 257–58; 276
Clement VII, Pope (Robert of Geneva), 295; elected at Fondi, 296
"Clementine," 296
Closed Valley, *see* Vaucluse
Clothing, lay, tax on clerics for wearing, 84
Clothing, 14th century, 92
Clovis, 21
Cluny, monks of, imposed on by Curia, 249–50
Code of Love, 146; 147
Colonna, Giacomo, calls Laura imaginary, 63; 201; Petrarch's letters to, 208, 209
Colonna, House of, helps to capture Boniface VIII, 9; 37; 55; 157; 170
Colonna, Stefano, 158; 170
Comminges, Jean de, 100
Companies, *see* Free Companies
Comtat Venaissin, 16; 45; 79; niece of Clement VI made *rectrice* of, 127
Conclave, attacked at Carpentras, 40; 47; 48; menu of, 219; tries to control Pope, 220–21; efforts undone by Innocent VI, 231; threatened by Roman mobs, 295–96;